MW01487012

ALL IN

THE PATHWAY TO PERSONAL GROWTH AND PROFESSIONAL EXCELLENCE

BRENT GLEESON

balance

New York Boston

Balance
Hachette Book Group
1290 Avenue of the Americas
New York, NY 10104
GCP-Balance.com
@GCPBalance

First Edition: December 2025

Balance is an imprint of Grand Central Publishing. The Balance name and logo are registered trademarks of Hachette Book Group, Inc.

The publisher is not responsible for websites (or their content) that are not owned by the publisher.

The Hachette Speakers Bureau provides a wide range of authors for speaking events. To find out more, visit hachettespeakersbureau.com or email HachetteSpeakers@hbgusa.com.

Balance books may be purchased in bulk for business, educational, or promotional use. For information, please contact your local bookseller or email the Hachette Book Group Special Markets Department at Special.Markets@hbgusa.com.

Print book interior design by Jeff Stiefel

Library of Congress Cataloging-in-Publication Data

Name: Gleeson, Brent author
Title: All in : the pathway to personal growth and professional excellence / Brent Gleeson.
Description: First edition. | New York : Balance, [2025] | Includes bibliographical references and index.
Identifiers: LCCN 2025007922 | ISBN 9780306836886 hardcover | ISBN 9780306836893 trade paperback | ISBN 9780306836909 ebook
Subjects: LCSH: Success | Self-actualization (Psychology) | Goal (Psychology)
Classification: LCC BF637.S8 G5337 2025 | DDC 158.1—dc23/eng/20250903
LC record available at https://lccn.loc.gov/2025007922

ISBNs: 978-0-306-83688-6 (hardcover); 978-0-306-83690-9 (ebook)

Printed in Canada

MRQ-T

1 2025

To my wife, Nicole—
my unwavering partner,
my greatest love,
and the one I am ALL IN for.

CONTENTS

PROLOGUE

My father died suddenly on Wednesday, September 20, 2023, in Dallas, Texas.

That week had begun like any other: I was on an early flight out of San Diego, heading to Dallas for a business trip. Monday was uneventful, filled with the familiar rhythm of airport terminals, Uber rides, and meeting agendas. By Tuesday afternoon, I was deep in discussions with a client, navigating the minutiae of the day's objectives, when my phone began vibrating incessantly in my pocket. At first, it was easy to ignore, but as the vibrations persisted, a subtle unease began to stir within me.

When the meeting finally ended, I stepped to the far corner of the conference room, its linoleum floors gleaming under the fluorescent lights, and pulled my phone from the front pocket of my jeans. I expected the usual: a barrage of irreverent group texts from college buddies or SEAL teammates. But life rarely unfolds as we expect, and in that fleeting moment, everything I knew as certain unraveled.

I found a series of text messages from my mom to my twin brother and me. The content was quite different from what I anticipated.

[4:22PM] Your Dad is in the Presbyterian Hospital ER. I was driving home from an event and came across him lying in the street with a crowd around him and a constable already there. They said he was apparently walking home from North Park shopping mall. This was not on his agenda today! He hit his head on the pavement. May have fainted. Paramedics said they would order a CAT scan and other tests. He was speaking a little but very dazed. Will keep you posted.

My heart quickened as I hastily texted my mom, letting her know I was in town and would head straight to the hospital. In the rush of this trip, I hadn't mentioned my visit to Dallas, my hometown and a city I frequented often, to her beforehand. Struggling to steady my emotions, I approached our VP of Programs, a thirty-year Navy SEAL veteran, and the client company's CEO, who were deep in conversation. As I delivered the heartbreaking news, the CEO, now a trusted friend, didn't hesitate. "Let's go. I'll drive," he said with quiet urgency, his love of fast cars suddenly a blessing.

With his NASCAR-worthy driving skills and a touch of divine intervention, we navigated the densely packed Dallas rush-hour traffic on Interstate 635 as if we were parting the Red Sea. I called my wife, Nicole, as soon as we were underway. We all prayed the entire drive. Ten minutes prior to my arrival, I received this text:

> **[4:58PM]** David has had a brain bleed and may have had a stroke and is in dire condition. Brain surgery ahead. The next minutes and hours are critical.

A deep pain burned in my chest. Throat tightened. Eyes welled with tears. Prayers continued at a more vigorous pace. Five minutes later, I received this message:

> **[5:03PM]** Just talked to the neurosurgeon. Not good. He probably won't survive.

I reread the text five times. Its impact was similar to the immense recoil of a Carl Gustaf M4 anti-tank weapon. For you civilians, that is a big-ass rocket launcher. There was no level of mental fortitude I could muster to keep the tears from streaming down my face.

The severity of my father's brain bleed made surgery impossible. Compounding this grim reality was the decision he had made in an advance directive—a do-not-resuscitate (DNR) order. The weight of the situation crashed over us, a devastating clarity settling in: These would be our final moments together.

Family members from across Dallas gathered at the hospital, seeking solace in shared grief, their hushed conversations blending with the sterile hum of the ward. I arranged a FaceTime call with Nicole and our four children, giving them a chance to say their goodbyes to "Poppsy." Though his eyes remained closed, he managed faint responses, whispering, "I love you, too," in those first, fleeting hours.

As midnight approached, I turned to the few who still lingered—my mom, my brother, his wife, and a couple of cousins—and assured them I'd take the first "watch." I urged them to rest at our family home, a short drive away, and promised to call if anything changed. By then, my father had slipped into complete unresponsiveness. We spoke to him anyway, clinging to the hope that he could still hear us through the silence.

Alone with my dad, a wave of restlessness and despair crashed over me, paired with an insatiable craving for a drink. I convinced myself—as I had so many times before—that alcohol would dull the sharp edge of reality, make the unbearable slightly more tolerable. It was a familiar vice, born from years of masking the scars of combat and the relentless demands of entrepreneurship. When the nurse returned for her routine check, I seized the chance to escape.

Crossing Greenville Avenue in the cool night air, I entered a dimly lit liquor store and hastily grabbed two small bottles of vodka and a handful of snacks. As I returned to the hospital, shame settled over me like a heavy cloak. What if, in those few moments, my father had passed? Quietly, I pleaded with God for forgiveness, grappling with the rawness of my choices.

Throughout the night, I sat crammed into an unforgiving hospital chair beside my father's bed. To fill the silence and honor his passion for military history, I played *Band of Brothers* on my phone, angling the screen toward him as though he could watch with me. The salty tang of tears mixed with the vodka on my lips as I quietly wept, spoke to him, and prayed. There, in the dim glow of the screen, I found a strange and solemn connection—a final communion between a son and his father, a former Marine whose love for history had shaped so much of who he was. And, yes, I know: Once a Marine, always a Marine.

At eight the next morning, my mom and brother returned to the hospital, their presence a quiet comfort in the heavy stillness of the hospital room. A dull, familiar headache had also joined me, a self-inflicted companion to the weight of waiting and grief. As the hours crept by, time seemed to stretch and contract, blurring the boundary between anticipation and inevitability. Then, at eleven o'clock, my father drew his final breath. The air seemed to shift in that instant, as though the universe itself paused to mark his passing. His earthly journey, though unfinished in the way all lives are, had reached its natural conclusion. He was called home—into the arms of eternity, where pain and struggle could no longer touch him. A profound stillness settled over the room, filled not with emptiness but with the quiet echo of a life well lived, a man deeply loved.

Upon learning of my dad's service in the Marine Corps during the Vietnam War, the hospital staff proposed a formal military ceremony to honor his veteran status. A dignified procession was organized, with his body respectfully covered in the American flag as he was transferred from the hospital to a vehicle destined for the funeral home.

The next day, I returned home to join my family and start the grieving process. Two weeks later, we returned to Dallas for Dad's memorial service. As part of my remarks, I recited Tecumseh's poem "Death Song":

> Live your life, so that the fear of death may never enter your heart. Trouble no one about their religion. Respect others in their views. And demand that they respect yours.

> Love your life. Perfect your life. Beautify all things in your life. Seek to make your life long and of service to others.

> Prepare a noble death song for the day you go over the great divide.

> Show respect to all people and grovel to none.

> When you arise in the morning give thanks for the light, for your life and strength. If you see no reason for giving thanks, the fault lies within yourself.

> When it comes your time to die, be not like those whose hearts are filled with the fear of death, so that when their time comes they weep and pray for a little more time to live their lives over again in a different way.

> Sing your death song and die like a hero going home.

A memorial service carries with it an intense sense of finality, a solemn acknowledgment that a chapter has closed. As guests began to depart, I felt the weight of loss mingled with a quiet peace, knowing my dad had found his eternal home. His life was a testament to devotion and determination—a husband, father, and successful real estate developer who poured his heart into everything he did. Yet, even as I celebrated his legacy, I felt the bittersweet sting of dreams left unfulfilled, projects left unfinished, and words left unsaid. His abrupt departure was a reminder of life's fragility, a reminder that urges us to live with intention, pursue our aspirations with urgency, and shape a life that reflects the depth of our love and the purpose of our days.

When my family and I returned home to San Diego, I made three transformative decisions:

1. To quit drinking—forever
2. To radically adjust my priorities
3. And to write this book

INTRODUCTION

As a Navy SEAL combat veteran, I have faced the sorrow of losing many brothers and the heavy burden of taking life. Yet, nothing compares to the aching finality of losing a loved one, especially a parent or a child. My father's passing became an unyielding reminder of life's delicateness and the certainty of death. His loss thrust mortality into sharp focus, compelling me to confront the impermanence of existence, the fleeting nature of time, and the precious threads that weave our lives together.

Death itself should not be feared—it is one of life's few certainties. What we should fear, however, is the quiet erosion of our spirit that comes with a life of mediocrity that is devoid of purpose. The true enemy is not life's swift end but the insidious decay born of regrets and missed opportunities—the slow, silent theft of our potential that leaves dreams to wither into forgotten whispers of what might have been.

The death of someone so central to our lives often ignites a serious reckoning that exposes vulnerabilities we'd rather ignore and provokes reflection on our choices, priorities, and the meaning we assign to each fleeting moment. My father's passing became precisely such a catalyst, urging me to pause and examine the trajectory of my own life, not merely through the lens of achievement at work, in relationships, and in faith but also through the greater question of impact. What am I building, and for whom? What meaningful initiatives am I pursuing that will enrich as many lives as possible and leave a positive mark on the world once I am gone?

In the stillness of this reflection, a question surfaced with piercing clarity: *Am I living my life so that the fear of death will never enter my heart?* The answer did not come easily, and I could not know it with certainty. Before sacrificing his life for his cause, American Christian missionary Jim Elliot declared, "When it comes time to die, make sure that all you have to do is die." So, this uncertainty became its own kind of truth—a call to action, a challenge to align my words and deeds with the values I hold most dear. It demanded that I pursue a life unburdened by regret, a life of purpose and authenticity, one in which every choice honors the gift of time.

This book is a journey through such questions and truths, a guide to embracing the finite nature of life as a force for extraordinary growth. It is about rejecting mediocrity, finding purpose, and living boldly so that when the end inevitably comes, it finds us fully alive.

GOING *ALL IN*

In the context of living a purpose-driven and fulfilling life, the concept of going *all in* involves wholeheartedly committing ourselves to pursuing only a few passions and aspirations but pursuing them with resolute dedication and determination. It involves fully immersing ourselves in endeavors that align with our purpose and values, which leaves no room for hesitation or doubt. Going *all in* means fully committing to the journey of growth by embracing challenges, taking bold and calculated risks, and breaking free from the confines of our comfort zones. It involves facing obstacles head-on with conviction, recognizing that these hurdles are not barriers but opportunities for innovation, resilience, and redirection. By leaning into adversity, we unlock new pathways for personal and professional development and transform challenges into catalysts of achieving our highest potential.

Living an *all in* life demands the alignment of mind, heart, and soul, anchored by a deep sense of self-awareness that discerns what truly matters and brings lasting fulfillment. It's about intentionally aligning actions with core values and aspirations and making choices that are not just meaningful but also transformative. No matter what you've dedicated yourself to—maybe it's your career or deepening your relationship with God and loved ones or committing to personal development goals that elevate your mindfulness, faith, health, or financial well-being—going *all in* requires steadfast commitment. It means embracing the full spectrum of the journey, with all its highs and lows, and fully engaging in the process of becoming the most heroic, grateful, and fulfilled version of yourself.

Ultimately, going *all in* is about living authentically and with conviction, refusing to settle for mediocrity or complacency. We are either moving forward or dying slowly. Why would we choose any other way of living than advancing in every area of our lives? So what if it involves embracing challenges and showing vulnerability? So what if the path is pockmarked with the potholes of fear and pain? On the journey to self-actualization and true consciousness, the concept of going *all in* serves as a beacon that guides us to unlock our boundless potential, declutter our lives, hone our focus, and craft a life teeming with clear purpose, deep meaning, and remarkable achievements.

The clock is ticking. It's time to take a look at your cards, put your chips on the table, and go *all in*.

HOW TO USE THIS BOOK

What unites Navy SEALs, Olympians, astronauts, renowned musicians, cancer survivors, thriving entrepreneurs, and history's greatest trailblazers? It is their commitment to purpose and their journey to discover excellence. Whether striving for greatness or mere survival, these individuals master the art of focus, eliminate distractions, and cultivate disciplined routines that drive them toward their aspirations. Their high-growth mindset—marked by resilience, adaptability, and the courage to embrace discomfort—sets them apart and allows them to thrive in the face of adversity.

Yet, they are not immune to life's challenges. Like us all, they encounter setbacks, failures, and unforeseen trials. What distinguishes them is their ability to transform obstacles into opportunities for growth through disciplined action and their clear sense of purpose. They declutter their lives, break detrimental habits, and embrace systems that foster consistency and progress. Pursuing their goals in this way, these individuals embody the transformation necessary for great success.

In this book, I share how you can integrate these principles into every facet of your life—from personal health and relationships to career obstacles, leadership challenges, and moments of quiet self-doubt—whatever your battlegrounds may be. You'll find stories and lessons drawn from history, modern science, and my personal experiences as a Navy SEAL, entrepreneur, and life-long student of growth. This is not a guide for those content with mediocrity but a call to action for anyone ready to embrace discomfort as a catalyst of transformation. It is for you if you are ready to pursue a life of meaning and impact.

As Hemingway famously remarked, "In order to write about life, first you must live it." This truth resonates deeply with me. To write this book, I committed to embodying the principles discussed within its pages and applying them rigorously in my own life. From refining my daily routines and eliminating bad habits to fully transforming my business and deepening my relationships, I've lived this framework. My hope is that, by sharing insights from my journey, you'll find the tools here to do the same.

My expertise is rooted in the lived experience of war, loss, love, marriage, raising four children, and building high-growth businesses. The process for achieving remarkable results I present here is anchored in rigorous scientific research and the collective wisdom of extraordinary leaders across generations. Any shortcomings in its presentation are my own. Any inaccuracies are mine to bear. But my aspiration is for you to unlock the transformative power of purposeful routines, intentional habit formation, commitment to systems, and a clear focus on what truly matters so that you can go *all in* on building the life and experiences you want.

Life is fleeting, and our time is finite. More significant still is where we place our attention in the moments we're granted. Why not use your time with intention? Let's commit to a life of meaning, purpose, and joy—a life that transcends mere existence and becomes a journey of growth, contribution, and impact. Living this way, we not only enrich our own lives but also illuminate a path for others and leave behind a legacy that inspires and endures.

With all this in mind, are you ready to go *all in*?

If so, let's begin.

PART 1

RELENTLESS ROUTINES

THE REMARKABLE RESULTS PYRAMID (RRP)

1

DRIVEN BY PURPOSE

The Psychology Behind Our Goals

*Do not let your fire go out, spark by irreplaceable spark in the hopeless
swamps of the approximate, the not-quite, the not-yet, the not-at-all.
Do not let the hero in your soul perish in lonely frustration for the life you
deserved and have never been able to reach. Check your road and the
nature of your battle. The world you desired can be won, it exists,
it is real, it is possible, it's yours.*

—AYN RAND, *THE FOUNTAINHEAD*

At twenty-three, I made a choice that would redefine my life, a decision that
would require an unflinching commitment to discipline, the demolition of
old habits, and the embrace of new rituals that would not only transform my
actions but also rewire my way of thinking. This step demanded I unlock latent
potential, forge resilience, and dedicate myself to the pursuit of challenges far
beyond the ordinary. As I would later realize, this decision illuminated the
immense power of intentionally crafted routines pursued with relentless vigor.
Routines are not only tools for habit formation but also gateways to purpose,
excellence, and the realization of ambitious goals.

Seated at my desk on the forty-second floor of the Trammell Crow Center, a high-rise that dominated the Dallas skyline, I drafted a letter that I knew
would leave my parents speechless. I revealed my decision to leave behind a
hard-earned role as a financial analyst—my first position after college—to

3

pursue an extraordinary path. I wasn't just planning to enlist in the United States Navy; I had set my sights on the most grueling special operations training program in the world. My goal was to become a Navy SEAL.

But let me be clear—this wasn't a random epiphany. The why behind my decision, shaped by pivotal experiences and encounters, had been quietly evolving over time.

During my undergraduate years at Southern Methodist University, where I earned degrees in finance and economics, my path seemed securely aligned with corporate ambition. Yet, my time spent studying English literature and criminal justice at Oxford University between my sophomore and junior years at SMU changed something in me. Oxford's tutorial approach to learning—with an emphasis on independent study, collaborative projects, and one-on-one mentorship—demanded intellectual rigor, disciplined routines, and a mastery of time management. The direct, often brutal feedback from professors brought alive in me a newfound appreciation for the intersection of accountability and personal growth, and my studies required a level of self-discipline that hadn't been expected of me before.

A few months into my sophomore year, I met Matt, a freshman at SMU who shared his dream of becoming a Navy SEAL with me. At first, I admired his conviction but dismissed his ambition as an improbable pursuit—a noble but nearly unattainable goal. *Good for him*, I thought, *but that's not for me*. And yet, his determination planted a seed by subtly challenging my understanding of what it meant to chase something truly remarkable. It wasn't an instant revelation, but over time, that seed took root and ultimately grew into a decision that would dramatically alter the trajectory of my life.

This is where my journey begins: a young man, stepping away from the predictable path, daring to chase something audacious, and discovering along the way the unparalleled power of discipline, purpose, and consistent pursuit.

My college years were a whirlwind of rugby matches, social antics (mostly legal in Texas), and occasional academic diligence. I captained the SMU rugby team for two of my four years on the team, likely because no one else wanted the job. During this time, Matt and I became close friends, and to my surprise, his seemingly wild ambition to become a Navy SEAL only grew stronger.

His compounding enthusiasm for the Naval Special Warfare organization piqued my curiosity. Intrigued, I delved into the available literature, which mostly centered on the SEAL community's history from World War II to Vietnam. I also read Richard Marcinko's book, *Rogue Warrior*. Discovering that all Navy SEALs could leap tall buildings in a single bound and bench-press five hundred pounds while sweating the sweet smell of toxic masculinity was compelling, to say the least. They breathed fire, stared down death with only a single glance, hypnotized the most beautiful women with a mere flip of the hair, and munched on glass without even lacerating their gums. These findings were incredibly inspiring. *Who are these demigods?!*

Nevertheless, I knew this fairy tale would never become my reality. I didn't know where to start even if I wanted to. But, I figured, maybe Matt had a chance. So, while I was diligently practicing the fine art of *fake it till you make it* as a financial analyst, I decided to lend Matt a helping hand and train with him while he completed his senior year at SMU and prepared to enlist in the Navy. I needed some balance in my life anyway. The effort would prove my love as a friend and support—of his insanely unattainable goal—and give me the opportunity to maintain a respectable degree of fitness. A win-win.

I spent time at work pretending to geek out over spreadsheets, meticulously organizing data, creating complex models, analyzing financial metrics, and desperately trying to remember the formulas for calculating P/E ratios. But I found myself frequently daydreaming about being a special operations superhero who would swoop in and single-handedly save the day in the event our office building was taken over by terrorists planning to steal millions in bearer bonds. Just like John McClane in the Christmas movie *Die Hard*. Maybe I, too, could become some version of a guy with a penchant for kicking ass and taking names! One can dream.

And then one day, it clicked. I would go *all in*.

✪

Before you embark on the journey to conquer your universe, before you muster the strength to overcome each obstacle along the way, it's essential to understand why you have chosen the goals that drive you. Our choices, in personal relationships, professional ambitions, faith, fitness, and finances, are rarely random. Instead, they stem from a deeper yearning, a desire to become more than we are today. Yet, this yearning does not promise comfort or a smooth path to fulfillment. It beckons us toward challenges, toward the storms of adversity that will only refine and strengthen our resolve.

We don't select our goals simply to get to the destination but for the transformation they demand. Meaningful pursuits test our limits and require us to face discomfort, fear, and doubt head-on. Adversity, rather than an unwelcome intruder, is an essential ally. Our aspirations often feel less like deliberate choices and more like a calling—a soft but persistent voice urging us to rise, to act, to persevere. It is through the labor, the discipline, and the relentless pursuit of these endeavors that we discover our core purpose.

As Michelangelo famously remarked, "If you knew how much work went into it, you would not call it genius." Greatness is forged in the crucible of effort and resilience. So, when doubt looms and the weight of the task feels overwhelming, remember that you are building strength for a life that matters. Let us embrace the work ahead.

THE TRANSFORMATIVE POWER OF ROUTINES

I mailed that momentous letter to my parents rather than delivering it in person—a deliberate choice to demonstrate the gravity of its contents. The day after sending it, I began crafting a disciplined training regimen for Matt and myself, one designed to cultivate transformative habits and eliminate distractions. This system wasn't just about physical preparation; it was about reshaping our identities and fostering an unrelenting commitment to the goal of becoming Navy SEALs. Every facet of my life was overhauled to singularly align with this pursuit.

As a former college athlete, I had long known the transformational power of disciplined routines and the intricate dance of balancing competing priorities. Yet, this new endeavor demanded far more than balance—it called for an unyielding, asymmetric focus, a mindset sharpened to optimize every ounce of cognitive bandwidth I had and channel it exclusively into what truly mattered.

By stripping away distractions and concentrating all my energy on specific, measurable objectives, I found a clarity that cut through the noise and a level of commitment that sustained my motivation. This deliberate focus not only illuminated the path forward but also provided the framework I would use to measure our progress and continually refine our pursuit.

One Sunday morning, I sat on my apartment balcony with a pen and legal pad, the kind my dad used obsessively in his career, and drafted this framework. I needed to analyze how I allocated my time and energy. By asking myself pointed questions related to my existing routines and priorities, I laid the foundation for a system of total focus that would ensure every effort going forward was aligned with achieving the extraordinary results Matt and I were looking for. I asked the following questions:

- Who in my social circle will support and guide me on this journey, and how can I reclaim time from activities that no longer serve my purpose?
- Can I adjust my work schedule to create additional time for preparation, or is leaving my job a necessary step toward my goal?
- Which current routines and rituals should be eliminated, refined, or intensified to align with my objective?
- How can I design evening and morning routines that optimize my energy, focus, and productivity?
- What dietary choices enhance my physical and mental performance, and which habits hinder my progress?

This pivotal step caused me to reflect deeply on the forces shaping my life and to identify the people, rituals, and resources that could propel me forward while showing the distractions I must shed and obstacles to be leaped along the way. Because a demanding work schedule consumed my days, I turned my focus to crafting purposeful morning and evening routines, well before I understood the science behind their regenerative power. History's great achievers—Marcus Aurelius, a Stoic philosopher and Rome's emperor from AD 161 to 180, among them—have long championed the value of predawn rituals. In *Meditations,* Aurelius captures this ethos: "At dawn, when you have trouble getting out of bed, tell yourself: 'I have to go to work—as a human being. What do I have to complain of, if I'm going to do what I was born for?'" Inspired by such wisdom, I began shaping routines to align my actions with my purpose.

My mornings began at 5:00 a.m., when I jolted myself to life with a cold shower—long before cold plunging swept into global vogue. The frigid water sharpened my senses and fortified my resolve. This was followed by light stretching and core exercises that awakened both body and focus. The next twenty minutes I devoted to reading material that broadened my mind and deepened my pursuits, and the period culminated with prayer and reflection that allowed me to clarify my intentions and set a purposeful tone for the day ahead. Not dissimilar to the "20-20-20 Formula" Robin Sharma presents in his incredible book *The 5AM Club*.

Evenings were equally disciplined. After work, I'd pack my gear, run four miles to the SMU natatorium, and complete rigorous swimming and calisthenics sessions designed to exceed the Navy SEAL training requirements. The night ended with another four-mile run home, a healthy dinner, and lights out by 9:45 p.m. Weekends followed a similar rhythm, with ten- to twenty-mile runs around White Rock Lake on Saturdays and light recovery on Sundays to prepare for the week ahead.

These routines, consistent and balanced, were not for show but for mastery. Discipline in the morning begins with discipline in the evening, because restorative sleep is the cornerstone of both mental and physical excellence. Through structured repetition, my daily habits became a system for transformation, a methodical path to achieving a purpose far greater than any single day's effort. Mastery, I realized, was not about grand gestures but about the quiet persistence of showing up, day after day, with unwavering focus and intent.

THE COMMITMENT

After a year of intense training, research, and introspection, I'd fully committed to this path. A timeline emerged, and Matt and I moved to Crested Butte, Colorado, to elevate the last bits of our training—literally. At high altitude, we pushed ourselves harder, running long distances carrying heavy logs, swimming in icy lakes, and scaling the region's tallest peaks. After six months, physically, mentally, and spiritually fortified, we returned to Texas, joined the US Navy, and embarked on the next phase of the journey.

I reached that milestone through relentless routines that helped me cultivate better habits, break free from detrimental ones, and automate difficult tasks. I had begun by not only striving for the goal but also embodying the mindset and actions of someone who had already achieved it. Engaging in this process built my willpower and mental resilience and cleared the way for a new identity to emerge. Just know that this approach requires caution: There's a difference between imagining the finish line prematurely and transforming yourself through consistent effort.

Fueled by commitment, we had developed systems that focused on time management, productivity, nutrition, sleep, and continuous learning. These systems emphasized small, daily improvements that compounded over time. The results were significant, though I could never have foreseen that they would ultimately lead me to war. Be careful what you wish for.

THE REMARKABLE RESULTS PYRAMID

It would be years later—a couple decades—before I grasped the significance of this metamorphosis from financial analyst to Navy SEAL and the implications of the framework I had designed to bring it about. I realized, with carefully crafted routines at its foundation, this framework could apply to all facets of life, psychological, neurological, and philosophical.

The implementation of the model certainly bore fruit as we secured admission into the SEAL training program. Yet, gaining entry paled in comparison to enduring the punishing crucible of training that awaited. Joining Basic Underwater Demolition / SEAL (BUD/S) Class 235 in the autumn of 2000, I was one among more than two hundred hopefuls. When the dust settled more than a year later, only twenty-three of us emerged triumphant, having earned the privilege of donning the revered Navy SEAL Trident pin. Then, we were assigned to our respective teams.

At that juncture, the conflict in Afghanistan was already in full swing, with murmurs of an impending war in Iraq spreading, too. In April 2003, my task unit of approximately forty SEALs from SEAL Team 5 became the first SEAL troop to be deployed to Iraq. Our mission: to undertake "capture or kill" operations targeting terrorists who harbored unimaginable malevolence. Leading up to that point and throughout the trials of rigorous training and multiple combat deployments, the validity of my original framework held. This is the progression:

Relentless Routines	→ New Habits and Beliefs	→
Transformed Mindset	→ New Identity and Deeper Resolve	→
Increased Commitment	→ Meaningful Connection to Purpose	→
Structured Systems	→ A Blueprint for Goal Achievement	→
Remarkable Results	→ Confidence and Continuous Improvement	

When you use this framework, what once seemed like a daunting goal is transformed into achievable milestones, footholds on the path to continuous growth. Each success is another rung on the ladder, lifting you ever upward. As your comfort zone broadens, challenges that once felt insurmountable become your new standard and are seamlessly integrated into your journey to excellence.

✪

Years later, I applied the principles I learned during my SEAL career to the realms of graduate school and entrepreneurship. They became the bedrock on which I built innovative tech companies and cultivated dynamic, high-performance cultures. The journey, marked by moments of intense stress, significant setbacks, and the ever-present shadow of uncertainty, was far from smooth. Yet, through it all, my single-minded commitment to continuous improvement and the transformative power of a growth mindset proved invaluable, indispensable, and guided each step forward so that I was acting with purpose and could face any hardships with resilience.

While leading my second company, a digital marketing and data analytics firm that earned a spot on the *Inc.* 500 list for three consecutive years, I launched a *Forbes* column called From the Battlefield to the Boardroom. One early article caught the attention of the president of Bank of America Merrill Lynch Asia Pacific, and he invited me to speak at the bank's global leadership summit in Hong Kong—a daunting yet tremendous opportunity that opened doors to repeat engagements with global organizations.

After selling that company, I authored my first book, *Taking Point: A Navy SEAL's 10 Fail-Safe Principles for Leading Through Change*, which offers a window into the transformative power of leadership and culture when navigating organizational change. This milestone led me to found a management consulting firm that specialized in talent development and employee engagement strategies for enterprise organizations that eventually evolved into my current organization, EXCELR8 (pronounced "accelerate"), a cutting-edge, AI-powered workforce technology software-as-a-service (SaaS) company. During this time, I was speaking to audiences exceeding fifty thousand annually, and I found the company's purpose: to more deeply explore human performance, behavioral science, and neuroscience in order to fuel groundbreaking innovations and drive meaningful impact in leadership and high-performance team development.

All of which prompted me to write my second book, *Embrace the Suck: The Navy SEAL Way to an Extraordinary Life*, which was published in December 2020, approximately nine months into the COVID pandemic. The culmination of these efforts, experiences, research, and trial and error is the framework you see in Figure 1–1.

The **Remarkable Results Pyramid (RRP)** is a proven framework for driving transformation—individual, team, and organizational—and achieving extraordinary outcomes. Each level of the pyramid builds on the one below, creating a powerful structure for growth and success. The journey begins with defining precise goals, whether in your career, relationships, health, or business—but the model is equally impactful even if your goals remain unclear. The beauty lies in its adaptability.

At the foundation of the pyramid are **relentless routines** and habit formation, where consistent action rewires neural pathways and turns intentional actions into automatic behaviors (habits) through repetition and reinforcement. As habits take hold, they transform your **mindset** and identity so that your self-concept becomes aligned with your goals. This fosters deeper **commitment**, which connects with your **purpose**: a clear why that enhances your motivation and resilience and continually points you in the correct direction.

Figure 1–1: *The Remarkable Results Pyramid (RRP)*

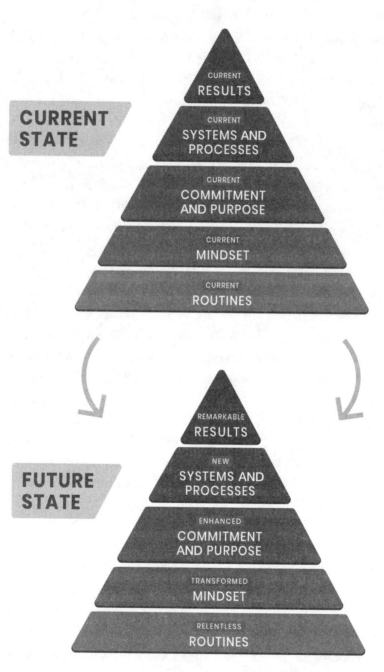

When you have a clear sense of purpose, you can design **systems** and **processes** that create structure, enhance efficiency, and optimize your efforts—transforming discipline into an everyday behavior on the path to achieving remarkable **results**. These results, however, are not the end goal—they're milestones. You can hop to the base of the pyramid and scale it again. The Remarkable Results process is ongoing so that you continually reinforce habits, refine systems, and move the goalposts farther out in an embrace of infinite growth.

Rooted in psychological principles, the RRP emphasizes consistency, identity, purpose, and systems as the foundation for success. Habits shape the neuroplastic brain by leveraging the power of structured routines so that anyone can harness the RRP to achieve extraordinary results and sustain long-term progress. You possess far more discipline than you may realize. This framework serves as a road map, helping you harness your courage and break the journey to remarkable results into clear, manageable steps.

WHO DARES WINS

The unorthodox is always unbreakable.

—SIR DAVID STERLING

A few months before I entered the Navy, I was seated at the far end of the bar at the Buffalo Rose Saloon in Crested Butte, the oldest bar in Colorado. The saloon's atmosphere was thick with history. I examined the intricate antler chandelier that hung above, quietly giving thanks to the fine beasts that so generously donated to the worthy cause of the lighting fixture. The air was filled with the rich scent of aged wood mingled with the aroma of grilled burgers and the faint hoppy trace of spilled beer. Patrons, a mix of locals and travelers, sat along the bar and at scattered tables, their low conversations blending into a comforting hum. The creak of the old wooden floorboards added to the saloon's charm.

I sat contemplating my journey to becoming a Navy SEAL. Matt and I had moved to Crested Butte to train for six months in extreme conditions prior to enlisting. There was only one thing on this odyssey we could control, and that was our level of physical and mental preparedness. As I scribbled our training regimen for the coming week in a notebook, the older man sitting next to me took notice.

"Excuse me, young man," he said, his voice carrying the gentle lilt of Yorkshire. "Are you an athlete? Crested Butte attracts a lot of athletes looking to train at high altitudes." His face was leathery and wrinkled, and bushy eyebrows accented eyes magnified by the wisdom that no doubt rested between his rather large ears.

Hesitantly, I replied, "Sort of. I'm actually training for a special operations selection program in the Navy."

A knowing smile spread across his face. "Ah, that's quite the journey. SEALs, I assume? I spent many years in a special operations regiment in the British Army. Have you heard of the Special Air Service, the SAS?"

"I've heard a bit," I admitted. "Weren't they originally involved in some pretty crazy operations back in World War II?"

"Indeed," he said, leaning in slightly. "One of the most daring campaigns was Operation Crusader in November 1941. Sir David Stirling, the founder of the SAS, conceived and led these outlandish operations. They aimed to destroy airfields and communication lines in North Africa, specifically targeting Axis airfields in Libya. Stirling and his small team of SAS operatives became experts in desert warfare and unconventional tactics. On a series of nighttime raids, they destroyed enemy aircraft and killed many Nazis deep in German-held territory. They had little to no support—completely on their own."

"How did they manage to pull that off?" I asked, intrigued. My dad was quite the military history buff, but my knowledge of how these conflicts in WWII extended to the northern regions of Africa was limited.

"They relied heavily on surprise and deception," the gentleman explained. "They'd drive long distances in the dark and often wear German uniforms to infiltrate enemy positions undetected. This was long before the luxury of night-vision goggles. They would strike swiftly and violently, like savages without mercy, and then vanish into the vast desert, evading enemy patrols. Despite formidable odds, they succeeded in blowing up countless enemy aircraft and significantly disrupted Axis operations."

"That's impressive," I said. "What motivated Stirling to create such an elite force? It was unlike any of its kind at the time, right?"

"Stirling was a visionary with a daring spirit," the old man continued. "He saw the flaws in traditional large-scale military raids, which he believed were too cumbersome and vulnerable to enemy retaliation. His revolutionary idea was to use small, highly trained teams to infiltrate behind enemy lines, strike multiple targets with precision, then escape before substantial opposition could be mounted."

"That sounds a lot like the tactics of modern special operations forces," I noted. "How in the world did he get the British military to support his idea?"

"It's quite a tale," the old man said, his eyes gleaming. "Undeterred by a parachuting accident that left him with a broken back, Stirling approached General Headquarters Middle East directly, bypassing the usual bureaucratic channels. He gained the support of General Sir Neil Ritchie, who authorized the creation of a new unit, 'L Detachment, Special Air Service Brigade.' Despite approval, senior officers were not wholly convinced that the brigade would have any lasting impact. But the detachment might marginally disrupt German operations for a short time and give the impression of a shadow force hunting Axis in Africa. That was their hope."

"I'm not surprised he faced a lot of skepticism," I said, laughing and signaling the bartender to bring us another round.

"Oh, absolutely," he replied with a nod. "Like all founders with radical ideas, he confronted extreme skepticism. But his persistence paid off. The SAS's early missions were plagued with difficulties and even significant casualties, but Stirling rapidly adapted his strategies. The new tactics were extraordinarily successful, allowing the force to significantly disrupt German logistics and communications in North Africa."

"It sounds like he was not only a military leader but also an entrepreneur in many ways," I observed.

"Exactly," the older gentleman said. "He was a disruptor in every sense of the word. His leadership style was unconventional but highly effective, characterized by personal bravery and rigorous training. Under his command, the SAS executed daring raids and destroyed hundreds of enemy aircraft, which contributed to the eventual Allied success in North Africa. His story is a testament to what one determined individual can achieve."

"What do you think drove Stirling?" I asked, legitimately curious. "Was it ego, a sense of challenge and purpose, service to his country, or something else?"

"We were told Stirling was driven by a deep sense of adventure and a desire to make a mark on the world," he reflected. "Some accounts suggest he sought to live up to his father's distinguished military career, but I believe his motivation stemmed from his experiences and visionary ideas about transforming the battlefield. He wasn't just building a legacy; he was transforming military strategy. His story is a reminder that resilience and success often result from facing and overcoming immense challenges."

"That's inspiring," I said, feeling a renewed sense of purpose and the courage to tackle the obstacles that lay ahead on the road to the SEAL program. "I guess, like Stirling, I'm looking for a way to test myself, to see what I'm truly capable of. Someone once told me that you can't get to third base with one foot still planted on second. Finding meaningful ways to push beyond our comfort zone a little each day can unlock magical opportunities that lead to lasting growth and change."

"And you will certainly discover what you are capable of soon." He chuckled, a slightly sinister smile spreading across his wrinkled face. "A strong, disciplined mind—which anyone can cultivate through daily practice—can drive us to achieve remarkable things. If you want to conquer this goal and live life to the fullest, care for your thoughts and actions as if they were your most prized possessions," the aging warrior said, raising his glass in a toast.

"Remember," he continued after our pint glasses clinked, "Stirling's motto was, 'Who dares wins.' Embrace the challenges ahead, and you'll find your own path to greatness. Readiness in life and on the battlefield is key. Just because the world is not engaged in any major conflicts at this very moment, history says opportunity lurks around every corner for a warrior's valor to be tested. Good luck on your journey, son. Accept every adversity as the gift that it is. On the battlefield of life, we are either winning or learning. It's that simple," he said, and his eyes welled with tears. The hand gripping his pint glass trembled slightly.

We touched glasses again, and each took a sip of beer while maintaining eye contact. He placed his empty glass on the bar, rose slowly, gathered his coat from a hook beneath the bar top, and patted me twice on the shoulder. And without another word he departed.

Back at the house later, energized and inspired, I told Matt about this unexpected encounter. Determined to continue the conversation, I returned to the saloon several times a week over the coming months, hoping to talk to the older gentleman once again and satisfy my now raging curiosity. I could glean so much wisdom from this man. What he had experienced. What he had seen and done. What memory had triggered his emotions in our final moment together. I never saw him again, but I never forgot what he said either.

✪

I reflect on this brief but life-altering exchange often. Clearly, I still think about it to this day. When we hear the stories of legendary military leaders, philosophers, extreme athletes, Nobel Prize winners, and successful entrepreneurs, they tend to spark in us enthusiasm, inquisitiveness, and motivation. Similarly, accounts of POWs and cancer survivors facing insurmountable challenges evoke our admiration and make us question our own degree of resilience.

But among all the stories of these extraordinary people, where do we mere mortals fit in? Is it conceivable that we, too, could attain such levels of greatness? Where would we begin? What will our contribution to the world be? If we were to take a chance and go all in, what obstacles might we face? What pain or setbacks would we experience? And what about misguided goals—if a goal is, or becomes, misguided, how and when do we know?

Let's clear something up first. Not everyone aspires to be a champion who is celebrated for their God-given talent, recognized for their diligent effort, or known as the "greatest of all time" in their chosen field. Neither do most people seek fame, title, or fortune. For many, the pursuit of immense wealth, public recognition, or the most expensive possessions holds little appeal. Instead, many of us gravitate toward more modest or private goals: simplicity, a good career, providing for our family, a minimalist lifestyle, inner peace, harmony, redemption or salvation, and everything in between. To be a great spouse or parent. A hard worker. A contributing member of society. Our ambitions may revolve around making a small yet meaningful and positive impact on others. And, of course, for many, going all in is about survival.

While one individual might dream of founding a tech start-up destined for a multibillion-dollar valuation, another might cherish a simpler existence, residing in a mud hut in Turtuk, India, sipping chai and tending a small flock of sheep. As we know, which paths we take in life can be quite unpredictable. The ambitious entrepreneur might face setbacks, make some bad decisions, and find themselves reading philosophy and playing golf within the confines of a minimum-security federal prison. The contemplative shepherd might experience a profound revelation, sell her flock, use the proceeds to buy a place in Silicon Valley, and unexpectedly rise as a tech mogul. Who knows? Life's outcomes are as varied as its beginnings. But initially, whatever path you take, your journey requires reflection, decision-making, and action.

Why would I leave a respectable job to voluntarily engage in mental, emotional, and physical torture in the Navy with only the reward of war and combat waiting patiently on the other side? Regardless of the path we choose—whether it involves academic pursuits, career decisions, marriage proposals, or base jumping from a hot-air balloon—determining the direction to go can pose a multifaceted and intimidating challenge. The struggle often stems from various psychological, social, and practical issues we face. The impetus to pursue specific goals is rooted in a complex interplay of intrinsic motivations, external influences, and personal aspirations. Whether we're driven by a desire for personal growth or we want to fulfill societal expectations, defeat our demons, or make a meaningful impact, our goals ideally should reflect our deepest values and aspirations.

And when we do decide to go all in, it is not uncommon for *negativity bias* to quickly follow. Negativity bias could also be described as fear; it's the second-guessing of our decisions as soon as we step on the battlefield of discomfort. This brain shortcut evolved as a survival mechanism and helped our ancestors quickly recognize and react to potential threats such as ravenous saber-tooth cats or bands of club-wielding marauders. As a result of negativity bias, we are more likely to remember negative, rather than positive, interactions, dwell on criticism, and respond more strongly to adverse events than to positive ones. Simply put, we spend more time focused on potential negative outcomes rather than executing on tasks we can control to bring about positive outcomes.

We allow negative thoughts to distract us from our *why*, or the reason we chose a particular path in the first place. With this in mind, how can we avoid the pitfalls of negativity bias? Should we first spend weeks or months in isolation defining our values and discovering our greater purpose? If so, how? Would that intensive process allow us to clearly see the correct path? Or is it through taking action that we uncover the pervasive truths about our passions—the greater meaning of life? I argue that considering our purpose and identifying our values play a significant role in understanding our why. But most people are unwilling to take even ten minutes a month to consider their actual goals, what they want from this short life and what purpose their existence truly holds. In my book *Embrace the Suck*, I provide the Personal Values Manifesto framework to help you define your values. The framework guides you through the process of identifying and distilling your core values into five or six meaningful words or phrases that are both actionable and measurable—a personal performance management system of sorts. Ideally, well-defined values become guiding principles that steer every decision you make and every action you take. But for how long should we sit and ponder? Is a camping trip in the desert with an ayahuasca ceremony really necessary?

Maybe. But we must not allow ourselves to be encumbered by the attitude that we will begin only when certain things are in order. "Once I have done X, then I will begin Y." "Once I 'find myself,' then and only then can I make strides toward my goals." "When everything slows down at work, then I can work on my relationships." "When I get that promotion, then I can refocus on being a better parent." No. Ideal conditions do not exist. Ever. Every moment we spend in this void robs us of the valuable time we could be spending changing the world. Yes, *changing the world.* Do not let planning and pondering turn into standard-issue procrastination.

Take action to begin the journey of discovery—it need not be bold action. It's often the smallest changes, the tiniest steps we take—supported by discipline, dedication, and follow-through—that drive us to achieve the most remarkable results.

As we pursue our goals, regardless of their magnitude, we navigate a journey of self-discovery, confront challenges, embrace successes, and experience moments of clarity. Through this process, we gain insights into what truly interests us, resonates with our values—or defines them—and inspires a sense of purpose deep within us. Each small step forward unveils new layers of understanding, whether we are trying to get in better shape, improve our marriage, earn a promotion, launch a business, purge the world of evil, deepen our faith, or kick the crap out of an incurable disease. Forward motion is key. But forward motion can be daunting, so let's take a look at that pesky nuisance we call fear.

THE BEAUTIFUL THING ABOUT FEAR

Courage is not the absence of fear, but the triumph over it.
—NELSON MANDELA

Constant training shapes the warrior, but combat is the true teacher. I became a gunfighter in a house in Iraq.

Bullets tore through the air and slammed into the wall behind us. With adrenaline surging, my teammates and I unleashed our own barrage of fire, the deafening bangs echoing in the tight quarters of the stairwell. But then, a dreaded *click*—my rifle jammed, rendering it useless.

In a heartbeat, training and instinct took over. Without pause, my right hand darted to the SIG Sauer P226 holstered at my hip, while my left hand swiftly lowered the malfunctioning rifle. With a seamless motion, I was back in the fray, sending rounds from my pistol to the intended targets.

"In the face of fear, remember your training, trust your instincts, and march forward with courage" is a popular military proverb. It encapsulates the essence of military training and the importance of remaining composed and resolute in the face of adversity. In combat, as in life, we do not rise to the occasion, we fall to the level of our preparedness. This is why Naval Special Warfare—the Navy Sea, Air, and Land (SEAL) and Special Warfare Combatant-craft Crewman (SWCC) organization—invests countless hours and resources in training, or, in corporate vernacular, in talent development. The public might assume SEALs spend all our time downrange hunting terrorists and the purveyors of evil deeds, when in actuality, we spend the majority of our time mastering our trade. Fine-tuning every detail of our craft. Maintaining peak performance of mind and body. As the Spartans believed, the more we sweat in training, the less we bleed in battle.

This is important to note as you begin to understand the purpose behind relentless routines. Building better habits through daily rituals ensures better outcomes. Yes, fear and discomfort are guaranteed. But they are blessings to be embraced and transformed into our very own superpowers.

✪

Characters in Frank Herbert's *Dune* used the "Litany Against Fear" as a mantra to maintain mental equanimity in the face of fear: "I must not fear. Fear is the mind-killer. Fear is the little death that brings total obliteration. I will face my fear. I will permit it to pass over me and through me. And when it has gone past, I will turn the inner eye to see its path. Where the fear has gone there will be nothing. Only I will remain."

Many world-renowned psychologists have explored the depths of the human psyche as it relates to fear, such luminaries as Sigmund Freud, John B. Watson, and Joseph LeDoux. I am inspired by Susan Jeffers, who is best known for her groundbreaking work in the field of psychology, particularly in how she helps individuals overcome fear and self-doubt so they can live more fulfilling lives. Her most profound work centers around the concept of fear and its impact on human behavior. In her best-selling book *Feel the Fear… and Do It Anyway*, Dr. Jeffers explores the idea that fear is a natural part of the human experience and that it can be transformed into a catalyst of personal growth and empowerment.

Through her research and teachings, Dr. Jeffers emphasizes the importance of embracing fear as a natural and inevitable aspect of life's journey. She advocates for a shift in mindset and perspective—a concept we will cover in great detail in Part 2—from one of avoidance and hesitation to one of courage, action, and resilience. By reframing fear as an opportunity for growth and self-discovery, Dr. Jeffers says, we are empowered to step outside our comfort zone, confront our fears head-on, and live with greater confidence, authenticity, and purpose. Dr. Jeffers died from a rare form of cancer in 2012, but her work continues to inspire millions of people worldwide to overcome their limiting beliefs and live life to the fullest.

Sometimes it's not as simple as we think to identify the root causes of fear. We may not be clear on why we hesitated or failed to take action at the right moment, why we didn't approach the beautiful girl in the room or failed to introduce ourselves to the keynote speaker at the conference. The list goes on. We avoid asking for help because it must mean we're weak, and we shy away from having difficult conversations and taking leaps of faith because we're afraid. We pause or an unforeseen obstacle crops up, and we cease moving forward. In that crucial split second, we hesitate on the battlefield—one weapon malfunctions, yet we don't reach for another. One resource dries up, yet we do not seek new opportunities. Why?

Fear is often fueled by a low tolerance for risk, by ambiguity, by uncertainty. An ancient philosopher once said, "Fear causes hesitation, and hesitation will cause your worst fears to come true." Wait, no, I think it was Bodhi, Patrick Swayze's character in the original version of *Point Break*, who said that. But my point is, we "what if" ourselves to death: What if I put myself out there and get rejected? What if I make a dramatic career shift and it ends in epic failure? What if I finally tell my boss that I will no longer tolerate his verbal abuse and get fired? What if I fling myself from that hot-air balloon and only then realize I forgot my parachute? What then?

Three Pillars of Fear

We must endure one of two inevitable pains in this life: the pain of action and discipline, or the pain of fear and regret. It's our choice. Here are a few reasons why we might find it difficult to choose a path, take action, or take even the first step toward any goal, for that matter. I refer to them as the Three Pillars of Fear. Although each of these reasons can be situational, consider which one you trend toward most frequently.

FEAR OF CHOICE: OVERWHELMING POSSIBILITIES AND INFORMATION OVERLOAD

The paradox of choice presents a seemingly limitless array of options—careers, lifestyles, and obligations—that leads to decision fatigue and disengagement. Too many choices can cripple us with cognitive dissonance, the mental discomfort of holding conflicting beliefs at the same time. The result is often *analysis paralysis*, where the abundance of information fuels endless deliberation with no action.

Social comparison, when we compare ourselves to others, amplifies indecision. Platforms like social media expose us to curated lives that tend to make us feel self-doubt. Stanford psychologist Carol Dweck highlights how certain individuals view others' success as barriers to their own success rather than as inspiration, so social comparison can further hinder action.

Overcoming Fear of Choice

Narrow your focus by leaning into your values. Create an environment that reduces decision fatigue and take decisive action. The sting of regret is far more enduring than the discomfort of moving forward in the face of fear. Run your own race, and measure your progress against your past self's progress, not others'. Growth lies in embracing your mistakes, learning from them, and pressing on.

FEAR OF COMMITMENT: COMMITMENT PHOBIA AND THE WHAT-IF SYNDROME

The fear of regret—making the wrong choices or missing out—can paralyze decision-making. Yet, the deeper regret often lies in never trying. At age sixty, would you rather say, "I tried and learned," or "I wish I had"?

Perfectionism compounds this fear because it stokes anxiety about finding the "perfect" choice. Inaction is the result despite the well-known truth: Perfection is unattainable. As we'd say in the SEAL Teams, "Good enough is good to go." Excellence is born from action, not endless deliberation.

Overcoming Fear of Commitment

The perceived consequences of failure—social, financial, or personal—can loom large. Yet failure is not final unless we stop moving forward. True growth comes from seeing setbacks not as defeats but as valuable lessons. Winning or learning—these are the only two options. So make your move.

FEAR OF UNMET EXPECTATIONS: SOCIETAL NORMS AND CULTURAL STANDARDS

External pressures put on us by family, cultural expectations, or societal norms often conflict with our passions. This dissonance between what we *should* do and what we *want* to do can stifle ambition. Imagine if Denzel Washington or J. K. Rowling had conformed to their skeptics' expectations. The world would have missed their brilliance.

Society's metrics of success—wealth, status, prestige—rarely align with individual definitions of fulfillment. Surrounding yourself with people who inspire you and share your values can counteract this pressure. Positive peer influence fosters alignment with your goals and aspirations.

Overcoming Fear of Unmet Expectations

Mentors and role models play a critical role in helping us navigate expectations. The right guidance opens pathways, prevents missteps, and inspires action. True mentors are those who invest selflessly in your success, expecting nothing in return. Introspection, deliberate action, and embracing risk are key to overcoming societal pressures. Surround yourself with uplifting influences and seek mentors who align with your values. Understanding that doubt and struggle contribute to growth will transform your hesitation into purposeful progress, helping you forge a path aligned with your truest self.

Even Alexander the Great had a mentor. You may have heard of him, some philosopher by the name of Aristotle. Aristotle tutored Alexander from the time Alexander was thirteen to sixteen and taught him a wide range of subjects, including philosophy, science, medicine, and literature. This education played a significant role in shaping Alexander's approach to leadership and conquest.

During Alexander the Great's conquests in what is now Afghanistan, he faced numerous challenges, including daunting mountain passes and fierce resistance from local tribes. In seemingly endless and extremely bold displays of leadership, Alexander often led his army from the front—riding days ahead of the siege train through the high mountain passes, ascending steep cliffs, climbing to dizzying heights despite precarious footing. He wore no fancy armor or even warm clothing. To lead, you have to bleed. Figuratively and, in some cases, literally.

Legend has it that, as Alexander's army approached the formidable cliffs of the Hindu Kush, his soldiers grew increasingly fearful of the treacherous terrain and the fierce warriors who awaited them. Despite trembling with fear, witnessing their courageous leader boldly forging ahead, his soldiers found the will to press on. Inspired by Alexander's unwavering determination and resolve, they overcame their fear and conquered the nearly insurmountable obstacles before them.

We win more when suffering is a team sport. It is no different in SEAL training or on the battlefield. Which is why the final line of the Navy SEAL Ethos states:

> Brave SEALs have fought and died building the proud tradition and feared reputation that I am bound to uphold. In the worst of conditions, the legacy of my teammates steadies my resolve and silently guides my every deed. I will not fail.

Stoicism is a school of philosophy with roots in ancient Greece. One prominent aspect of Stoic philosophy is distinguishing between what is within our control (our thoughts, attitudes, and actions) and what is not (external events, outcomes, and the actions of others). We must understand and accept that some things are beyond our control.

A key Stoic teaching related to fear is the concept of *apatheia*, which is often translated as "freedom from passion" or "imperturbability." Stoics believed that through rational self-discipline and philosophical reflection, we could achieve a state of inner calm and tranquility, even in fear-inducing situations. This involves cultivating a mindset of acceptance, resilience, and courage, as well as practicing techniques such as negative visualization (imagining worst-case scenarios to prepare yourself mentally—although I recommend using this one sparingly) and focusing on the present moment rather than worrying about the future. This exact mindset is one of the fundamental drivers of success for students navigating the early weeks and months of SEAL training—especially Hell Week.

Throughout the years, I've remained committed to giving back to the community that gave so much to me. As part of this commitment, I've mentored numerous SEAL hopefuls through the savage training and selection process, which is widely regarded as one of the most challenging military programs worldwide. On one occasion, I reached out to my friend and former BUD/S classmate David Goggins, a retired SEAL turned globally acclaimed extreme athlete. I sought his words of encouragement for a mentee who had tragically lost his mother to a brain aneurysm that suddenly burst just a week before he began his training. My mentee's class was a few weeks into the first phase of training and two days away from Hell Week, the brutal trial designed to filter out those who are not all in. True to form, Goggins responded with a message that encapsulates the mindset that employs negative visualization and being fully present in each moment. He said:

> Please tell him that my words will make no difference when he is more cold and miserable than he could ever imagine. Men don't get many chances to show their grit! You need to pray for bad weather!
>
> Pray for the coldest water! Pray for a broken body! You should want the worst-case scenario in all aspects of Hell Week! Pray for it to be so hard that only your boat crew makes it all the way through! They make it through because you lead them through the worst Hell Week ever!
>
> You have to become the devil to get through Hell! This is all about your mindset! If you are hoping for the best-case scenario in Hell Week, you are not ready! Know that no one can endure what you can. Not because you believe in yourself. But because you have trained harder than anyone alive!
>
> You might think this is a motivational speech! Well it's not! This is my mentality before I tackle any challenge! Hell Week is not for the weak! It's for that person looking for the beginning of his soul! You want to see where most people end, and you begin! Be that guy; when everyone is in pain and miserable with their heads hanging low, you're the one smiling! Not a friendly smile, but one that says, "You think this pain can hurt me?!"
>
> This is your time to start creating the man you want to be! You can't make that man in a soft environment! You must be willing to suffer more than any other man! Not because you have to, but because you want to!
>
> I leave you with this: Many people are looking for hard shit to prove themselves, but once the hard shit comes, the reality is too much to bear. Be watching for "the look"! You will know it once you see it! It looks like their soul is leaving their body.
>
> It happens during deep suffering, when a person can no longer handle the mental pain and suffering of what they

thought they could do. The key word is "thought" they could do! After you see the look, quitting is very near.

My question to you is this: What are you going to do when you are cold and miserable? What are you going to do when your body is broke as hell and you have fifty hours left? What are you going to do when your boat crew starts to quit and you feel alone? What are you going to do when it won't stop raining and you can't get warm? I don't know what you're going to do. But you asked me for my advice, so here's what I did: I prayed to God to make it worse! Mindset!

Go to war with yourself!

Ultimately, Stoic philosophy encourages individuals to confront their fears with rationality, courage, and acceptance and to recognize that fear often arises from our perceptions and judgments rather than from the external world itself. Stoics believed that by cultivating our inner strength and resilience, and reframing our perspective, we could overcome fear and achieve a state of inner peace in any circumstance.

THE PRINCIPLES OF GOAL SELECTION

There is nothing noble in being superior to your fellow man;
true nobility is being superior to your former self.
—ERNEST HEMINGWAY

We must caution ourselves against unquenchable ambition. Going all in doesn't mean pursuing every opportunity with reckless abandon but rather focusing on the most significant goals and actions. Our core resources—time, talent, and energy—are finite, particularly time. Talent can be developed; energy, replenished. But time...we get what we get. So, before plunging into the unknown, it's crucial we scrutinize our motivations.

Consider Diana Nyad, renowned for long-distance swimming. She embodies a remarkable blend of ambition, talent, resilience, and just the right touch of bold eccentricity. Her decision to pursue the seemingly impossible goal of swimming from Cuba to Florida at the age of sixty-four was driven by a combination of personal passion, resilience, and a desire to challenge the limitations of age. Nyad made several attempts over a thirty-five-year period from 1978 to 2013, but even after failing to complete the swim in previous attempts, Nyad was determined to achieve her lifelong dream and prove that age should not be a barrier to pursuing ambitious goals. She completed the swim without a shark cage on September 2–3, 2013.

Despite facing numerous obstacles, including challenges in fundraising and resource allocation, jellyfish stings, strong currents, and extreme fatigue, Nyad remained undeterred in pursuit of her goal. Her determination and steadfast belief in her ability to succeed sustained her throughout the grueling journey.

Additionally, Nyad saw this swim as an opportunity to inspire others and demonstrate the power of perseverance and resilience in the face of adversity. By publicly documenting her journey and sharing her story with the world, she hoped to encourage people of all ages to pursue their dreams and push beyond their perceived limitations. Once again, a common theme emerges: The key to success involves unyielding goal pursuit and giving to others along the way.

But was there something more fueling this decades-long quest? Nyad has spoken openly about experiencing trauma in her early life, including childhood sexual abuse by her coach, which may have contributed to her resilience and determination to overcome other challenges later in life. While it's difficult to determine the precise impact trauma may have had on Nyad's pursuit of her goal, it's likely that those hardships helped shape her character and served as a catalyst for her relentless drive to succeed.

Ultimately, Nyad's decision to embark on this extraordinary challenge came from a deep-seated desire to prove to herself and others that age should never be a barrier to achieving greatness. Her remarkable feat serves as a testament to the indomitable human spirit and the power of perseverance in chasing one's dreams.

✪

In the lively Delta Sky Lounge at JFK Airport, amid the hum of conversation, clinking glasses, and hurried travelers, I found a quiet corner with a team member, a behavioral psychology PhD, to reflect on the day's meeting with Delta executives. We had time before our flight, so I delved into a question that had been on my mind: What drives people to pursue specific goals, and how can leaders tap into these motivations to elevate employees' performance?

"Why do we go after some goals and not others?" I asked. "Really, what are the core drivers of those choices?" I was eager to connect his insights to both my personal growth path and the workforce performance and collaboration software we were developing.

"It's actually pretty complex," he began. "One foundational theory is Deci and Ryan's self-determination theory, which highlights individuals' three core needs: autonomy, competence, and relatedness. When these are met, motivation and well-being soar. For leaders, understanding this can dramatically improve engagement."

He explained autonomy as the need for control over our actions, competence as the drive for mastery, and relatedness as the desire for connection. Together, these elements create intrinsic motivation. "Align goals with these needs, and you unlock commitment and satisfaction," he said.

We explored how expectations and perceived value also influence goal pursuit, referencing Victor Vroom's expectancy theory and Albert Bandura's concept of self-efficacy, our belief in our ability to succeed. "Self-efficacy grows through mastery experiences, observing others' successes, and encouragement," he said, and then emphasized the role of self-efficacy in resilience.

I asked him about procrastination, and he pointed to temporal motivation theory, which explains why people often delay tasks: As deadlines approach, the perceived value of completing the task increases, which creates a sense of urgency. He elaborated, "People tend to prioritize immediate rewards over distant ones, which is why procrastination happens. To combat this, setting clear deadlines and offering incremental rewards can help people maintain focus and motivation."

As we walked through the bustling airport to catch a flight back to San Diego, I pressed further: "What principles can guide goal setting and help leaders and individuals make better choices?"

He outlined six actionable principles:

1. **ALIGNMENT WITH VALUES AND PASSIONS:** Goals rooted in personal values create deep meaning and drive. When your goals align with who you are, motivation is intrinsic.

2. **SPECIFICITY AND CLARITY:** Clear, measurable goals provide direction and focus. If an objective or milestone can't be actioned or measured, it is not a goal.

3. **FEASIBILITY AND REALISM:** Achievable milestones build momentum, but lofty goals—if wrapped in realistic plans—can stretch potential.

4. **SUSTAINABILITY AND LONG-TERM IMPACT:** Visualizing the lasting effects of your goals fosters resilience and ensures you choose goals that align with your broader life aspirations.

5. **BALANCE AND DIVERSITY:** When you pursue goals across various aspects of life—career, relationships, health—your motivation is maintained and burnout is prevented.

6. **SOCIAL SUPPORT AND ACCOUNTABILITY:** Sharing goals and seeking regular feedback significantly increase the likelihood of success.

"Ultimately, it's about aligning actions with deeper motivations and crafting disciplined systems to sustain momentum," he said as we reached the gate.

As I stepped onto the jetway, a renewed sense of clarity coursed through me. These principles weren't just theoretical insights but also a call to action that would guide my journey while also providing innovative solutions for the software my company was developing. Goals, much like life itself, demand we have clear vision, discipline, and purpose. It is the harmonious blend of meaningful aspirations and deliberate action that transforms dreams into impactful achievements.

✪

Setting meaningful goals demands a balance of ambition, realism, and perseverance. Although the journey may be fraught with fear and uncertainty, it is in those initial, deliberate steps that growth and transformation begin. Fear, far from being a barrier, can serve as a compass, pointing us toward opportunities for personal and professional development. By embracing the risks inherent in reaching our aspirations, we build resilience and adaptability—qualities that propel us forward, even in adversity.

True success lies not merely in reaching the destination but also in the transformation we undergo along the way. Each courageous step, no matter how small, is a testament to our determination and capacity to grow. Purpose is the force that sustains us in this pursuit; purpose guides us through chaos and fuels our progress when the way forward feels unclear. Achieving the most meaningful milestones is about embracing discomfort, facing fear, and committing to something greater than ourselves.

GOING *ALL IN*

TO ACCESS YOUR ALL IN WORKSPACE, VISIT APP.EXLR8.AI/ALL-IN

WHAT DRIVES MY GOALS?

Reflection
In this chapter, we explored the psychology behind goal setting, emphasizing that our aspirations are rarely random. They often emerge from a blend of personal values, external influences, and a desire for growth. From Diana Nyad's relentless pursuit of successfully swimming across from Cuba to a founder's realization that they are the leader their organization needs, the question isn't just *what* you want but *why* you want it.

Action
Reflect on your deepest motivations. Why are you pursuing your current goals? Write down three to five key drivers for each goal. Are the goals aligned with your values and purpose? If not, consider how you might realign your goals to reflect what truly matters to you.

HOW DO I RESPOND TO FEAR AND UNCERTAINTY?

Reflection
Fear is an inevitable companion on the journey to achieving meaningful goals. It's not the absence of fear but how we respond to it that defines our success. Whether it's the Navy SEAL Ethos of embracing adversity or our fear of criticism and failure, the most transformative outcomes arise when we lean into discomfort.

Action

Identify one fear or source of hesitation that's holding you back from pursuing a goal. Write it down and dissect it: What's the worst that could happen if you face it? How might overcoming this fear contribute to your growth? Develop a small action step to confront it head-on and reframe it as an opportunity.

ARE MY GOALS DESIGNED FOR SUSTAINABLE SUCCESS?

Reflection

Goals that align with your intrinsic motivations, embrace long-term impact, and consider balance are more likely to lead to self-fulfillment. As highlighted in this chapter, lofty ambitions like Diana Nyad's ocean swim or Alexander the Great's conquest of the Hindu Kush require vision and sustainability to ensure their pursuit doesn't lead to burnout or misaligned priorities.

Action

Evaluate one of your major goals. Does it balance ambition with realism? Does it consider diverse aspects of your life—health, relationships, career, personal growth? Adjust your plan to include milestones that celebrate progress, foster balance, and account for the support system you need to stay on track.

2

PASSION, PAIN, AND THE POWER OF PURPOSEFUL ROUTINES

Masters of industry, thought leaders of society, and heroes of civilization live challenging lives. Some of the hardships they must face stem from the inevitable ebbs and flows of human existence. Yet much of their journey is meticulously crafted with purposeful intention. They endure, work through pain, and relentlessly push their limits to master their mind, body, and spirit. Their ambition knows no bounds, their drive is ceaseless, and their determination remains ferocious as they strive to fully realize their grandest potential—all in pursuit of causes greater than themselves. The primary way all great history makers unlock their superpower is through well-crafted routines that sharpen their focus and unleash their passion.

The Latin root of the word *passion* means "to suffer," and extraordinary individuals are willing to suffer for their visions, ideals, and aspirations. They endure suffering to enhance their skills and they make sacrifices to achieve greatness, often experiencing immense anguish intentionally as they perfect their craft and resist temptations. Their suffering isn't just personal; they bear it for the betterment of others.

When we fail to harness our potential, we are robbing the world of the immense value our greatness can bring. A lack of discipline is an act of disrespect to ourselves and those who rely on us. We all have a responsibility to develop and share our God-given talents for the greater good.

I AM THE MASTER OF MY FATE

I am the master of my fate. I am the captain of my soul.
—WILLIAM ERNEST HENLEY

Late on a quiet Monday evening at SEAL Team 5 headquarters in Coronado, California, the energy of unparalleled performance lingered in the air. I had just checked in that morning; I was the new guy then, grappling with equal parts excitement and apprehension. Although the grueling training of BUD/S was behind me, it was clear that my journey was far from over. Standing in my cage—a small, chain-linked storage area—I was lost in thought as I organized my newly issued gear when a familiar voice broke my focus.

"Hey, brother! Just checked in?" It was Mathew, a seasoned SEAL and former instructor from my recent training days. Shirtless, sweat glistening after a rigorous workout, his thoroughly tattooed frame exuded the confidence of a warrior who had been forged in adversity. The type of formidable presence that says to terrorists, "You're not the bad guys, we are."

"Making it here is just the beginning," he said, shaking my hand in the kind of firm, knowing grip that carries the weight of experience. I asked what he meant, eager to understand. "Training prepares you for continuous improvement," Mathew explained. "In the Teams, we hold ourselves accountable—extreme ownership is the standard. We never stop learning or striving for excellence."

My eyes landed on one of Mathew's tattoos: INVICTUS was etched boldly on his forearm. When I asked about its significance, his tone turned reflective. "It means 'unconquered.' It's a reminder of my faith in God and the inner strength He gives us—inspired by the poem by William Ernest Henley." He recited its final lines: "*I am the master of my fate / I am the captain of my soul.*"

Those words resonated deeply with me and capture the ethos of the SEAL Teams—a commitment to face adversity with resolute resolve. To remain disciplined. To grow continuously. "It's not just about tactics," Mathew said. "We train our minds as much as our bodies. Every challenge shapes us, every mission sharpens us. It's a way of life."

He shared more as our conversation unfolded. Pointing to another tattoo, a Spartan shield on his shoulder, he said, "It's a nod to the Spartans, their unyielding discipline and their ethos of service. They trained incessantly, not just for their own survival but also for the greater good of their people. That's our purpose too—to protect those who can't protect themselves."

Mathew's words were a powerful reminder that excellence isn't a destination but a process, an enduring pursuit of betterment. "We dominate the battlefield because we never accomplish anything alone, as you know from your training. We're a brotherhood. And in the worst of conditions, it's the legacy of our teammates that steadies our resolve and guides our every deed. Welcome to the Teams," he said. Then he turned and walked down the corridor.

As Mathew's footsteps faded, the gravity of his words settled over me like a weighty cloak. His message was a call to action and a reminder of the immense responsibility I now carried. The path ahead would demand far more than physical skill or brute strength; it would require the unshakable discipline of continuous improvement, unyielding resilience to endure the trials, and the humility to trust in the brotherhood that would stand beside me.

Alone in my cage, surrounded by the tools of a warrior's trade, I felt the burden of this path press against my chest. This was no ordinary commitment—it was a covenant. A pledge to something far greater than myself. There was no room for hesitation; the mission, the Naval Special Warfare community, and the legacy of my teammates demanded nothing less than my absolute best.

THE FIVE TRUTHS ABOUT
HABIT-BUILDING ROUTINES

There is nothing outside of yourself that can ever enable you to get better, stronger, richer, quicker, or smarter. Everything is within.
—MIYAMOTO MUSASHI

Consider Miyamoto Musashi as another example of how routines lead to success. He was essentially the Tom Brady (the GOAT) of the samurai hundreds of years ago. Musashi, born in 1584 in Japan, is celebrated as a legendary swordsman, strategist, and philosopher. His life and teachings have influenced martial arts, military strategy, and the broader cultural landscape of Japan. Musashi was born into a samurai family in Harima Province, where his father, Munisai, an accomplished martial artist, likely provided his initial training. From an early age, Musashi demonstrated an exceptional aptitude for swordsmanship. At the age of thirteen, he fought his first duel and defeated a samurai named Arima Kigei. This marked the beginning of his *musha shugyō*, or warrior's pilgrimage, aimed at honing his skills through real combat experiences, similar to the *agoge* of Sparta. Musashi engaged in numerous duels and reportedly won all by employing unconventional techniques and psychological strategies that bewildered his opponents. At age thirteen, most of us were complaining about having our braces tightened and stressing about being late to soccer practice. Not Miyamoto. He was slicing and dicing his way to glory town!

One of Musashi's most famous duels took place in 1612 against Sasaki Kojiro, a swordsman known for his formidable skill and use of the long sword. Musashi defeated Kojiro using a wooden sword fashioned from an oar after intentionally arriving late to the duel as a way to disrupt Kojiro's focus, demonstrating Musashi's mastery of psychological warfare. As he matured, Musashi expanded his focus beyond martial prowess. He delved into philosophy, strategy, and the arts, emphasizing Bushido, the way of the warrior, and integrating martial arts with broader spiritual and philosophical principles.

In 1645, Musashi wrote his magnum opus, *Go Rin No Sho* (*The Book of Five Rings*), a penetrating treatise on strategy, tactics, and philosophy structured around five books named after the elements: Earth, Water, Fire, Wind, and Void. So, before we dive into the five truths of habit-building routines, let's look at Musashi's five core principles. By understanding Musashi's approach to strategy and self-mastery, we can draw parallels to the art of creating routines that are not only practical but also deeply aligned with our purpose and personal growth.

The Book of Earth

The Book of Earth teaches the importance of mastering foundational skills before advancing, a principle deeply rooted in the samurai's discipline. This approach emphasizes the necessity of grounding oneself in the basics, of both personal growth and professional success.

In life, this means focusing on core values and habits such as discipline and self-care to create a solid base for tackling complex challenges. In work, it highlights the value of mastering fundamentals, such as coding basics for a software developer or understanding consumer behavior for a marketer, to build expertise and adaptability. This foundational mastery requires patience, humility, and resolute refinement.

Like Musashi's insistence on perfecting basic stances and strikes, the pursuit of excellence lies in repetition and continuous learning. Building a resilient base allows us to face challenges with confidence, grow incrementally, and achieve lasting success.

The Book of Water

The Book of Water draws parallels between the adaptability of water and the need for flexibility in life and work. Musashi's metaphor emphasizes the importance of flowing with change rather than resisting it.

This principle applies equally to all areas of life, emphasizing the need for adaptability and openness as foundational traits. In our personal lives, it encourages us to embrace new experiences, seek creative solutions, and foster resilience in the face of adversity. Professionally, adaptability is indispensable to thriving in industries shaped by rapid advancements and constant evolution.

Emotional and mental flexibility—remaining composed under pressure, valuing diverse perspectives, and collaborating effectively with others—are also vital. By embodying the fluid and transformative nature of water, we can navigate life's challenges with creativity and grace, unlocking opportunities for growth and success in both personal and professional realms.

The Book of Fire

The Book of Fire highlights the power of decisiveness and focused action. In battle, hesitation can be fatal.

In life, inaction often leads to missed opportunities. This principle teaches us to approach challenges assertively, make bold decisions, and act with purpose. In our work, this means taking initiative and being proactive, even in uncertain circumstances. It also involves understanding the psychological dynamics of confrontation—knowing when to stand firm and when to deescalate. The *Book of Fire* encourages us to channel focused aggression and inner determination to push through obstacles with resilience and a tenacious drive for excellence.

The Book of Wind

The Book of Wind emphasizes the value of understanding broader strategies and perspectives. To refine his own techniques, Musashi critiqued other schools of swordsmanship, demonstrating the importance of learning from diverse approaches.

Avoid narrow-mindedness and seek broader context. In business, leaders must stay informed about market trends, competitor strategies, and emerging opportunities. Interdisciplinary knowledge fosters collaboration, innovation, and adaptability. By continuously learning from various perspectives, we can anticipate challenges and develop more effective strategies.

The Book of Void

The Book of Void delves into the spiritual and philosophical dimensions of mastery. It explores the concept of emptiness, which is when we cultivate clarity and shed preconceived notions to see situations as they truly are. This state of mental openness fosters creativity and innovation.

Mastery, Musashi argues, transcends technique; it's about internalizing skills to the point they become intuitive, spontaneous actions. This applies across fields, from the scientist solving complex problems instinctively to the musician expressing emotion beyond mere notes. In relationships and leadership, clarity and intuition enable effective decision-making and deeper connections.

The Book of Void teaches that true fulfillment lies in this balance of mastery, creativity, and clarity. By embracing emptiness and intuitive action, we achieve growth, deepen our relationships, and find greater purpose in our pursuits.

✪

Miyamoto Musashi's life and methodologies exemplify the indefatigable pursuit of excellence, the integration of physical and spiritual disciplines, and the timeless principles of strategy and fortitude. His legacy as a legendary swordsman and philosopher continues to resonate, offering valuable insights into the nuances of the human condition.

THE FIVE TRUTHS OF HABIT-BUILDING ROUTINES

On the battleground of self-mastery, world-class willpower isn't an inherent gift but a skill honed through persistent practice. Picture personal discipline and willpower as a muscle, growing stronger with each stretch and exertion. The samurai would deliberately craft hardships to forge unbreakable discipline. In the same fashion, special operators intentionally pursue hardship and the disciplined daily practice of their most important skills in pursuit of their core mission: continuous improvement.

As the Navy SEAL Ethos states:

> We demand discipline. We expect innovation. The lives of my teammates and the success of our mission depend on me— my technical skill, tactical proficiency, and attention to detail. My training is never complete. We train for war and fight to win. I stand ready to bring the full spectrum of combat power to bear in order to achieve my mission and the goals established by my country. The execution of my duties will be swift and violent when required yet guided by the very principles that I serve to defend. Brave men have fought and died building the proud tradition and feared reputation that I am bound to uphold. In the worst of conditions, the legacy of my teammates steadies my resolve and silently guides my every deed. I will not fail.

Even the strongest willpower requires moments of rest and recovery, because it can flag over time. True victory is attained through steadfast consistency; honoring your commitments cultivates a sense of self-respect. The dedication demonstrated in private practice inevitably reflects in public performance. The essence of self-discipline lies in the continual practice of challenging yet essential tasks, even at the height of discomfort. For it is in this crucible that true warriors are forged.

So, here is a fundamental truth about cultivating high-performance habits: Effective routines—relentlessly pursued—play a fundamental role in building good habits and breaking free from bad ones because they provide structure for and reinforce desired behaviors. Here are some key fundamentals.

Habit-Building Truths: A Practical Guide to Transformation

TRUTH 1: CONSISTENCY

Consistency is the foundation of habit formation. Regularly repeating actions ingrains them into the brain's neural pathways, making behaviors automatic and reducing reliance on willpower. For example, a morning workout initially requires effort but over time becomes second nature. Similarly, starting the workday with your most challenging task—after a purposeful morning ritual—ensures priorities are addressed with maximum energy and focus. Consistent routines anchor discipline, conserve mental energy, and set the stage for sustained personal and professional growth.

TRUTH 2: CUE-ROUTINE-REWARD LOOP

The cue–routine–reward cycle, a concept rooted in behavioral psychology and popularized by Charles Duhigg in *The Power of Habit*, explains how habits form and are reinforced. This cycle begins with a **cue**, a signal or trigger that prompts the behavior. The **routine** is the action or activity itself, and the **reward** is the satisfying outcome that reinforces the behavior, encouraging its repetition.

Consider this cycle in practice: waking up to an alarm (cue), completing a morning workout (routine), followed by enjoying a cup of coffee or meditation session (reward). Over time, the brain associates the cue with the reward, making the routine automatic. This process not only builds consistency but also reduces reliance on willpower. Whether you are building personal wellness routines, improving work productivity, or refining a specific skill, this cycle provides a framework for creating habits that endure and drive purpose.

TRUTH 3: ENVIRONMENTAL DESIGN

The concept that your environment shapes your habits, which has existed for centuries but has been more recently popularized by James Clear in *Atomic Habits*, emphasizes how external surroundings influence internal actions. A well-designed environment reduces reliance on willpower by aligning your surroundings with the behaviors you want to cultivate and eliminating distractions.

For example, creating a distraction-free workspace fosters productivity; laying out workout gear the night before sets a visual cue for exercise. Stocking your kitchen with nutritious foods while keeping unhealthy snacks out of sight supports better eating habits. Similarly, disabling phone notifications or using apps to limit screen time minimizes distractions. Thoughtfully designing your environment creates a feedback loop in which positive behaviors feel natural and reinforce habits that align your actions with your goals.

TRUTH 4: GRADUAL PROGRESSION

"Slow is smooth, and smooth is fast." This saying is the foundation of the training methodology in the SEAL Teams. Effective habit formation thrives on incremental progress. By setting small, achievable goals and consistently building on them, you expand your comfort zone, foster confidence, and create a foundation for lasting growth.

A shining example of this is British Cycling's transformation under Dave Brailsford. His philosophy of seeking 1 percent daily improvements—whether in bike aerodynamics, rider nutrition, sleep quality, or even the comfort of their pillows—led to unprecedented success. Pillow comfort is essential for SEAL Teams' success on the battlefield too!

These seemingly minor adjustments, which compound over time, turned a historically underperforming team into world champions and led to multiple Tour de France victories and Olympic gold medals. Gradual progress activates the brain's reward system with each small win, strengthens neural pathways through repetition, and embeds sustainable habits that lead to extraordinary results.

TRUTH 5: FEEDBACK AND REFLECTION

Constructive feedback drives continuous improvement. Positive reinforcement activates the brain's reward system, motivating further progress. Reflection helps refine routines, identify areas for improvement, and adapt strategies. High performers embrace feedback to ensure their efforts align with their goals. They hone their focus while celebrating incremental successes. This iterative process transforms habits into lifelong strengths.

THE TAKEAWAY

Mastering these truths empowers you to create habits that stick, break free from unproductive cycles, and achieve meaningful change. Through consistency, intentional design, incremental progress, and thoughtful reflection, you can build a foundation for personal and professional excellence and pave the way for a life of purpose, strength, and success.

My original intent with this book was for me to serve as a living testament to transformation, assuring readers that the frameworks I present are both authentic and deeply rooted in lived experience. As I perform the final edits to this book, I stand at the fifteen-month milestone of my lifelong sobriety journey. While writing, I meticulously redesigned my morning routine and daily rituals and wove back in elements of my rigorous preparation for the Navy. The evolution has been life-changing: My energy levels, mental clarity, productivity, stress management, relationships, and leadership skills have all ascended to new heights.

My marriage is flourishing, and I am fully present with my children, despite the demands of my work. At my company, I have pinpointed critical opportunities in our business strategy and spearheaded a complete transformation. We've shifted from traditional management consulting to pioneering an AI-powered collaboration and performance enhancement SaaS platform that is set to revolutionize the workforce technology industry. With significant capital raised, we are now aggressively executing our go-to-market strategy. By the time this book is published, we will have been in operation as a SaaS company for over a year. My vision for both my personal life and professional endeavors has never been clearer. And I say this with deep humility and a rather deep sense of regret: Could I have achieved these personal and professional transformations earlier? Could I have sidestepped the pitfalls and preserved relationships that suffered along the way? Most likely, yes.

Yet, all this began with the simple yet powerful act of breaking bad habits and building more effective routines. This journey underscores the immense power of consistent, incremental improvements and the immense impact they can have on every aspect of our lives.

Now, with a newfound understanding of how harnessing the power of routines can transform our lives and work, it's time for profound introspection. We must take a deep dive into auditing our existing routines, scrutinizing how we spend our time and evaluating the positive, neutral, and negative impacts of our current rituals. This self-audit is not just an exercise but also a pivotal step toward consciously crafting a life of remarkable results and lasting fulfillment.

The path to unlocking our fullest potential is not forged overnight but through the deliberate design of our daily lives. As we've seen, the great masters and heroes of history achieved remarkable feats by embracing purposeful routines that sharpened their focus and unleashed their passions. Their discipline was about personal excellence and contributing something greater to the world. By breaking free from detrimental habits and establishing empowering routines, we honor ourselves and those who depend on us.

GOING *ALL IN*

TO ACCESS YOUR ALL IN WORKSPACE, VISIT APP.EXLR8.AI/ALL-IN

ARE MY CURRENT ROUTINES SUPPORTING THE PERSON I WANT TO BECOME?

Reflection
The stories of SEALs, Spartans, and great thinkers like Musashi remind us that routines shape identity. Your daily habits—how you start your mornings, approach work, and spend your evenings—either build momentum toward your goals or create barriers. Reflect on whether your routines align with the person you aspire to become or whether they need recalibration. Are your actions each day pushing you closer to excellence or holding you back?

Action

Conduct a self-audit. Write down your daily routines and evaluate their impact. Label each habit as "positive," "neutral," or "negative." Then, identify one negative habit to replace with a more productive one. For example, swap mindless social scrolling with twenty minutes of reading or a morning walk to set a productive tone for the day.

HOW DO I HANDLE SETBACKS OR BREAKDOWNS IN MY ROUTINE?

Reflection

Even the most disciplined individuals, like Navy SEALs and world-class athletes, encounter setbacks. What sets them apart is their ability to adapt and recommit. Setbacks aren't failures but opportunities to refine your approach. When routines falter, do you spiral into guilt and inaction, or do you analyze what went wrong and reengage with intention?

Action

The next time you miss a routine or encounter a setback, pause and reflect. Ask yourself: What caused the disruption? What adjustments can I make to prevent it in the future? Implement one small change—whether it's setting an earlier bedtime to ensure a productive morning or placing a reminder on your calendar for critical habits.

AM I PRIORITIZING INCREMENTAL PROGRESS OVER PERFECTION?

Reflection

Mastery doesn't come from grand gestures but from small, consistent actions repeated over time. Whether it's the 1 percent improvements philosophy or the patient practice of Musashi's swordsmanship, incremental progress builds the foundation for greatness. Are you setting manageable goals that allow for steady growth, or are you chasing perfection, only to feel overwhelmed?

Action

Identify one long-term goal and break it into smaller, actionable steps. For instance, if you aim to improve fitness, start with a twenty-minute daily walk rather than a full marathon training regimen. Celebrate each small win to build momentum. Remember: Slow is smooth, and smooth is fast. Consistent progress, no matter how small, compounds into extraordinary results.

These insights remind us that purposeful routines are not just about productivity—they are a statement of who we are becoming. With each deliberate action, you are carving a path toward the best version of yourself.

3

UNLOCKING OPPORTUNITY

A Routines Reality Check

In our ceaseless hunt for success, we often overlook the most fundamental aspect of our lives: where we invest our time and energy. Imagine if every minute of your day was intentionally organized to optimize your talents and make progress toward your goals. Reflecting on and analyzing our daily routines can unlock the opportunity for game-changing transformation and guide us to redesign our lives for optimal success in both personal and professional spheres. So, let's embark on a journey of self-discovery, one that will challenge you to scrutinize the habits that shape your existence and envision a life where each action is a deliberate step toward your most desired outcomes.

As we delve into the intricacies of our daily routines, we uncover the subtle ways in which our choices either propel us toward greatness or hinder our progress. By thoughtfully evaluating where we invest our time and energy, we can identify the patterns that serve us and those that don't. This process of introspection is not merely about productivity; it is about aligning our lives with our deepest values and passions. Through this conscious redesign, we can create a harmonious balance that fuels our ambitions, enriches our lives, and leads to a state of fulfillment and sustained achievement. Let us take this opportunity to reimagine our routines to craft a life that is not only successful but also deeply meaningful.

As Winston Churchill said, "Success is not final, failure is not fatal. It is the courage to continue that counts." So, let's go.

WHAT GOT YOU HERE WON'T GET YOU THERE

The best time to change is when you don't have to.
—MARSHALL GOLDSMITH

My legs dangled freely from the open door of the UH-60 helicopter, a gust of wind tousling my shaggy hair as we glided effortlessly over the ever-changing landscape. Sand dunes stretched out like waves frozen in time, punctuated by clusters of mud huts and patches of palm groves. With gloved hands, I adjusted my headphones, the familiar strains of "Bodies" by Drowning Pool literally drowning out the hum of the aircraft's engines. Each small movement was deliberate, every sense heightened by the rush of adrenaline coursing through my veins. I cradled my M4 rifle effortlessly in my arms. Subconscious pregame habits unfold as we move closer to our target. Hands grazing pieces of gear. Fingers finding rifle magazines, grenades, and radio cables, all meticulously stowed in their respective well-conceived homes for easy access. No willpower tapped. No conscious effort required. These simple, repeated routines had transformed into purposeful habits over time. Habits that shaped my identity as a warrior, that fostered a deep sense of purpose and emotional connectivity to mission and team. I would protect the teammates to my left and right at all costs. Even if my own life was required.

As the music pulsed in my ears, I mentally rehearsed each step of the mission plan with precision. The mantra of the Navy SEAL Ethos echoed in my thoughts, reminding me of the responsibility resting on my shoulders. The lives of my teammates and the success of our mission depended on my technical skill, tactical proficiency, and close attention to detail. In the world of special operations, training is a constant, unending pursuit of excellence. And the cycle is never complete. We can't afford to wait for the need for change to rear its ugly head. We are in a perpetual state of transformation, making incremental improvements daily. This progression compounds our capabilities, ensuring that by the time our adversaries believe they have adapted to our tactics, we have already evolved far beyond. Through this continuous evolution, we maintain a decisive edge, always staying a step ahead and redefining the battlefield.

Yet, beneath the veneer of confidence lay a silent acknowledgment of the unknown. Despite our rigorous training and reputation as the world's most feared operators, none of us had experienced the crucible of combat. The spec-ter of uncertainty loomed large as we prepared to face the realities of war. We were trained to be the best, yet untested in the chaos of battle. Tonight, as we pre-pared to descend into the unknown, the questions lingered. Would our training hold true? Would we emerge victorious, or would we confront challenges beyond our training and preparation? We had to assume what the engineer and Air Force captain Edward A. Murphy once reportedly said: "Anything that can go wrong will go wrong." This philosophy became, as you know, Murphy's law. The reality of our circumstance would soon unveil itself.

The familiar call crackled over the radio, "Two minutes out." Instantly, everyone snapped to alertness and passed the message along with a simple hand gesture—two fingers raised for all to see. It's a mesmerizing experience to both witness and be part of—elite warriors preparing to execute their craft with pre-cision. "Thirty seconds out," the voice called over the radio moments later.

Imagine yourself sitting at the open door of a Black Hawk as it hovers over a battlefield marked by uncertainty and volatility. The world around you slows down. You see your teammates seemingly in slow motion moving with delib-erate precision, hear the helicopter rotors spinning above you as if they are somewhere off in the distance, and feel the adrenaline igniting every fiber of your being. The distinct scent of engine fuel swirling in the warm air finds every olfactory receptor in your nose. It's a smell that signals the brain that it is time to go to work. Every moment is detailed and drawn out so you can take in the entire scene with heightened clarity. Such intense focus ensures you are fully prepared for whatever lies ahead, giving you the perception of more time to assess, decide, and act. There is no past. No future. Only the beauty of being in the present moment.

This feeling is called *tachypsychia*, and for a special operator, it is a potent tool that enables you to operate with heightened efficiency and effectiveness in the most critical moments. For special operators, the remarkable response of our bodies and minds to stress and danger is not just a survival mechanism but also a testament to our training and readiness for the challenges each day would bring as we stepped onto our respective battlefields.

Even in that heightened state, my mind journeyed back to the early morn-ings and late evenings I'd spent honing my skills. Despite the years of meticulous

Figure 3–1: *Routines and Habits: Impact and Purpose Matrix*

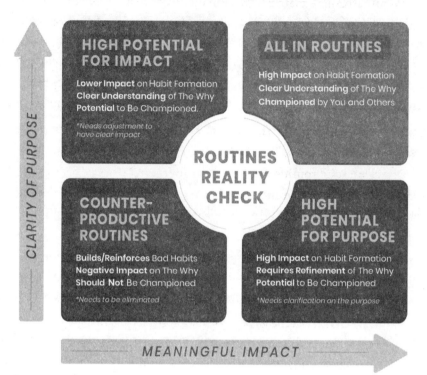

planning, the design and execution of purposeful routines, and ultimately the complete transformation of my identity, I couldn't ignore the questions pulsing in my mind: How did I actually get here? How did I really transform from a young college-educated financial analyst into, well, a warrior? An untested warrior, but a warrior by job description nonetheless. Intrinsically, I comprehended the processes and actions that transpired at every juncture. Yet, the questions lingered. What was the profound sense of calling that lay beneath it all? And how did I make that calling a reality?

This rapid reflection continued back to my senior year of college, when our training regimen began to take shape. Matt and I had turned the covered patio of the house I was renting with three other SMU seniors into an outdoor workout space, complete with a whiteboard bearing a two-by-two matrix. I adapted the BCG growth-share matrix from a finance class to analyze how we invested our time. On the vertical axis was "Clarity of Purpose," and on the horizontal, "Meaningful Impact," under the title "Routines and Habits." (See Figure 3–1.)

I explained the quadrants to Matt, starting with the upper right for routines with clear value and high impact—our **All In Routines**. The upper left was for efforts that added value but required refinement. These were labeled **High Potential for Impact**. The bottom right captured activities that seemed impactful but that lacked a clear purpose—**High Potential for Purpose** routines. These are solid routines but require a bit more clarity as to the why. The bottom left was labeled **Counterproductive Routines**—anything that stood in the way of success. Drenched from a grueling twenty-mile run around White Rock Lake, we pondered the framework that would become a tool for clarity and accountability in shaping our future.

The goal was to evaluate how we spent our time so that we could prioritize high-impact routines, refine those with potential, and eliminate bad habits and time-wasting activities. At the whiteboard, we sorted everything into quadrants. Our rigorous workouts, focused knowledge building, and dietary habits landed in the upper right as **All In Routines**. The upper left held routines that needed optimization, while the bottom right exposed actions we initially thought were valuable but now questioned. They still had potential. Finally, we turned to the empty bottom-left quadrant—the repository for distractions and bad habits.

"We need to list what has to go, now," I said, and surprisingly, it felt liberating. Excessive social outings, bad dietary habits, and activities that left us feeling drained made the list. With a red marker, we struck through the quadrant, committing to erase these habits. We then elevated our most impactful routines and attached measurable goals to track their progress over the next two months.

Suddenly, I snapped back to the present as the helicopter banked sharply to the port side and came to an almost complete standstill in the air. Moments later the fast rope hit the ground, and with it, the weight of all our preparation crystalized. This was the crucible, the moment where discipline and resilience would be tested. As the roar of the helo blades filled the air, I found clarity: Nothing mattered but the present moment. That was the purpose of all the work—to thrive in the now.

WHAT AM I FISHING FOR?

It is not the length of life, but the depth of life.
—RALPH WALDO EMERSON

On a tranquil early morning in Nicaragua, I walked along the beach as the sun rose over jungle-covered hills and cast golden light across the ocean. A welcome break from responding to messages in Slack and hacking away at my ClickUp to-do lists. The rhythmic waves and distant calls of birds created a serene backdrop. I noticed an old fisherman preparing his gear with deliberate care. His weathered face and wiry frame spoke of a lifetime spent at sea. I greeted him with a *buenos días*, and to my surprise, he responded in perfect English.

Curiosity piqued, I asked, "What are you fishing for today?"

He paused, considering my question as he secured a net. "Mostly snapper, mackerel, and tuna. Sometimes we get lucky with something bigger."

"I see. Do you go out every day?"

"Almost every day." He glanced out at the ocean as if it were an old friend. He asked me, "Are you here on vacation?"

"Yes, I'm here with my family. We wanted to experience the beauty of Nicaragua again. We came here last year and fell in love with the tranquility."

His smile broadened, the lines on his face deepening. "It's a beautiful place. How long are you staying?"

"Ten days," I said. "I once lived in a small seaside village in Africa near a fisherman and his family at a different time in my life. He said to me, *'Wanaume wengi wanavua samaki maisha yao yote bila kujua kwamba si samaki wanawatafuta.'* In Swahili this means 'Many men go fishing all their lives without knowing that it is not fish they are after.' What does that mean to you, if you don't mind me asking?"

His eyes took on a distant look, memories surfacing. "I've been a fisherman for almost fifty years, since I was a boy. It's hard to imagine." The old fisherman paused, his eyes reflecting the deep orange hues of the early-morning sun. He looked at me thoughtfully before saying more.

"That saying, my friend, holds a deep truth," he began. "Fishing is often seen as a quest for fish, but for many of us, it's about something of greater meaning. When a man casts his line into the water, he's not just hoping for a catch. He's seeking peace, connection, and sometimes, answers to questions he doesn't even know he has."

He continued, his voice a mix of gravel and wisdom, "In my many years at sea, I've come to realize that the act of fishing is a meditation, a way to escape the chaos of the world and find solitude. It's about the journey, the patience it teaches, and the respect for nature it instills."

A sense of calm washed over me. The fisherman looked to the horizon and elaborated, "This saying teaches us that often what we seek is not what we truly need. Fish are a metaphor for our desires and goals. We spend our lives chasing after them, thinking they will bring us fulfillment. But true fulfillment comes from understanding the deeper purpose behind our actions."

I removed my baseball cap and ran my fingers through my sweaty hair. The cool ocean breeze wafted over me.

He turned to me, his gaze piercing yet kind. "This lesson applies to all walks of life. Take you, for instance," he said, making an assumption about me as he looked me up and down. I began to feel self-conscious in my brand-name T-shirt and running shorts in the presence of this sage in worn clothing. "You strike me as a businessman or maybe an entrepreneur of some kind. We get a lot of tourists like you here, which we greatly appreciate. I might assume that early in your career you were probably chasing success, wealth, and recognition, thinking these things would make you happy. But you probably discovered that it's the pursuit of these things, the growth, the challenges, and the connections you make along the way that bring true satisfaction. Am I right?"

Indeed, his words resonated deeply within me. I found myself reflecting on my own journey: the start-ups I had launched, the speeches I had given around the globe, the countless meetings to secure capital, the deals both won and lost, the triumphs and sorrows, and the unyielding quest for success. The true rewards were not in the accolades or the financial gains but in the relationships I nurtured, the skills I developed, and the profound personal growth I experienced. It was my wife, my children, and the beautiful, fleeting moments lived fully in the present that held the true essence of my life's journey. But there were things, of course, that he did not yet know about me.

The fisherman continued, "In life, we must learn to see beyond the immediate goals and understand the deeper meaning of our pursuits. When you fish, it's not just about the catch. It's about the calm of the water, the patience you develop, and the stories you gather. Similarly, in your career and personal life, it's about the journey, the lessons learned, and the impact you have on others."

The early dawn cast a soft glow over the beach as we continued our conversation. He looked at me closely, his gaze lingering on the tattoos covering my upper arms and shoulders.

"You weren't always a businessman, were you? Military, maybe?" he asked, his eyes narrowing with a hint of curiosity.

I was a bit stunned by his perceptiveness. "Yes," I replied, "I joined the Navy right before 9/11."

"What did you do in the Navy? I assume it wasn't fishing!" he chuckled, which made the crow's feet stand out at the corner of each eye.

"Naval Special Warfare. The SEAL Teams," I said, wondering if he would know what that was.

The fisherman nodded knowingly. "I assume, then, that you have seen war and death. You've experienced pain, loss, and had to delve into the basic human instincts required for survival."

I took a deep breath and unexpectedly welled with emotion, memories flooding back, surprised at how forward he was being. "Yes, I've been through my share of experiences. Not compared to some, but enough. The training was brutal, and often the missions even more so. The bonds we formed were unbreakable though."

The fisherman listened, his weathered face reflecting a lifetime of understanding. "I can only imagine survival in war teaches you many things about life. It strips away the superficial and brings out the core of who you are. You've faced the darkest parts of human nature and come out stronger. Yes?"

I nodded, my thoughts turning inward. "Absolutely. Those experiences instilled in me resilience, discipline, personal accountability, and the importance of staying grounded. They also made me deeply appreciate the simple, beautiful moments that often go unnoticed—the things we take for granted every day. It made me realize how much time we waste on meaningless activities and pointless routines. Sometimes, the present moment is what is most important."

He nodded, and I continued, "I've lost many friends to war and the personal aftermath that comes with it. Their work here was done, as decided by God, and many left behind young families. I've spent countless hours questioning why they were taken instead of me. It's a shared burden among us—the lives they didn't get to live, the children they didn't get to see grow up and start their own families."

At this moment, I felt as if I was no longer speaking to a stranger but to a part of myself. The fisherman, sensing the depth of my pain, stood and placed a comforting hand on my shoulder. "It's in these reflections that we find our true selves," he said softly. "Your journey, with all its trials and tribulations, has shaped you into a man who understands the value of life and the importance of meaningful pursuits. This awareness is your strength, and it will guide you through whatever lies ahead."

His words offered solace, reminding me that despite the hardships, there is beauty and purpose in every moment. This encounter, on a quiet beach at dawn, was giving me a renewed sense of clarity and a deeper understanding of the path I was on.

The fisherman smiled, a hint of pride in his eyes. "Those lessons have shaped you into the man you are today. They are the foundation on which you build your life, your family, and your businesses. Just like fishing, it's not just about the catch; it's about the journey, the patience, and the connections you make along the way."

I was impressed. Quickly changing the subject and gesturing toward him with the hat in my hand, I offered, "You must have some fond memories and possibly crazy stories yourself."

He chuckled, a deep, throaty rumble that hinted at the wealth of experiences he carried. "Oh, I have stories. Even stories of survival."

I sensed the weight of his words, understanding that beneath the surface of his calm demeanor lay tales of the sea's unpredictability, of battles fought against nature's fiercest elements. His life, like mine, had been a series of challenges and triumphs, each day a testament to human perseverance and resilience.

As the sun rose higher, I felt a deep connection with this man, united by our shared respect for survival and the sea. Curious, I asked if he would share a remarkable story of resilience.

After thinking a moment, he began, "Have you heard of José Salvador Alvarenga and Ezequiel Córdoba?" When I shook my head, he continued, recounting their harrowing tale.

In 2012, Alvarenga and Córdoba set out on a two-day fishing trip off the coast of Mexico, only to be caught in a storm that left them adrift for 438 days. "They faced unimaginable challenges," the fisherman said, describing their endless hunger, the scorching sun, and the bone-chilling nights. Survival required ingenuity—crafting makeshift fishing gear, collecting rainwater, and rationing supplies. These routines gave them purpose and control amid chaos.

"And how did they keep hope alive?" I asked.

He smiled knowingly. "Hope isn't passive; it's active. They created daily routines, shared stories, and marked time, finding meaning in even the smallest actions." Tragically, Córdoba did not survive, but Alvarenga continued, driven by the necessary routines they'd designed. More than a year later, he was rescued near the Marshall Islands, having drifted over six thousand miles.

The fisherman paused, his words heavy with meaning. "Their story reminds us that routines anchor us. They bring strength, structure, and hope, even in the face of overwhelming odds."

We said our goodbyes and I walked home. His tale stayed with me, a testament to the resilience found in purposeful action. The rhythmic sound of the waves mirrored the steady routines that had carried Alvarenga through his ordeal. Two truths emerged: (1) Purpose and mental resilience are not innate but are cultivated one small, deliberate act at a time. (2) Each moment is a gift to be appreciated fully. In reflecting on how we spend our time, we must pause to ask ourselves, What am I truly fishing for?

A FEW LIFE LESSONS FROM THE SAGE OF PHILLY

Lost time is never found again.

—BENJAMIN FRANKLIN

The walk back to the beach house offered a moment of quiet reflection on my conversation with the fisherman. His profound wisdom stood in striking contrast to the seemingly simple life he appeared to lead. Yet, I realized how misguided it is to equate simplicity with insignificance, as though a person's trade, lifestyle, geographic location, or relationships could define the complexity of their existence. Many do not lead such lives out of necessity but by choice—a deliberate decision to focus on mastering a few essential tasks, nurturing meaningful relationships, and refining those pursuits with intention and care, day after day. What an extraordinary way to live, dedicating oneself to excellence in the seemingly ordinary.

As I gazed at the lush jungle spilling over the steep hillside a mile ahead and cascading down to the rocky barriers that shielded it from the crashing waves, I was drawn into the sea's enduring mystery and intrigue. Its unfathomable depths and untamed power have always captivated me. For years in my previous career, the cold, shadowy underworld of the ocean was a familiar refuge, a sanctuary from which we emerged to deliver swift justice to those who sought to harm the defenseless. Yet, above all, it is the ocean's timeless rhythm that has always mesmerized me, lulling me into a meditative state.

I felt a renewed curiosity about how history's great figures balanced discipline and routine in their lives. Often, we celebrate their remarkable achievements without delving into the broader impact of their ambitions—both positive and otherwise. In my studies, I had come across the fascinating life of Benjamin Franklin, one of the Founding Fathers of the United States. I'm sure you've heard of him. But many are unaware of how he truly lived.

His days began at 5:00 a.m. with quiet self-reflection: "What good shall I do this day?" This question set a purposeful tone for his day, aligning his mind with his goals. The early hours were spent planning, reading, and setting objectives, creating a road map for his activities. This period of quiet contemplation and strategic planning was crucial, providing clarity and direction. The rest of the day's schedule went as follows:

8:00 A.M.–12:00 P.M.: Focused work, conducting experiments, writing, or engaging in his various enterprises

12:00 P.M.–2:00 P.M.: Break for lunch; time for personal reflection and to recharge

2:00 P.M.–6:00 P.M.: Return to focused work

His evenings, from six to ten, were spent in introspection, asking himself, "What good have I done today?" Essentially, he performed a daily debrief that allowed him to assess his accomplishments, identify areas for improvement, and plan for the next day, ensuring a seamless transition between days. Dedication to this routine is likely what enabled Franklin to achieve his now famous kite experiment in 1752, in which he demonstrated that lightning is a form of electricity.

Franklin's daily routines, a cornerstone of his success, enabled him to embody the values of diligence, purpose, and continual self-improvement. His life serves as a testament to the power of structured routines in achieving remarkable accomplishments and leaving a lasting legacy.

The Thirteen Virtues of Poor Richard

In his quest for personal excellence, Benjamin Franklin architected thirteen virtues that would serve as a blueprint for his disciplined life and ambitious pursuits. These principles, meticulously chronicled in his autobiography, were more than lofty ideals—they were the cornerstone of a routine designed to align his values with his actions; they shaped his identity and elevated his impact. Franklin's virtues are as relevant today as they were in the eighteenth century, offering timeless wisdom to anyone striving for purpose, productivity, and personal growth in a fast-paced, modern world.

TEMPERANCE: CLARITY THROUGH MODERATION

Franklin's focus on temperance—moderation in food and drink—remains strikingly relevant in this era of overindulgence. Today's equivalent might be reducing alcohol intake and rethinking binge-watching or mindless scrolling on social media. By curbing overconsumption, whether of calories or content, we free our minds and bodies to operate at their peak, foster clarity and judgment, and reserve energy for what truly matters.

SILENCE: THE POWER OF PURPOSEFUL SPEECH

In a world dominated by noise—notifications, meetings, and endless chatter—Franklin's call for meaningful communication is a clarion reminder to prioritize substance over sound. Being intentional about our words fosters deeper connections and ensures our interactions add value, whether in personal relationships or professional collaborations.

ORDER: A BLUEPRINT FOR PRODUCTIVITY

Franklin's emphasis on organization is tailor-made for the modern age of digital calendars and task management tools. By assigning everything its place and time, we reduce decision fatigue and stress, which leaves more bandwidth for creative and strategic thinking. Order is not just tidiness; it's a commitment to efficiency.

RESOLUTION: FOLLOW-THROUGH IN A DISTRACTED WORLD

Franklin's dedication to accountability—firm decisions paired with disciplined follow-through—is an antidote to modern procrastination. It reminds us to see through commitments, whether that's launching a business or simply finishing the book gathering dust on the nightstand.

FRUGALITY: INTENTIONAL LIVING

In a consumer-driven culture, Franklin's frugality resonates as a call for mindfulness in spending and resource management. It's not about deprivation but about focusing resources—time, money, and energy—on what truly aligns with our values and goals so that we can leave behind the clutter that distracts us.

INDUSTRY: MAXIMIZING TIME AND EFFORT

The principle of industry is a nudge to make the most of each moment. Whether we are dedicating uninterrupted time to a project or carving out space for self-care, Franklin's ethos of purposeful action helps us cut through distractions and stay aligned with our bigger picture.

SINCERITY: BUILDING TRUST THROUGH INTEGRITY

In a world increasingly skeptical of authenticity, Franklin's call for sincerity—honesty and integrity in our words and actions—strengthens relationships and builds trust. Whether in leadership or daily interactions, sincerity fosters an environment where collaboration and mutual respect thrive.

JUSTICE: EQUITY AND FAIRNESS

Franklin's focus on justice reminds us of the importance of fairness, both to others and to ourselves. In today's interconnected world, this might mean honoring commitments, advocating for equity, or simply ensuring that our actions contribute positively to the lives of those around us.

MODERATION: BALANCE AMID EXTREMES

From work-life balance to managing emotions, Franklin's virtue of moderation is a timeless guide to maintaining equilibrium. In an age of extremes—workaholism, on one hand; escapism, on the other—it's a call to center ourselves so that intensity doesn't give way to burnout.

CLEANLINESS: A FOUNDATION OF WELL-BEING

Cleanliness for Franklin wasn't just about hygiene but also extended to the external environment. In modern life, this might mean decluttering both physical spaces and mental ones—creating a workspace that inspires focus or engaging in digital minimalism to reduce mental noise. Practicing mindfulness to clear the mind and refocus.

TRANQUILITY: COMPOSURE IN CHAOS

Franklin's call for tranquility is more relevant than ever in a world of constant demands and minor irritations. Whether it's managing the frustration of a traffic jam, navigating workplace challenges, or managing the chaos of the home front, cultivating composure ensures we maintain emotional discipline and mental clarity.

CHASTITY: RESPECT AND RESPONSIBILITY

Franklin's virtue of chastity underscores the importance of respecting oneself and others in all forms of relationships. In modern terms, this translates into fostering connections that are meaningful and rooted in mutual respect, avoiding exploitation or superficiality.

HUMILITY: LEARNING FROM GREATNESS

Inspired by figures like Jesus and Socrates, Franklin's humility reminds us to remain open to learning and to recognize our limitations while valuing the wisdom of others. This principle is a call to approach life with curiosity, respect, and the courage to evolve.

Franklin's thirteen virtues represent a holistic approach to living with purpose and integrity. They are not relics of the past but tools for the present—guides to crafting routines that foster growth, align actions with values, and drive extraordinary outcomes. By embracing these virtues, we can build lives of meaningful progress, transforming everyday actions into catalysts for achieving our loftiest goals.

WARNING ORDER: SUCCESS AT WHAT COST?

Benjamin Franklin, often hailed as the "First American," left an indelible mark on science, politics, and literature by pioneering advancements like bifocals, conducting groundbreaking studies on electricity, and playing a pivotal role in securing American independence. However, his relentless ambition often came at a personal cost. His betrayal of his brother James, despite profiting from his print shop, and his prolonged absences from his wife, Deborah, even during her illness, reveal a recurring pattern of placing professional pursuits and self-interest above loyalty and family obligations.

Franklin's life illustrates the tension between ambition and meaningful connections. Although his disciplined routines and drive led to monumental achievements, they also highlight the cost of neglecting personal bonds. His story reminds us that true success requires balance, that we must focus not only on achievement but also on nurturing relationships and honoring the journey alongside the destination.

Being all in means committing fully while ensuring we don't sacrifice life's greatest treasures along the way. Analyze your routines to ensure that you are avoiding the unintended consequences of neglecting things (and people) that matter.

✪

Reflecting on how we spend our time and energy unlocks the insights necessary to transform our lives with intention. Purposeful routines are not merely about productivity; they are frameworks that build sound habits and maximize cognitive bandwidth. By investing each moment with intention, we create a harmonious balance of personal growth, professional success, and meaningful relationships. This chapter invites you to reevaluate your habits, uncover the patterns that shape your existence, and take control of the actions that propel you forward.

True fulfillment is found in the milestones we reach along the way in the journey we embrace. By fostering discipline and crafting intentional routines that shape our thoughts and actions, we deepen our commitment to growth in every area of life. Each deliberate step elevates the ordinary into extraordinary progress. This is how a meaningful life is built, moment by moment, through the conscious choices we make each day.

GOING *ALL IN*

TO ACCESS YOUR ALL IN WORKSPACE, VISIT APP.EXLR8.AI/ALL-IN

AM I SPENDING TIME ON WHAT TRULY MATTERS?

Reflection

Time is your most valuable resource, yet it often slips away unnoticed. As Benjamin Franklin reminds us, "Lost time is never found again." Consider how much of your day is spent on activities aligned with your core values and aspirations versus those that are merely distractions. Are your routines fostering growth and building good habits, or are they holding you back?

Action

Conduct a "routines audit" for one week. Track your activities and categorize them into All In Routines, High Potential for Purpose, High Potential for Impact, and Counterproductive Routines. Identify one area where you can reduce wasted time and redirect it toward something that aligns with your goals.

DO MY ROUTINES REFLECT THE PERSON I WANT TO BECOME?

Reflection

Routines are powerful because they shape your identity. Benjamin Franklin's daily habits and his thirteen virtues demonstrate the transformative potential of disciplined living. Ask yourself: Do my current habits align with the person I aspire to be, or are they reinforcing behaviors that detract from my highest potential?

Action

Choose one existing routine to refine or elevate. For example, if you spend time on social media every morning, replace it with a habit such as reading, journaling, or exercising. Start small—shift just ten minutes daily—and build consistency to create a ripple effect in your life.

AM I BALANCING AMBITION WITH RELATIONSHIPS AND WELL-BEING?

Reflection

Success often demands sacrifices, but as Franklin's life shows, a ceaseless search for achievement can strain relationships and personal well-being. Balance doesn't mean compromising ambition; it means ensuring that your journey uplifts you and those who depend on you. Are you nurturing meaningful connections while striving for success?

Action

Schedule intentional time for relationships and self-care. Dedicate a nonnegotiable slot each day to connect deeply with loved ones, reflect, or recharge. Use this time to strengthen bonds or realign with your values. Balance is not an afterthought—it's the foundation of sustained achievement.

Every step you take with intention shapes the life you aspire to lead. Embrace the power of purposeful routines, for they are the foundation of the extraordinary life you are capable of creating.

4

HOW RELENTLESS ROUTINES TRANSFORM YOUR WAY OF THINKING AND DOING

M astery and habit formation share a common truth: They demand time, discipline, and commitment. Phillippa Lally's groundbreaking research at University College London reveals that forming a new habit takes an average of 66 days, though the timeline can range from 18 to 254 days depending on individual differences and situational contexts. Similarly, Malcolm Gladwell's popularization of the "10,000-hour rule" emphasizes the necessity of deliberate practice over long periods of time to achieve mastery. Together, these philosophies highlight the importance of sustained effort, persistence, and incremental progress in achieving both excellence and habit transformation.

Building habits, like honing skills in a given craft, is not an all-or-nothing pursuit but a continuum of daily actions. Missing a step or skipping a day does not undo the process; it's the consistency over the long term that counts. This approach mirrors the disciplined routines of Spartan warriors, samurai, and Olympic athletes, whose rigorous training and intentional actions shaped not only their skills but also their identities. Mastery, in this sense, is about more than the outcome: It's about aligning your daily routines with your ultimate vision and embracing the transformative journey.

By intertwining clear goals with intentional practice, mindful recovery, and celebrated milestones, you can unlock hidden potential and reframe challenges as stepping stones to greatness. Whether you are striving for personal breakthroughs or collective team success, these principles form the foundation for extraordinary achievement. Embrace the path with patience and dedication, knowing that every purposeful action compounds over time and can propel you to the highest expressions of your potential.

THE SCIENCE OF HABIT FORMATION

Habits are formed when the brain encodes simple cues and routines as automatic responses to save effort, so we can focus on more complex actions.

—B. F. SKINNER

In the complex tapestry of human behavior, habits weave together the intricate patterns of our daily lives, silently shaping who we are and who we become. Habits, whether we realize it or not, are the invisible architects of our success or failure. And for high performers—from elite athletes and business moguls to ancient warriors and historical icons—harnessing the power of habits has been instrumental in transcending obstacles, building resilience, and achieving greatness. Understanding the science of habit formation allows us to improve our personal and professional lives and redefine our identity by intentionally shaping our behavior. Previous chapters briefly touched on habit formation, but let's dive a bit deeper now.

At its core, a habit is a behavior that, through repetition, becomes automatic. Habits are formed when the brain identifies a routine that leads to a reward and encodes this behavior as something worth repeating. This is known as the **habit loop**, which consists of cue, routine, and reward and was popularized by Charles Duhigg, a Pulitzer Prize–winning journalist. The concept of the habit loop synthesizes ideas from various fields, including psychology and neuroscience, to explain how habits form and how they can be altered.

In *The Power of Habit*, Duhigg describes the habit loop as follows:

- CUE: A trigger that initiates the habit. It can be an emotional state, a time of day, an event, or anything that sets off the habitual behavior.
- ROUTINE: The behavior itself, which can be physical, mental, or emotional.

- **REWARD:** The positive reinforcement that encourages the behavior to be repeated in the future. This could be a feeling of pleasure, a tangible reward, or a sense of accomplishment.

Duhigg's work builds on earlier research by psychologists and behaviorists such as B. F. Skinner, who studied behavior modification and operant conditioning. Duhigg's habit loop provides a simple, actionable approach to understanding and changing habits, making it widely applicable in personal development and business practices.

During the soul-grinding crucibles of Navy SEAL training, I came face-to-face with the principles of psychology that B. F. Skinner pioneered, particularly operant conditioning. Skinner's work, which revolves around reinforcement, punishment, and behavior shaping, mirrors much of what we went through in our rigorous programs. Naval Special Warfare's warrior-forging environment, like the controlled settings of Skinner's famous experiments, is designed to push individuals through repetitive reinforcement until behaviors become automatic. This process of habit formation, of turning deliberate action into instinct, is what transforms citizens into warriors capable of executing extraordinarily complex tasks under the most extreme pressure.

In Skinner's theory, *positive reinforcement* strengthens a behavior by presenting a reward after a desired action. I vividly remember the small—and extremely rare—but significant moments of positive reinforcement during Basic Underwater Demolition / SEAL (BUD/S) training. A simple nod from a stone-faced instructor for maintaining a flawless room—a bed with every corner squared with military precision—was a reminder that excellence in small tasks paved the way for mastery in more complicated missions. It was these meticulous habits, like keeping our gear in pristine condition, that laid the groundwork for far more intricate skills later in training, from urban combat to undersea warfare.

In SEAL training, just as in Skinner's experiments, *negative reinforcement* also played a major role—in fact, it was the norm for us to be subjected to aversive conditions as a way to strengthen our habit of outstanding performance under pressure. From being forced to remain wet, cold, and covered in sand day and night, to doing thousands of push-ups and burpees and going days without sleep, every moment of negative reinforcement was by design, specifically crafted to develop mental fortitude and physical resilience. *Punishment* had a distinct purpose in our training, too, acting as a swift deterrent to any deviation from the high standards expected of us. *Negative punishment*, in Skinner's terms, involved removing something desirable, like personal time or sleep, as a consequence of mistakes. These experiences were designed not to break us but to teach us there are consequences to failure. The lesson: Be relentless in improvement and avoid complacency at all costs. When you know your mistake will lead to further physical and mental strain, it drives you to find the strength to adapt quickly and improve.

Skinner's mice learned to press a lever to avoid shocks. We were drilled endlessly in tactics, not just to perform them but also to internalize them so deeply that they became instinctual responses to stress. For example, when I first began learning close-quarters battle (CQB), the mechanics felt stiff and awkward—just like the initial strides you make in breaking bad habits. But over time, through constant repetition and reinforcement, these movements became second nature. The routine became the reward itself, as mastering these tactics gave us the confidence and precision to execute flawlessly in combat.

But the most fascinating aspect of SEAL training, much like Skinner's theory, is the concept of habit formation through consistency and reinforcement. The repetition of the smallest tasks built up to more complex operations becoming habit, not unlike Skinner's "shaping" process, where you build on a small behavior by reinforcing it at each step until the full desired action is achieved. In SEAL training, that meant escalating from simple tasks to life-or-death battlefield skills, such as orchestrating demolition, executing air assaults, or engaging in urban combat.

The key takeaway from Skinner's work and SEAL training is that our habits are powerful tools for success. *Keystone habits*—those core practices that influence the most important behaviors—were critical in preparing us for the battlefield. Discipline is paramount to building keystone habits. Maintaining my gear to standard wasn't just about having a clean weapon but also about having the discipline to ensure that I was always combat-ready. That discipline transferred to other areas of my profession, driving me to perform under the harshest of circumstances, whether during multiday sniper overwatch missions or intense capture-or-kill operations.

High performers across all disciplines rely on keystone habits to drive success and foster resilience. These foundational practices create a ripple effect and influence multiple aspects of life and performance. As B. F. Skinner's research on reinforcement shows, transforming simple routines into deliberate, reinforced actions builds psychological resilience and equips individuals to navigate even the toughest challenges.

For example, athletes often adopt structured morning rituals, starting with visualization or mental rehearsals followed by tailored warm-ups that prime both body and mind for peak performance. Similarly, military leaders implement high-intensity fitness routines paired with rigorous mission rehearsals to cultivate discipline and readiness for high-pressure situations. Keystone habits like these, combined with daily reflection—a staple among elite units and high-performing teams for evaluating performance and driving improvement—create a foundation for sustained excellence. By embedding such practices into our lives, we ensure that success becomes a predictable outcome rather than a rare achievement.

Over time, when we perform the same actions in response to the same cues and receive the same rewards, our brain encodes this loop, making the behavior automatic. Once ingrained, a habit no longer requires conscious effort or thought. This efficiency is one reason habits are so impactful—they free up mental space for more important decisions. Special operators and professional athletes train so rigorously each day so that the most important actions and behaviors become automated and their cognitive capacity to think strategically while performing complex tasks is liberated.

Keystone Habits in Action

Keystone habits are not theoretical constructs—they are essential tools that define the lives of elite performers. Physical training, a hallmark of SEAL life, is about fitness but also forms a cornerstone of mental toughness and operational readiness. Through unrelenting conditioning, SEALs develop the grit to perse-vere under the pressure of extreme physical and psychological demands. More-over, the SEAL approach to habit stacking—pairing small, consistent actions like repetitive training with painstaking preparation rituals—creates a seam-less system of excellence. These practices are not standalone; they're part of a deeply integrated framework that ensures precision, discipline, and the abil-ity to perform under pressure, aligning perfectly with our ethos: "If knocked down, I will get back up every time. I am never out of the fight."

The takeaway for anyone seeking to level up is this: Keystone habits have the power to transform lives, no matter the arena. Whether you start the day with a structured routine, such as reading or journaling, to set the tone for accomplishment or integrate regular exercise into your day to fuel both mind and body, these habits create a foundation for resilience, focus, and long-term success. They're not reserved for elite warriors or high-stakes operators—they're accessible tools for anyone ready to elevate their performance and achieve meaningful, lasting change. Let's dive into how you can identify and leverage your own keystone habits to unlock your full potential.

The Power of Habit Stacking and Autosuggestion

Athletes are perhaps the most vivid example of how intentional habits fuel greatness. Every gold medal, championship title, or record-breaking feat is underpinned by a web of carefully honed routines designed to optimize phys-ical performance, mental resilience, and strategic execution. Growing up, I witnessed this firsthand: My dad, a collegiate swimmer, instilled in my twin brother and me the discipline and structure of training from an early age, even to the point of scheduling private swim lessons at our house with former Olym-pians. It's no wonder I often find myself drawn to swimming as the perfect met-aphor for the power of habits. In a sport where every fraction of a second counts, success isn't about talent alone but about the commitment to perfecting the details.

From a young age, Olympic swimmer Michael Phelps's coach, Bob Bow-man, ingrained in him a set of prerace routines that conditioned his body and mind for peak performance. Before every race, Phelps followed the same series of actions: stretching in a specific way, listening to the same music playlist, and visualizing every stroke of his race. These routines became second nature, helping him remain calm and focused in high-pressure situations. Over time, these small, deliberate habits culminated in his record-breaking winning of twenty-three Olympic gold medals.

Beyond his physical routines, Phelps also practiced habit stacking, a technique wherein one habit is built on top of another. For example, Bowman would instruct Phelps to visualize a perfect race every night before bed and every morning after waking up. By pairing the act of visualization with daily routines like waking and sleeping, Phelps created a habit loop that trained his mind to focus on success every day.

This is where autosuggestion comes into play. Autosuggestion is a psychological technique in which individuals influence their subconscious minds through repeated positive affirmations, mental imagery, or self-directed thoughts. Elite athletes use autosuggestion as a tool to enhance their performance, boost confidence, and maintain focus under pressure.

The process involves intentionally repeating specific positive phrases or vividly visualizing success—whether it's winning a race, executing a flawless play, or triumphing over a challenge. When we consistently feed these types of messages into our subconscious mind, they can replace negative or self-limiting beliefs with constructive, empowering thoughts. This type of mental conditioning enables athletes to stay focused, reduce anxiety, and build mental resilience.

For instance, a sprinter might repeatedly visualize crossing the finish line first or affirm "I am fast and powerful" before stepping onto the track. Admittedly, I used to scoff at this sort of thing, dismissing it as psychological fluff. But here's the truth—it works. Autosuggestion aligns the body and the mind with the goal of peak performance by embedding the belief that success is not just possible but also inevitable. I've had the privilege of witnessing this in its most intense form: the nightly transformation of the world's elite warriors as they prepare for a mission. Each individual follows their own ritual, immersing themselves in both conscious focus and subconscious visualization. Meticulously rehearsing every detail of their execution, embedding precision and readiness into their mental framework. Each operator's deliberate mental conditioning is not just preparation but the foundation of battlefield superiority.

Moreover, autosuggestion helps athletes navigate high-pressure moments because the repeated positive affirmations create a sense of control and preparedness. Over time, the practice becomes second nature, leading to consistent improved performance, especially in high-stakes situations. The effectiveness of autosuggestion lies in its ability to harness the power of the mind to enable anyone to actualize their goals through focused, positive mental reinforcement.

Athletes, elite warriors, and high performers in every field remind us of a universal truth: Greatness results from deliberate, disciplined habits and mental conditioning. The tools they use—meticulously rehearsed routines, habit stacking, or the transformative power of autosuggestion—are accessible to all of us, like a blueprint for achieving our own goals. When we commit to intentional habits and align our minds with our aspirations, we cultivate not only the skills but also the belief that success is inevitable. The power of these practices transcends the arena, the battlefield, and the pool—they are the foundation for mastering any challenge and realizing our full potential.

Transforming Bad Habits Through Productive Routines

We all have habits—both good and bad—that shape the course of our lives. The key to self-improvement lies in identifying counterproductive habits and replacing them with ones that propel us forward. James Clear, author of *Atomic Habits*, likens habits to compound interest: They accumulate over time, and even the smallest adjustments can yield monumental impacts.

Take, for example, the all-too-common habit of checking social media immediately upon waking. The cue is clear: the phone easily within reach on your bedside table. The routine? Scrolling through notifications, messages, or feeds, which often leads to wasted time and a reactive, distracted mindset. The reward? A quick hit of dopamine from the updates, likes, or engagement you see. Although this habit might feel harmless, it often sets a tone of distraction and stress for the rest of the day.

To transform this habit, keep the same cue and reward but change the routine. Replace the scrolling with a constructive activity, such as journaling a quick gratitude list, reviewing your goals for the day, or reading a few pages of an inspiring book. The reward remains the same—a sense of stimulation and engagement—but now it's tied to an action that aligns with your personal growth and priorities.

By focusing on small, incremental changes, anyone can leverage the habit loop to escape negative patterns. Habit stacking can amplify this transformation. For example, if you want to build a habit of daily mindfulness, pair it with an existing habit like brewing your morning coffee. Use the act of waiting for the coffee to brew as a cue to take a few deep breaths or practice a brief meditation. By anchoring new habits to established routines, you reduce the mental effort required in making positive changes, and the new habit stack is easier to sustain over time.

Prisoners of War: Resilience in Captivity

The transformative power of habits has been demonstrated even in the direst of circumstances, such as during captivity. Prisoners of war, subjected to physical and mental torture, have used simple daily routines to preserve their sense of identity and humanity.

Admiral James Stockdale's experience during the Vietnam War serves as one of the most compelling examples of mental fortitude, leadership, and the power of habits in extreme adversity. Captured during the war and imprisoned for more than seven years in the infamous "Hanoi Hilton" prison, Stockdale endured torture, isolation, and harsh conditions that could have broken even the strongest of men or women. Yet, what set Stockdale apart was not only his leadership abilities but also his mental and physical habits he cultivated to survive and support his fellow prisoners.

One of Stockdale's most important routines was communicating with fellow prisoners, a lifeline that connected him to those he was leading through an unimaginable hell. Using a system of tapping—a rudimentary form of Morse code—Stockdale and other prisoners could send messages to one another by tapping on the walls of their cells. This form of communication became a habit that served as a psychological anchor. For Stockdale and his fellow prisoners, maintaining communication was not just about passing information but also about sustaining a sense of solidarity and purpose. Through the constant repetition of this behavior, the prisoners reaffirmed their unity and maintained a form of human connection in the face of unimaginable isolation.

In addition to communication, Stockdale developed a habit of reframing his circumstances through what later came to be known as the "Stockdale paradox," which he described as the ability to balance steadfast faith that he would eventually prevail with the brutal acceptance of his current reality. This mental framework relied on the cultivation of daily habits that fostered resilience: focusing on what he could control, engaging in deliberate mental exercises to fortify his will, and balancing short-term expectations with a long-term vision of freedom. This form of mental discipline was neither accidental nor a fleeting reaction; it was a daily practice that Stockdale honed with intention, and it enabled him to endure and ultimately thrive in the face of overwhelming hardship.

Physical habits also played a key role in Stockdale's survival. Exercise, even in the confines of a small cell, became a disciplined routine. Stockdale and other prisoners used calisthenics to maintain their physical health. These routines were critical for maintaining their bodies and for reinforcing a sense of control and normalcy in an environment where both had been stripped away. Each exercise, however small, contributed to a larger psychological framework in which control over one's actions, no matter how limited, provided an antidote to the helplessness that imprisonment could breed.

Stockdale's leadership was also defined by his commitment to maintaining these habits, not only for himself but also for those around him. He made it a priority to support his fellow prisoners by encouraging them to adopt similar routines of communication, mental discipline, and physical exercise. It was not about making grand gestures but rather about instilling daily habits that empowered the men to survive collectively. By encouraging these shared routines, Stockdale transformed his role from a passive prisoner to an active leader, ensuring that his comrades could withstand the psychological and physical strains of captivity.

Stockdale's habits—communication, mental resilience, and fitness—were instrumental in his survival, but they also point to the broader power of keystone habits. For Stockdale, communication was a keystone habit that reinforced the sense of community for the prisoners and increased their mental strength and resilience. Once communication was established, it became easier to cultivate the other habits of mental discipline and physical exercise together. Similarly, the daily practice of mental fortitude created a mindset that allowed Stockdale to keep faith in eventual liberation, even in the darkest moments.

This is an important lesson for anyone seeking to transform bad habits into productive ones. The key lies in maintaining the cue and the reward while altering the routine. This concept extends beyond daily routines and into the realm of transformative leadership. High performers use keystone habits to transform their personal challenges into opportunities for growth in themselves and others. Stockdale's story illustrates how high performers—no matter their profession or position in life—use keystone habits to overcome adversity. These habits, small and repetitive, aren't only about skill building or routine maintenance but also about identity transformation. The repetition of positive habits gradually rewires our perception of adversity so that we become adaptable and use our creativity to face obstacles with strength. Stockdale didn't merely survive prison; through his habits, he embodied the resilience and leadership required to bring the others through it as well.

Stockdale's story offers a profound insight into the science of habit formation. Habits—when well cultivated—are far more than repeated activities: They are the building blocks of our identity and the framework through which we navigate the world. Whether we are enduring years in a prison camp, excelling in elite sports, building a high-performing team at work, or leading a nation, the daily practices and rituals we commit to shape our capacity to overcome challenges and succeed. By leveraging keystone habits, habit stacking, and the cue–routine–reward loop, we take control of the road map to achieving desired outcomes. We become the masters of our fate, and the captains of our soul.

The Science of Habit Formation in Teams

The principles of habit formation apply as much—if not more—to teams as they do to individuals. When teams form habits, they align their individual actions to create a collective rhythm that propels shared goals forward. But let's not sugarcoat it: Getting a group of people with varying motivations, personalities, and priorities to adopt a unified habit can feel like herding caffeinated cats through a laser pointer convention. Yet, when done well, the results are transformative.

Phillippa Lally's research on individual habit formation provides a solid foundation for understanding team dynamics. The average of sixty-six days for an individual to embed a new habit is a starting point, but let's throw in the delightful chaos of office politics, deadlines, and the never-ending stream of competing priorities. Suddenly, the timeline becomes…elastic. For teams, how much time it takes a habit to form can be even greater, depending on team size, organizational culture, and the complexity of the habit being formed.

But here's the catch: The underlying mechanism of habit formation remains the same. Teams, like individuals, require a **cue**, a **routine**, and a **reward** to establish habits. The challenge is ensuring that these components resonate collectively, not just individually, across the team. Here are two fundamental habits that support team success.

MAKING COLLABORATION THE NORM

Consider a team that struggles with collaboration. Their meetings often resemble WWE matches instead of productive discussions, and everyone's idea of "working together" is tackling their part of the project in a silo and assuming someone else will handle the rest. This is followed by flawless finger-pointing when deadlines are missed and work quality suffers.

To instill collaboration as a team habit, start with a **cue**: a standing agenda item in every meeting that requires brainstorming and shared input. The **routine** could be a structured process wherein team members discuss their contributions openly, assign tasks collaboratively, and commit to specific next steps. The **reward**? Visible progress on shared goals, public acknowledgment during meetings, and maybe even the elusive promise of eliminating an unnecessary meeting that could be replaced by an email or quick phone call.

The result? Over time, the team begins to expect collaboration as the default behavior, and the former lone wolves may even start sharing their snacks during the afternoon slump. Or not. Progress, not miracles.

EMBRACING FEEDBACK

Feedback culture is another area where teams benefit from habit transformation. Let's imagine a team where feedback is treated like an awkward middle school dance—everyone knows they should participate, but nobody wants to be the first to step forward.

A simple **cue** might be setting aside five minutes at the end of each meeting for feedback reflections. The **routine** could involve a structured framework, such as "What went well?" and "What could we improve next time?" In the military, we call this debriefing, a process foundational to rapid learning and continuous improvement. The **reward**? A noticeable improvement in team performance, fewer passive-aggressive comments, and perhaps the exhilarating thrill of an actual compliment from that perpetually grumpy senior manager.

As the habit forms, team members begin to associate feedback not with criticism but with growth. Suddenly, feedback isn't something to be endured—it's actively sought out. Okay, maybe not suddenly. Let's call it a "gradual evolution with occasional setbacks."

The Challenges of Team Habits

Here's the reality: Teams aren't blank slates, and embedding new habits often requires overcoming entrenched behaviors. There's always *that one person* who clings to "how we've always done it" as though the process was etched in stone tablets atop Mount Sinai. For these individuals, direct communication and clear incentives are essential. For example, if your team's new routine involves daily stand-ups designed to build habits around prioritization, highlight how this practice improves efficiency and eliminates the need for other meetings. Or, if all else fails, promise coffee, donuts, and stock options. Bribery: the oldest form of motivation.

The Role of Leadership in Team Habit Building

Leaders play a critical role in reinforcing team habits. They must act as the chief habit architects, creating environments that make the desired behaviors almost impossible to avoid. A leader who shows up late to meetings while preaching punctuality might as well tattoo HYPOCRITE on their forehead. Conversely, a leader who models the desired habit—whether it's active listening, task delegation, or effective communication—becomes a living cue for the team.

Take, for example, a leader who wants the team to adopt new project management software to streamline workflows. If they actively use the tool themselves to assign tasks, update progress, and share timelines, the team is far more likely to follow suit. The reward? Increased efficiency and fewer midnight Slack messages that read, "Hey, just circling back on this!"

Building Habits for a Shared Identity

When teams establish habits, they're not only optimizing workflows but also creating a collective identity. The habits a team adopts say, "This is who we are and how we operate." A marketing team that habitually conducts the routine of creative brainstorming sessions is living the identity of an innovative, forward-thinking unit. Similarly, a sales team that habitually celebrates small wins builds an identity rooted in camaraderie and motivation.

Intentional Design, Remarkable Results

The process of forming team habits isn't always smooth—it's messy, filled with false starts, and occasionally derailed by the boss's "urgent" requests. But with intentional design, patience, and reinforcement, teams can develop habits that not only improve performance but also redefine how they work together.

In the end, the beauty of team habit formation lies in its ability to transform individuals into a cohesive organism that can achieve far more than any one individual could alone. So start small, stay consistent, and don't forget the donuts.

ENVIRONMENTAL IMPACT ON HABIT FORMATION AND IDENTITY

The soul becomes dyed with the color of its thoughts, and the mind is shaped by the environment it dwells in. Choose your surroundings wisely, for they will sculpt the habits that define your life.
—INSPIRED BY MARCUS AURELIUS

Every aspect of our environment molds us—shaping our thoughts, behaviors, and ultimately our destiny. The people we surround ourselves with influence our values and aspirations, the places we frequent inspire or constrain our growth, and the media we consume quietly rewires our beliefs. Our routines and habits, the rhythms of our days, form the invisible architecture of our lives. Every choice, no matter how small, becomes a brushstroke on the canvas of who we are and who we are becoming.

Several years ago, our work at EXCELR8 took me to Mumbai. In partnership with one of our client companies, a large pharmaceutical organization, we were engaged to run a three-day leadership offsite session for sixty senior leaders and managers. The focus was on strategic alignment, productivity, and implementing better practices for delegation and accountability. At the conclusion of the final day, knowing I had several hours before my flight, the client graciously hired a driver to take me on a guided tour of Mumbai. The leadership event was held at the Taj Lands End, a superb waterfront hotel, and at 4:30 p.m., I was picked up in a 2021 Mercedes-Maybach S-Class for a two-hour evening tour of the city.

I felt quite special to say the least. The driver was a young man in his early thirties. I soon discovered he also had a postgraduate degree from the Indian Institute of Technology Madras, one of the most prestigious technical schools in India. As we navigated the bustling streets of Mumbai, filled with the sounds of honking horns, vendors calling out their wares, and the intense aroma of street food—a vibrant tapestry of smells, reflecting the city's diverse cultural and culinary heritage—the driver pointed out various sites and monuments.

Not long into our journey, he asked, "So, what brings you to Mumbai?"

"My company has been collaborating with senior leaders at a major pharmaceutical firm to focus on enhancing leadership performance and foster strategic alignment. These leaders are exceptionally intelligent and deeply committed to their work, yet many grapple with challenges such as maintaining discipline, optimizing time management, boosting productivity, and navigating tough decisions. To address these pain points, we've been guiding them in crafting transformative routines and shaping cultural experiences that instill lasting habits, which will empower them to excel both individually and as a cohesive leadership team."

"That reminds me of Dr. Sudhir Kakar, a famed Indian psychologist. His work in cultural psychology and human performance is remarkable," he said.

"Dr. Kakar? I've read about him. His insights on the influence of culture on human behavior are fascinating. Can you tell me more about his work?" I asked, once again immensely impressed with my guide's intellect.

"Certainly. One of my family members knew him well. He was born in Nainital and initially studied mechanical engineering and business before his interest in human behavior led him to psychoanalysis at the Sigmund Freud Institute in Germany."

"Impressive. From my limited knowledge, it seems his research also looks at how environmental factors play into human performance. Are you familiar with this area of his work?" I asked, reflecting on the early days of my military training, where the environment was meticulously designed to stimulate the mind and body to elevate our ability to overcome insurmountable obstacles. Through deep pain and immense suffering of course. But nevertheless.

"Dr. Kakar suggests that our surroundings and routines are crucial. For example, in his book *Shamans, Mystics, and Doctors*, he examines traditional Indian healing practices and highlights the importance of the healer–patient relationship and the environment in the healing process. Social relationships and community bonds are vital in shaping individual behaviors and cohesion in groups."

"So, the environment and our routines are as influential as our psychological construct it seems," I said. "Napoleon Hill was an American author born in 1883 and best known for his world-famous book *Think and Grow Rich*. He said, 'You are the average of the five people you spend the most time with.' Hill emphasizes the idea that the people around us significantly shape our mindset, our habits, and ultimately our success. He believed that surrounding yourself with driven, positive, and successful individuals can inspire growth and achievement, whereas negative influences can hinder progress. This idea aligns with his broader teachings on the importance of environment and association in shaping one's destiny," I shared.

He nodded, a thoughtful expression on his face.

"I've explored this a bit," I continued. "The psychology of shared energy and influence stems from social contagion theory and collective intelligence. Interactions between individuals amplify energy, spark creativity, and foster new ideas, partly because mirror neurons drive subconscious mimicry, helping us build connection," I explained.

"Exactly," he said. "By addressing underlying psychological conflicts and integrating them with cultural narratives, individuals—and teams—can achieve more profound and lasting changes in their behavior and performance," my intelligent driver wisely explained.

"That idea aligns with the tools and features we've designed into our performance improvement and collaboration software," I said, "and what we teach in leadership development programs. High achievement stems from well-designed routines and environments—and leaders—that nurture our goals and values."

"Absolutely. It's amazing how interconnected these principles are. Our surroundings and habits truly shape our potential."

As we made our way back to the hotel, passing bustling markets and historic landmarks, I reflected on the importance of environment, routines, and influences in shaping our ability to achieve greatness. Our conversation about Dr. Sudhir Kakar's work underscored the importance of environmental design to achieve exceptional outcomes in all areas of life and work.

As discussed in this chapter, the work of behavioral psychologists like B. F. Skinner, Charles Duhigg, and Dr. Sudhir Kakar sheds light on habit formation and human behavior. Skinner's operant conditioning explains how reinforcement shapes automatic responses; Duhigg's habit loop—cue, routine, reward—provides a practical framework for building and altering habits. Dr. Kakar adds depth by emphasizing the role of cultural and environmental influences. These principles are evident in the disciplined routines of elite performers in every realm, where daily practice transforms behaviors into instinctive excellence. Purposeful, well-designed routines align our daily actions with our long-term aspirations, automate success, and free mental energy for higher challenges. By crafting habits that reflect our values, we build the foundation of our identity. Extraordinary outcomes come through consistent, intentional action.

GOING *ALL IN*

TO ACCESS YOUR ALL IN WORKSPACE,
VISIT APP.EXLR8.AI/ALL-IN

HOW DO MY CURRENT HABITS SHAPE MY IDENTITY?

Reflection

Your habits are not just actions—they're the building blocks of who you become. As Charles Duhigg explains in *The Power of Habit*, every habit follows a cue–routine–reward loop that becomes automatic over time. Reflect on your current habits. Do they align with the person you aspire to be? Are they shaping an identity you're proud of?

Action

Identify one unproductive habit you want to change. Start by breaking it down into its cue, routine, and reward. Replace the routine with a more positive action that leads to the same reward. For example, replace mindless social media scrolling with a brief mindfulness practice.

ARE MY ROUTINES DRIVING INCREMENTAL PROGRESS TOWARD MY GOALS?

Reflection

Phillippa Lally's research shows that habit formation takes an average of sixty-six days but the length of time can vary depending on the behavior and the context. Habit building is not an all-or-nothing endeavor; the process thrives on gradual, consistent progress. Are your routines designed to foster incremental growth, or do they feel overwhelming and unsustainable?

Action

Choose one keystone habit that supports your goals. Commit to practicing it daily for at least two months. Track your progress to stay motivated, and celebrate small milestones along the way to reinforce the behavior. For example, if your goal is improved fitness, start with a manageable workout routine and gradually increase intensity.

HOW DOES MY ENVIRONMENT
SUPPORT OR HINDER HABIT FORMATION?

Reflection

Dr. Sudhir Kakar emphasizes that our surroundings significantly shape our behavior. Your environment can either reinforce positive habits or act as a barrier to change. Consider how your physical space, social circles, and mental cues influence your habits. Are they conducive to building the life you want?

Action

Optimize your environment to support your desired habits. For example, if you want to read more, place a book on your bedside table as a visual cue. Align your surroundings with your goals to make positive habits easier to sustain.

PART 2

MINDSET TRANSFORMATION

THE REMARKABLE RESULTS PYRAMID (RRP)

5

UNDERSTANDING MINDSET

Harnessing Habits to Redefine Identity and Elevate Performance

Mindset is the foundational framework of attitudes, beliefs, and thought patterns that shapes how we perceive challenges, seize opportunities, and approach our goals. It governs how we see ourselves and interact with the world, influencing every decision and action. Far from being fixed, mindset is dynamic and can be deliberately cultivated through disciplined routines, purposeful actions, and continuous reflection. By embracing a growth-oriented mindset, individuals can overcome limiting behaviors, unlock their potential, and align their lives with their deepest values and aspirations.

At its core, mindset is the driver of self-mastery. It empowers us to persevere through adversity, pivot in the face of change, and maintain fixed focus on meaningful goals. A purposeful mindset transforms daily actions into deliberate steps toward excellence, making success a predictable outcome rather than a fleeting possibility. By intentionally shaping our mindset, we can redefine who we are, embrace continuous improvement, and achieve extraordinary outcomes in every area of life.

The journey to transformation begins in the mind. In this chapter, we explore how intentional habit formation, anchored in well-designed routines, can fundamentally reshape our beliefs and elevate performance in all we do. We'll continue to examine how the mind forms habits through the elegant mechanism of cue, routine, and reward and, more importantly, how those habits shape a new way of thinking. The interplay of these elements doesn't merely create behaviors—it rewires the way we approach challenges, embrace opportunities, and, ultimately, define ourselves.

This is the transformative power of mindset: the ability to intentionally direct our thoughts and actions toward achieving our highest potential. This isn't just the domain of the extraordinary. Whether you're working to escape unproductive habits, cultivate new routines, or elevate your personal and professional lives to new heights, the principles in this chapter are universally applicable.

MONKEY SEE, MONKEY DO

It is not the strongest of the species that survive, nor the most intelligent, but the one most responsive to change.
—CHARLES DARWIN

As humans, we adapt to the world around us in two ways: through intentional action and through responding to the external forces that demand change. Both pathways offer important lessons about mindset and the routines that shape who we are. In this section, we explore a captivating story that bridges these concepts—a tale of survival, identity, and the undeniable influence of our environment.

The story you are about to experience provides a dual lens into the mechanics of habit formation and mindset shift. On one hand, it highlights how necessity forces us to develop new routines and ways of thinking to adapt to life's unpredictable circumstances. On the other, it reminds us that we have the power to consciously shape our environments and routines to unlock new potential even in the face of adversity. Whether driven by choice or circumstance, these transformative experiences underline a universal truth: Our identity is not fixed; it evolves with every habit, routine, and mindset we adopt.

Several months ago, the pastor at our church shared the story of a girl from Brazil who was lost in the jungle and allegedly raised by monkeys—a tale that captures the imagination and offers an unparalleled view of how environmental factors shape identity. Although the case of Marina Chapman, one of the better-known examples of feral children, provides much of the inspiration for a portion of this chapter, the broader narrative highlights the immense impact that environment and routine have on human behavior, thought patterns, and identity formation. We possess the power to consciously build our beliefs, rituals, habits, and, ultimately, our identity, all with the intent of clearly defining our purpose, creating the life we want, conquering the goals we set, and bringing more joy and fulfillment into our lives, and the lives of others.

The Jungle Takes Over

The extraordinary story of Marina Chapman, as detailed in her memoir *The Girl with No Name* (2013), is based entirely on her recollections and perspective. Although her account provides an incredible narrative of survival and resilience, it is important to acknowledge that the story has not been independently verified in its entirety. As such, it should be approached with an open mind that recognizes the challenges inherent in corroborating events that took place in such isolation and under such extraordinary circumstances.

Marina was born in Colombia around 1950. At the age of five, she was kidnapped from her family; after a failed ransom attempt, she was abandoned deep in the Amazonian jungle. The sweltering heat, combined with the constant hum of insects, became the soundtrack of her isolation. The thick tree canopy blocked much of the sunlight, and the moist air was filled with the pungent scent of decaying leaves and rich, wet earth.

Marina, bewildered and terrified, wandered aimlessly for days, unsure whether anyone would ever come for her. She became weak from hunger, and every sound—the rustling of leaves, the screeches of animals—sent her heart racing. Her identity was that of a frightened child lost in an unfamiliar and dangerous environment. Survival instincts soon took over, and she drank from puddles and ate whatever she could find, fruits, nuts, and insects. Fortunately, none of these caused her great harm.

Then, something extraordinary happened: She encountered a troop of capuchin monkeys. Known for their intelligence and complex social behaviors, the monkeys initially frightened Marina. Over time, however, she observed them, learning how they found food, communicated, and survived in the hostile environment. Through imitation, she adapted to their ways, gradually shedding her human identity and adopting the routines and behaviors of the capuchins.

For several years, this troop of monkeys was her family. She learned to climb trees, find food, and navigate the dense jungle. Her survival depended on her ability to integrate into this environment, and she succeeded. Her life changed once again after approximately five years in the jungle when she was discovered by hunters. The men, rather than rescuing her, sold her to a brothel in the city of Cúcuta.

At the brothel, Marina faced new forms of danger and exploitation. However, the survival instincts she had honed in the jungle enabled her to escape before being fully ensnared in the sex trade. Fleeing to the streets, she lived as a beggar, surviving by her wits and resourcefulness. Life as a street child brought its own hardships, but Marina endured, finding ways to adapt and survive.

Eventually, she found a semblance of stability when she was taken in by a family. Though they treated her more like a servant than a child, this period allowed Marina to reconnect with the human world and relearn language and social norms. In her late teens, her life took another turn when a kind neighbor helped her move to Bogotá, where she worked as a maid. This shift exposed her to a more supportive environment and allowed her to build an empowered sense of identity.

Marina's life improved further when she moved to the UK, where she eventually married and started a family. With the encouragement of her children, particularly her daughter Vanessa, she shared her story in *The Girl with No Name*. Her life is a testament to resilience, adaptability, and the human spirit's ability to survive and thrive in even the harshest conditions.

CHANGE YOUR MIND, CHANGE THE GAME

Human beings can alter their lives
by altering their attitudes of mind.
—WILLIAM JAMES

Marina's story reminds us that identity is neither fixed nor immune to change; it's a malleable construct shaped by the environments we inhabit and the routines we adopt. Human beings are adaptive creatures—and remarkably impressionable, like fresh Play-Doh. We tend to quickly take the shape of our surroundings before hardening into habits and thought patterns. Marina didn't wake up one day and think, *You know what? Monkeying around in the jungle sounds like a solid life plan.* No, the jungle dictated her priorities, and her identity shifted to ensure her survival.

For the rest of us living with thermostats and grocery delivery, our environment may be less dramatic but no less influential. The mind is subtly rewired by the people we spend time with, the content we consume, and the routines we practice daily. Ever notice how you start using the same phrases as your coworkers or humming that terrible pop song you swore you hated? That's environmental determinism at work—an invisible hand nudging you into patterns you didn't consciously choose. But here's the kicker: If your environment can shape you unwittingly, imagine what could happen if you designed your environment intentionally.

Transforming your way of thinking—and ultimately, your identity—doesn't mean you need to swap your coffee mug for a protein shake and start journaling at sunrise while blasting motivational podcasts. Instead, it's about being acutely aware of how your routines and surroundings influence your sense of self and then using that awareness to engineer a better version of you. And remember, you don't have to *change* your identity to achieve success. It's not about becoming someone else but about being the best version of yourself in the environment you choose to create. As Robin Sharma puts it, change is scary at first, messy in the middle, but gorgeous at the end. And if you mess up? Well, that's just part of the beautiful chaos of being human. So go ahead, design your environment, embrace the mess, and watch your identity—and your life—transform.

In *Atomic Habits,* James Clear masterfully illustrates that the true power of habit formation lies in its ability to reshape our identity. He shifts the focus from achieving specific goals to embodying the type of person you aspire to become. Instead of merely setting a goal to run a marathon, Clear suggests adopting the identity of a "runner." With this shift, daily actions—such as lacing up your sneakers, executing your training regimen, choosing nutrient-rich meals, and prioritizing recovery—flow naturally because they align with the core of who you believe yourself to be. The concept transcends athletics: If your goal is to rise to a senior leadership position, immerse yourself in the identity of an executive. Study how successful leaders think, act, and learn. Ask yourself, "What would a senior executive do in this situation?" Over time, these intentional habits not only mirror but also solidify the identity you seek, transforming aspirations into reality.

Some of our EXCELR8 team members were running a breakout session for founders and CEOs at a large conference in Las Vegas earlier this year. During one of the discussions, the founder of a rapidly growing cybersecurity company shared something I found to be so insightful. She said, "My company is still small but rapidly growing. One of my goals is for us to grow from $50 million in revenue to $100 million over the next three years. And I have found myself spending less time on the actual strategy and tactics required to fulfill that vision—as they are pretty clear and our team can definitely execute. Now I spend a significant portion of each day focusing not on what I need to do but on *who* I need to become as the CEO of an organization that size." It was such a simple yet incredibly profound statement that I asked her to repeat it to the group.

Marina's story, James Clear's insights, and the wisdom shared by the cybersecurity founder all converge on a singular, transformative truth: Who we become is a product of the environments we shape and the identities we embrace. The power to craft an intentional identity lies in our ability to align daily habits with the person we aspire to be, whether that's a thriving CEO, a disciplined athlete, or a more grounded individual. True transformation isn't about reaching a single milestone or adopting someone else's persona; it's about evolving into the best version of yourself, one deliberate choice at a time. Embrace the process, lean into the mess, and watch as the person you are aligns seamlessly with the future version you envision.

The Dance of Determination: How Misty Copeland Mastered Her Mindset

Misty Copeland's journey to becoming the first African American principal dancer at the American Ballet Theatre (ABT) is a testament to the transformative power of mindset. Her story illustrates how resilience, routine, and a strong belief in self can overcome seemingly insurmountable odds. In Copeland's evolution, from humble beginnings to performing on the grandest stages in the world, we see the interplay of intentional habit formation, adaptability, and a mindset that matured in tandem with her craft.

Misty's story begins far from the polished floors of ABT. Born in Kansas City, Missouri, in 1982, she grew up in San Pedro, California, as one of six children in a family that struggled financially. For much of her childhood, Misty lived in cramped motel rooms, grappling with instability and uncertainty. Yet, even in this environment, glimpses of what would later define her—a natural grace and an instinctive drive to move—shone through.

Copeland didn't discover ballet until she was thirteen, an age considered "too late" by industry standards. Most professional dancers begin training as toddlers, their pliés and pirouettes nurtured from the moment they can stand. But when Misty attended her first ballet class at a local Boys & Girls Club, taught by Cindy Bradley, it was clear she was extraordinary. Her natural ability to mimic complex movements, coupled with a rare athleticism and elegance, stunned everyone in the room.

Despite her raw talent, Misty's entry into ballet was far from seamless. She faced skepticism not only because of her late start but also because of her race. Ballet, traditionally dominated by white dancers, held rigid ideals of what a ballerina should look like—ideals that Misty's muscular frame and skin color challenged. External skepticism mirrored her own internal insecurities, creating an uphill battle that would test the limits of her resolve.

Building the Foundation: Routines That Built Resilience

One of the earliest lessons Misty learned was the importance of routine. Under Cindy Bradley's guidance, she adhered to a disciplined practice schedule. Every day, Misty would wake up early, attend school, and then dedicate hours to perfecting her technique in the ballet studio. These were not the routines of a recreational dancer—they were the rituals of someone intent on defying the odds. Ballet, for Misty, became more than an art form; it became her anchor, a source of structure and stability in an otherwise chaotic life.

Her routine was physical but also deeply psychological. Misty began to internalize the idea that mastery required talent and relentless effort. She embraced the mindset that setbacks weren't roadblocks but opportunities for growth. When a movement felt impossible, she would break it down into smaller components and practice each element until it felt natural. This iterative process mirrored her evolving mindset: Challenges, no matter how daunting, could be overcome through deliberate, focused action.

The Evolution of Mindset: From Student to Pro

As Misty's talent blossomed, so, too, did her mindset. When she earned a scholarship to train at the prestigious San Francisco Ballet School, she found herself in an entirely new world—one filled with both opportunity and heightened pressure. She was surrounded by dancers who had been training since childhood, whose technical precision seemed light-years ahead of hers. It was there that Misty faced her first true test of mental fortitude.

Rather than succumbing to self-doubt, Misty leaned into the discomfort. She doubled down on her routines, arriving early and staying late to practice. She adopted the mindset of a professional long before she became one, emulating the behaviors of the dancers she aspired to succeed. This intentional alignment of habits with her identity—she embraced the role of a professional rather than a student—allowed Misty to bridge the gap between where she was and where she wanted to be.

However, the path was not without setbacks. Injuries, a constant threat in the physically demanding world of ballet, forced Misty to confront her limits. During periods of recovery, she recalibrated her routines, shifting her focus to rehabilitation and mental preparation. These moments, though painful, taught Misty the value of adaptability. She began to see setbacks not as failures but as detours—temporary pauses that offered opportunities for reflection and growth.

The Breakthrough: Mastery Through Adversity

Misty's breakthrough moment came when she joined the American Ballet Theatre in 2000 as a member of the corps de ballet. Yet, even as she ascended the ranks, she continued to face barriers. The ballet world's narrow standards of beauty and performance often left Misty feeling like an outsider. Critics would comment on her physique and label her "too athletic" or "too muscular" for classical ballet. These judgments could have shattered her confidence, but instead they fueled her determination.

It was during this period that Misty's mindset underwent a significant shift. She stopped trying to conform to the expectations of others and began embracing her unique strengths. She realized that her powerful frame, far from being a liability, was an asset that allowed her to perform movements with extraordinary precision and force. This reframing of her self-perception—seeing her differences as advantages rather than shortcomings—became a cornerstone of her mindset.

To reinforce this shift, Misty crafted routines that celebrated her individuality. She incorporated cross-training that blended traditional ballet exercises with strength training and Pilates into her regimen. These routines not only enhanced her physical capabilities but also reinforced her belief in her potential. Each day in the studio became an affirmation of her identity as a trailblazer—a dancer who refused to be confined by outdated norms.

Lessons from Setbacks: Rewriting the Narrative

One of the most defining moments in Misty's career came in 2008, when she was diagnosed with six stress fractures in her tibia. For a dancer, such an injury could be career ending. The months of recovery that followed were some of the darkest in Misty's life. Stripped of the ability to dance, she wrestled with feelings of helplessness and fear.

Yet, even in this challenging period, Misty's mindset proved resolute. She used her time away from the stage to focus on her mental and emotional growth. She journaled extensively, reflecting on her journey and reaffirming her goals. She sought mentorship from other dancers who had overcome similar injuries, learning from their experiences and adopting new strategies for recovery. This period of introspection and learning not only healed her body but also deepened her sense of purpose.

When Misty returned to the stage, she was not the same dancer who had left. She was stronger, both physically and mentally. Her routines had evolved to include preventive care, such as stretching and meditation, to protect her body and mind. Her performances, infused with newfound confidence, captivated audiences and critics alike. The adversity she had faced had not diminished her—it had permanently upgraded her excellence.

Redefining What's Possible

In 2015, Misty Copeland made history as the first African American woman to be promoted to principal dancer at the American Ballet Theatre. This achievement, a personal victory, heralded a seismic shift in the world of ballet. Misty's success challenged the industry's long-held stereotypes and opened doors for dancers of all backgrounds.

Even at the pinnacle of her career, Misty continued to refine her mindset and routines. She understood that success was not a destination but a continuous process of growth and learning. She became a vocal advocate for diversity in ballet, and she used her platform to inspire the next generation of dancers. Her work extended beyond the stage, too: She authored books, mentored young artists, and collaborated with brands to promote inclusivity.

Mindset as a Catalyst for Change

Misty Copeland's story is more than a tale of individual triumph; it's a testament to the transformative power of mindset. Her journey underscores that greatness is not reserved for the chosen few but is accessible to anyone willing to commit to intentional action and being resilient. By cultivating routines that aligned with her goals and embracing setbacks as opportunities for growth, Misty redefined her identity and reshaped an entire industry.

Mindset is not a fixed trait but a dynamic force we can nurture and evolve. Whether on the stage, in the workplace, or in our personal lives, the principles that guided Misty—discipline, adaptability, and belief in self—are universal. They are the tools that allow us to transcend our circumstances, rewrite our narrative, and step into the fullest expression of our potential.

As Misty herself once said: "I will not be ignored. I will not be silenced. I will not be discouraged. I am here to stay." And with that mindset, she danced her way into history.

✪

Whether you're surviving in the jungle, enduring captivity, rising to stardom in the exclusive world of ballet, or navigating the complexities of modern life, the principles of habit formation remain the same. Our identities are shaped by the small, repetitive actions we take every day, and by consciously choosing the habits that align with the person we want to become, we can transform our lives.

The stories of extraordinary individuals like Marina Chapman, Misty Copeland, Admiral Stockdale, and Michael Phelps offer examples of how habits can shape identity and lead to success. But these principles apply just as readily to everyday people striving to improve their lives. Whether it's making a good living, mastering a craft, or simply becoming a better version of yourself, the key lies in the habits you form and the consistency with which you practice them.

By understanding the science behind habit formation, such as Skinner's operant conditioning and Duhigg's habit loop, and by applying these insights to your own life, you can unlock your potential and achieve greatness in whatever field you choose. And just like Navy SEALs, who prepare for the battlefield by honing their habits, you can prepare for the challenges of work and life by cultivating routines that begin to shift the way you think, behave, and act.

Our identities are not fixed; they are malleable constructs shaped by our environment, routines, and the habits we cultivate. This chapter highlights how deliberate action enables us to align our behavior with the person we aspire to become. Transformation isn't about completely reinventing who we are but designing environments and habit-building routines that foster growth. Through small, consistent actions, integrating keystone habits, and intentionality, we build the scaffolding that bridges the gap between our current selves and our highest potential. Keystone habits empower us to shape our lives with purpose and clarity.

GOING *ALL IN*

TO ACCESS YOUR ALL IN WORKSPACE, VISIT APP.EXLR8.AI/ALL-IN

HOW DOES MY ENVIRONMENT SHAPE MY IDENTITY?

Reflection
Marina Chapman's story demonstrates the transformative impact of one's environment on identity. Although most of us won't find ourselves adapting to life in a jungle, our daily environment—the people we surround ourselves with, the media we consume, and the spaces we inhabit—exert a powerful influence on who we are.

Action
Take a close look at your surroundings. Do they reflect the person you want to become? If not, consider small changes—spending more time with people who inspire you, decluttering your workspace, or creating routines that encourage growth. Remember, intentional environments breed intentional outcomes.

ARE MY ROUTINES ALIGNED WITH THE IDENTITY I ASPIRE TO?

Reflection
Misty Copeland didn't just adopt habits; she created routines that aligned with her vision of becoming a world-class ballerina. Her training, mental preparation, and adaptability were all rooted in this alignment.

Action
Think about the habits that define your daily life. Are they reinforcing the identity you want to build, or are they holding you back? Start by identifying one small habit that can serve as a keystone—such as dedicating ten minutes each morning to planning your day or ending each evening with reflection—and build from there.

HOW DO I RESPOND TO SETBACKS?

Reflection
Both Marina Chapman and Misty Copeland faced significant obstacles, yet their responses defined their journeys. Marina adapted to survival, and Misty reframed injuries and criticism as opportunities for growth.

Action
Reflect on how you react to challenges. Do you see them as failures or as stepping stones? Begin reinterpreting setbacks as moments to learn, adjust, and refocus. Write down one recent challenge and list three things you learned from the experience to reinforce this mindset shift.

6

MINDSET MASTERY

Unleashing Growth, Steadfastness, and Your Highest Potential

Mindset is far more than a passive mental state; it is the active engine that drives growth, adaptability, and the realization of our highest potential. A mindset well mastered fuels resilience in the face of adversity, sharpens our ability to navigate change, and unlocks the untapped reserves of our capabilities.

The all in mindset is a transformative force that can shape our identity and the behaviors and habits that define our success. Serving as the lens through which we interpret the world, our mindset determines how we respond to challenges, seize opportunities, and perceive our own power. By intentionally cultivating the all in mindset, we can reframe obstacles as catalysts for growth, annihilate self-imposed limitations, and align our beliefs with our greatest aspirations. This shift enables us to cultivate steadfastness, adopt habits of excellence, and create meaningful, lasting transformation. With *mindset mastery*, we gain the tools to turn setbacks into stepping stones, bridge the gap between who we are and who we aspire to be, and pursue not just a life of achievement but one of deep fulfillment.

MASTER YOUR MIND, MASTER YOUR LIFE

The mind is everything. What you think, you become.

—BUDDHA

In AD 705, a broken yet unyielding man named Justinian II defied the odds in one of history's most astonishing comebacks. To truly understand his extraordinary journey to reclaim Constantinople, it's essential to learn about the man behind the scars and the deep resolve that fueled his mindset and ferocious tenacity. Born in AD 668, Justinian II, the son of Constantine IV, ascended to the Byzantine throne in 685 at the young age of sixteen, inheriting an empire still struggling to maintain its dominance. From early on, he exhibited the traits of a determined and ambitious ruler. He was an ambitious emperor, willing to take risks to expand and solidify the empire and the Heraclian dynasty that had ruled Byzantium for generations. Justinian was a skilled tactician and a leader who didn't shy away from enforcing stringent policies to strengthen his realm.

Early in his reign, Justinian II made serious attempts to restore the power of the Byzantine Empire, showing a level of tenacity akin to that of his namesake, the legendary Emperor Justinian I. He spearheaded military campaigns to stabilize the empire's borders, consolidated church power, and attempted to implement tax reforms. However, his policies often came at the expense of various groups, which led to widespread dissatisfaction. We've all seen this movie before.

However, this same ambition and determination to impose his will on the empire also sowed the seeds of his downfall. Justinian II's tax policies were particularly unpopular with the aristocracy, military, and the general populace. His heavy-handed approach and authoritarian rule alienated many of his political allies and created a powerful coalition of enemies. In 695, a coup was orchestrated by Leontius, a general who seized the throne.

To ensure that Justinian could never reclaim power, his captors inflicted a brutal punishment: cutting off his nose and splitting his tongue, which earned him the nickname *Rhinotmetos*, which translates to "the Slit-Nosed" or "the Nose Cut." Such physical mutilation served a political purpose, because disfigured individuals were banned from becoming emperor in the Byzantine tradition. It was also a symbolic act meant to strip Justinian of his claim to the throne and permanently remove his capacity to rule. He was exiled to Cherson, an ancient Greek colony founded on the rugged coast of the Crimean peninsula, where he would live the remainder of his life in obscurity and shame, a once-proud emperor reduced to a disfigured exile.

By the time of Justinian II's exile in the late seventh century, Cherson was part of the Byzantine Empire and served as a strategic point on the northern coast of the Black Sea for controlling trade routes and exerting influence over the surrounding regions and peoples, including the nomadic tribes to the north and the Khazar Khaganate to the east. The city's location made it relatively isolated and a suitable place for exiling political prisoners.

Yet, the mutilation that was meant to end Justinian's aspirations only steeled his resolve and provided the impetus for his vengeful rise. The cruelty he faced seemed to ignite an even fiercer drive for retribution and reclamation of the throne. Despite his physical limitations, Justinian's spirit remained unbroken. For ten years, he plotted his revenge, gradually gathering a following among exiles, discontented factions, and those loyal to his cause.

In 704, Justinian made a daring escape from Cherson. Understanding that failure meant certain death, he capitalized on his connections and local support. Through his network, he became aware that the governor of Cherson had received orders to assassinate him, which prompted his urgent escape attempt. As word spread of his potential demise, Justinian persuaded a group of loyal supporters and locals to assist him. Under the cover of darkness, he managed to evade the guards, secure a small vessel, and flee the city. He traveled covertly across the Black Sea to reach the Khazars, who were neighboring allies. The Khazars were a Turkic people who had established an expansive trading and military empire. Upon arrival, he sought refuge with the Khazar ruler, Busir Glavan, who offered him protection and a place to regroup. To cement this alliance, Busir Glavan married his sister to Justinian. This move provided Justinian with both safety and political support, as he began to build a network that could aid him in reclaiming the Byzantine throne.

However, the story didn't end there. Even in Khazar territory, Justinian's life was imperiled when the Byzantine emperor Tiberius III tried to have him assassinated. But Justinian, ever resourceful, caught wind of the plot and fled once again—this time to Bulgaria, where he would gather a military force, a crucial step toward reclaiming his throne. He sought sanctuary and alliance with the Khan of the Bulgars, Tervel. The Bulgars, fierce rivals of the Byzantines, saw opportunity in aiding Justinian's cause, and Tervel agreed to help. With the support of the Bulgar forces, as well as Slavs and other disaffected groups from within the Byzantine Empire, Justinian amassed a force that would help him fulfill his vision.

The year 705 marked Justinian II's bold return to the heart of the Byzantine Empire. His plan to retake Constantinople was a blend of military strategy and audacity. Sailing once again across the Black Sea, he reached the city that had been the seat of his power. However, Justinian faced a nearly impregnable fortress: Constantinople's massive walls and defenses were among the most formidable in the world. Knowing a frontal assault would be doomed to failure, he relied on cunning rather than force—the Navy SEAL within him emerging. SEALs prefer both, but you get the idea.

By Water Beneath the Walls

In his incredible book on the history of Naval Special Warfare, *By Water Beneath the Walls*, my former SEAL teammate and close friend Ben Milligan references Justinian II's assault on Constantinople as an example of resilience and strategic ingenuity in military history. Milligan highlights this pivotal event to underscore the complexities of leadership in the face of insurmountable odds.

So, Justinian searched for a vulnerable entry point into the city that would allow him to bypass the main defenses. He identified an unguarded section of the city's infrastructure: The aqueduct of Valens, which ran beneath the city's walls and supplied Constantinople's water, offered a discreet and unexpected route into the heart of the city. Justinian and a small band of special operators stealthily approached this waterway at night. (Who knows, maybe they even applied face paint made of animal fat, charcoal, and ox excrement to blend into the dark of night and deliver a psychologically menacing blow to the enemy.) They moved quickly and quietly, navigating the dark, narrow confines of the aqueduct—all without the aid of night-vision goggles. The aqueduct was not heavily patrolled or defended because it was not considered a strategic entry point for invaders. This lack of vigilance of the city defenders provided the perfect opportunity for Justinian and his lethal gang of marauders. Emerging from the aqueduct inside the city

walls, Justinian's men infiltrated Constantinople and quickly dispersed to predetermined areas in the city with the goal of sowing confusion and undermining the
city's defenses before a coordinated response could be organized.

The operation was a stunning success, showcasing Justinian's strategic brilliance and determination. The audacious use of the aqueduct allowed him to
bypass the city's renowned defenses entirely, which turned the odds in his favor.
His return marked a dramatic reversal of fortune: from an outcast and deposed
emperor to a conqueror reclaiming his throne.

Once back on the throne, Justinian II's vengeance knew no bounds. Those
who had betrayed him faced brutal retribution. His nemesis, Leontius, and the
usurper who had followed him, Tiberius III, were captured, paraded through
the streets of Constantinople, and brought to the Hippodrome of Constantinople, the central arena where public events and spectacles took place. There,
before the gathered crowd, in an act of retribution and as a demonstration of
his regained power, Justinian personally oversaw their execution by beheading,
which served as a warning to any potential rivals or usurpers and was consistent with Justinian's harsh, merciless approach to ruling after his restoration. In
his second reign, Justinian II showed even greater resolve to fortify the empire's
power and secure his legacy. However, his ruthless pursuit of revenge and absolute control once again stirred unrest.

Ultimately, Justinian's ruthless methods and unyielding thirst for power
sparked discord and fear and led to yet another rebellion in 711. This time, he
could not escape his fate, and he was eventually captured and executed, and
thus ended the tumultuous life of one of Byzantium's most defiant rulers.

We've uncovered three undeniable truths about Justinian II: (1) he was neither kind nor beloved as a ruler, (2) his actions were driven by an intense thirst
for revenge and unbridled ambition, and (3) he possessed an extraordinary
degree of fortitude—as misguided as it may have been. Despite his flaws, his
story underscores the weighty impact of mindset on resilience and the ability
to pursue goals with intense focus. Justinian's life is a testament to defiance and
determination, a saga of enduring humiliation and physical disfigurement only
to rise again with ruthless tenacity. What was meant to destroy him became

the fire that fueled his resolve, and personal tragedy changed into the driving force behind reclaiming the power he believed was his destiny. The mutilation, far from rendering him powerless, transformed him into a determined warrior with a singular focus. It's a bit like placing an employee on a performance improvement plan—albeit without the brutality of nose removal and tongue splitting (HR would have a fit!). But the concept is the same: When someone is given harsh, direct feedback or is stripped of their power, the truest test is how they respond. Justinian's response was not just to survive but to come back in a fierce, calculated way.

His story stands as a testament to the crucible of environmental adversity and hardship fostering the metamorphosis of mindset and the evolution of identity. His capacity to endure oppressive humiliation, excruciating pain, and isolation rested on a mental framework that redefined challenges as opportunities to assert his power and indomitable will. This unyielding perception of himself as the rightful emperor became both his anchor and his compass, driving every action and reinforcing a singular, unshakable purpose. Remarkably, he sustained this steely resolve for over a decade—a span of time during which many would have succumbed to despair or the belief that their moment had irretrievably passed. Yet, there are those rare individuals who refuse to yield and tirelessly persevere until the mission is complete.

But such tenacious pursuit of a goal is not without peril. Ambition untethered from self-awareness can become destructive, not only to oneself but also to those who stand in the shadow of such unrelenting drive. The critical balance lies in discernment: The cause must be just, the ambition tempered by wisdom, and the awareness of when to let go present. Without this balance, the pursuit—no matter what it is—risks devolving into obsession that leaves collateral damage in its wake.

In the realm of habit formation and identity transformation, Justinian II emerges as an extraordinary example of how unfaltering resilience and an unshakable belief in the mission can defy even the harshest odds. Just as habits are forged through deliberate, repeated actions aligned with a deeper purpose, Justinian's journey coalesced from a sequence of decisions and maneuvers shaped by his singular goal: reclaiming the throne. His steadfast resolve created a mindset impermeable to defeat—a force capable of penetrating fortifications, shattering resistance, and seizing power against a tide of resistance. Whether or not he really wore ox excrement as camouflage (as I hope he did), he embodied the spirit of one wholly committed, completely undeterred—he was unequivocally *all in*.

Justinian's return to power transcended the physical act of reclaiming a throne: It was a masterpiece of psychological warfare (largely against himself), a testament to the transformative power of an unconquerable will. His triumph underscores an undeniable fact: Those who dare to align their behaviors with a deeply felt purpose, redefine their identity, and stand resolute in the face of adversity can achieve feats that others deem impossible. His story is a call to embrace resilience and deliberate action as tools for reshaping our destiny.

WHO AM I NOW? WHO DO I NEED TO BECOME?

We are not what happened to us,
we are what we choose to become.
—CARL JUNG

Let us revisit the concept of identity, not as a fixed label but as a dynamic framework—one that can be intentionally shaped to align with our ambitions and unlock our highest potential. Understanding identity is pivotal to crafting the routines, environments, and learning experiences that empower us to grow into the person we aspire to be, a continually evolving version of ourselves. Whether we aim to refine who we are or undergo a profound transformation to achieve the extraordinary, identity serves as both the foundation and the compass, guiding us steadfastly toward our goals.

Erik Erikson was a renowned psychologist best known for his theory of psychological development, which outlines eight stages of identity and psychological growth across the human life span. His work, particularly the idea of "identity versus role confusion," highlights how individuals continuously shape their sense of self by resolving challenges at key life junctures. We need not explore each stage in detail, but it is worth noting that identity, as Erikson describes it, is dynamic and influenced by the interplay of personal experiences, relationships, and the environments we inhabit. This foundational understanding empowers us to intentionally craft our identity—not by waiting for circumstances to define us but by actively designing routines and systems that foster growth and resilience.

The transformative power of identity lies in its inherent malleability. By cultivating deliberate routines, shaping purposeful environments, and committing to continuous learning, we can align our daily actions with the identity we aspire to embody. For instance, fostering a growth-oriented mindset requires immersing ourselves in relationships, settings, and practices that challenge and inspire us. Similarly, developing habits rooted in discipline and perseverance strengthens our internal narrative, reinforcing the belief in our resilience and adaptability amid life's challenges. These intentional efforts empower us to overcome fear, self-doubt, and limiting beliefs and allow us to shape a persona capable of achieving extraordinary results.

Ultimately, the journey of identity transformation is about crafting a life in alignment with our values and vision. It is not enough to let life's stages passively shape us; we must actively seize the opportunity to define who we are and who we aim to be. By embracing this philosophy, we empower ourselves to face adversity with clarity, pursue our ambitions with resolve, and leave an enduring mark on the world.

The Nordic Alchemist:
Magnus Nilsson's Journey to Mindset Mastery

In the hinterlands of Jämtland, Sweden, where winters grip the landscape with unrelenting ferocity for months and the sun's warmth feels like a distant memory, a culinary revolution unfolded. At its epicenter was Magnus Nilsson, a chef whose journey is as raw and elemental as the harsh Nordic wilderness that shaped his vision. From humble beginnings to global acclaim, Nilsson's story is one of resilience, identity, and the pursuit of mastery—a perfect embodiment of the philosophies explored in this chapter on mindset mastery.

Magnus Nilsson's story begins in the Swedish countryside, where he was born in 1983. Growing up, his connection to food was forged not in the bustling commercial kitchens of a metropolis but in the simplicity of rural life. His family hunted, fished, and foraged and lived in harmony with the land. These formative experiences etched an appreciation for nature's cycles into Nilsson's psyche, yet they also planted the seeds of restlessness.

From an early age, Magnus felt torn between the rugged simplicity of his surroundings and an unshakable ambition to create something extraordinary. At just sixteen years old, he left home to train as a chef in Åre, a nearby ski town. Though talented and determined, Nilsson found himself battling doubts about his abilities and his place in the culinary world. These insecurities propelled him to push harder, to immerse himself in the meticulous discipline of a fine dining chef.

In his early twenties, Nilsson set his sights on Paris, the mecca of haute cuisine. Working under celebrated chefs such as Alain Passard at L'Arpège, he refined his skills and absorbed the artistry of French gastronomy. Yet the experience left him questioning his identity. The rigid perfectionism of the Parisian kitchens clashed with the untamed spirit of his Nordic roots. He realized that to find his true voice, he would need to step away from the traditions he had once revered. This pivotal moment of introspection became the foundation of his culinary philosophy. He began to grasp that true mastery doesn't come from simply imitating greatness but from reconciling skill with authenticity.

After several years in France, Nilsson returned to Sweden, hoping to integrate his skills with his heritage. His homecoming, however, was anything but triumphant. Struggling to find his footing, he took a position at a wine import company—an ironic detour for someone whose culinary ambitions had once burned so brightly. At his lowest point, Nilsson considered abandoning the kitchen altogether. The weight of perceived failure, exacerbated by an internal dialogue steeped in self-doubt, pressed heavily on him.

But within this crucible of disillusionment, Nilsson found clarity. He realized that his struggle stemmed not from a lack of talent but from an unwillingness to conform to anyone else's definition of success. The world didn't need another French-trained chef trying to replicate Michelin-starred formulas—it needed authenticity. This epiphany set the stage for what would become one of the most innovative culinary ventures of the twenty-first century.

FÄVIKEN: A BEGINNING AND AN END

In 2008, Nilsson stumbled on an opportunity that would transform his career: the chance to helm a modest restaurant located on a twenty-four-thousand-acre hunting estate in the remote village of Järpen. At first glance, this seemed an unlikely venue for culinary greatness. For any restaurant aiming for fame and success, location isn't just important but is the difference between being the new hotspot or being the best-kept secret no one can find. Remote from urban centers and presenting logistical challenges, this was hardly the type of establishment destined for international acclaim. But for Nilsson, it was a blank canvas—a place where he could distill his vision into its purest form.

Drawing on his rural upbringing and his experiences in Paris, Nilsson crafted a menu that celebrated hyper-local ingredients and ancient Nordic techniques. Dishes at Fäviken were as much about storytelling as they were about sustenance: reindeer hearts smoked over juniper branches, scallops cooked in their shells over an open flame, and wild herbs foraged from the surrounding forests. Each plate was an ode to the land, prepared with a precision that elevated the rustic to the sublime.

Yet Fäviken's success was anything but overnight. Nilsson faced frequent obstacles—unpredictable weather, logistical nightmares, and the skepticism of diners accustomed to more traditional fine dining experiences. He poured himself into the work, often to the point of extreme exhaustion. The long hours and rigorous pace tested his physical and mental resilience, but Nilsson refused to compromise. He understood that greatness demanded skill, unyielding discipline, and an ability to embrace hardship as a necessary component of growth.

He welcomed the idea that purposeful suffering—whether it was the grueling labor of fermenting vegetables over harsh winters or the emotional toll of navigating self-doubt—was essential to creating something meaningful. For Nilsson, every obstacle was an opportunity to refine his craft and deepen his connection to his work.

This mindset echoes a philosophy central to this book: The pain of discipline today is far preferable to the regret of unfulfilled potential tomorrow. Nilsson's journey illustrates that mastery is not about avoiding discomfort but about leaning into it, transforming challenges into catalysts for growth. The lessons he learned at Fäviken extend far beyond the kitchen and offer a universal blueprint for anyone striving to achieve remarkable results in any area of their life.

By the mid-2010s, Fäviken, having earned two Michelin stars, had become one of the most sought-out dining destinations in the world, attracting food enthusiasts from around the globe. Yet, behind the accolades, Nilsson faced an internal reckoning. The pursuit of perfection had taken its toll, leaving him physically and emotionally drained. He began to question whether the sacrifices required to sustain Fäviken's success were worth the cost.

In 2019, at the height of his career, Nilsson made the shocking decision to close Fäviken. For many, this move seemed counterintuitive, even reckless. But for Nilsson, it was an act of self-preservation and a testament to his commitment to living authentically. Stepping away allowed him to focus on his family, explore new creative pursuits, and reconnect with the joy of cooking outside the constraints of a high-pressure environment.

LESSONS FROM NILSSON'S JOURNEY

Magnus Nilsson's story is a masterclass in mindset mastery and the art of continuous improvement. His ability to navigate identity crises, embrace purposeful suffering, and maintain an unrelenting focus on his vision offers applicable lessons for anyone seeking to unlock their highest potential.

Authenticity as a Compass

Nilsson's success was rooted in his refusal to conform to external expectations. By aligning his work with his values and heritage, he created something truly unique.

The Power of Resilience

In the face of adversity, Nilsson demonstrated that resilience is not about avoiding hardship but about enduring it with purpose and grace.

The Importance of Self-Awareness

Recognizing when to pivot—whether it's stepping back from a demanding project or redefining goals—is as crucial as the pursuit of excellence itself.

The Courage to Begin

Nilsson's journey reminds us that every great achievement starts with a single step, often taken in the shadow of uncertainty and fear.

Magnus Nilsson's life and career embody the principles of growth, resilience, and self-actualization. His story is a testament to the transformative power of mindset and the importance of staying true to one's values, even in the face of overwhelming challenges (and success). As we reflect on his journey, we are reminded that the path to greatness is not linear—it is a winding trail marked by trials and triumphs on the way to greater authenticity. Nilsson demonstrated that mindset mastery is not an endpoint but a continuous journey. Whether we are creating a culinary masterpiece, building a business, or navigating life's complexities, the infinite edge of improvement awaits those who dare to begin, endure, and evolve. Nilsson's legacy is the challenge to step boldly onto our own battlefield, armed with resilience, purpose, and an unshakable belief in what we can achieve.

✪

As Carol Dweck says, "Becoming is better than being." This idea reflects the belief that identity and ability are not fixed but can be shaped and developed with effort and perseverance. A growth mindset, unlike a fixed mindset, opens the door to evolution because it emphasizes continuous learning over static achievement and enables us to rewrite the narrative of who we are and who we can become.

The intentional transformation of mindset has far-reaching impacts. At work, it drives innovation and resilience; in relationships, it fosters empathy and openness; and personally, it propels us toward a life rooted in progress rather than perfection. As we align with our potential, we inspire others to embrace growth, creating a ripple effect that fosters mutual transformation in families, teams, and communities. Ultimately, mastering our mindset transcends personal success because it builds an ecosystem of collective progress, fulfillment, and lasting impact.

GOING *ALL IN*

TO ACCESS YOUR ALL IN WORKSPACE,
VISIT APP.EXLR8.AI/ALL-IN

HOW DOES MY CURRENT MINDSET SHAPE MY ABILITY TO OVERCOME CHALLENGES AND PURSUE GROWTH?

Reflection
Justinian II and Magnus Nilsson remind us that resilience and a growth-oriented mindset can turn even the most daunting obstacles into stepping stones to success.

Action
Identify one challenge you're currently facing and consciously reframe it as an opportunity to grow. Write down three actions you can take today to approach it with renewed determination and focus.

WHAT STEPS AM I TAKING TO DESIGN ROUTINES AND ENVIRONMENTS THAT SUPPORT MY HIGHEST POTENTIAL?

Reflection
Magnus Nilsson's intentional creation of Fäviken as a space to honor his heritage while pursuing culinary mastery demonstrates the power of designing environments that align with purpose.

Action
Audit your current routines and environments. Identify one habit or element that is holding you back and replace it with a practice or setting that propels you toward your goals.

HOW CAN I TAKE THE FIRST STEP TOWARD PERSONAL OR PROFESSIONAL TRANSFORMATION TODAY?

Reflection
This chapter emphasizes the importance of starting now, even when the path ahead seems uncertain. Magnus Nilsson's bold decision to leave Paris and forge his unique culinary identity serves as a reminder of the courage required to act.

Action

Choose one goal you've been delaying. Break it into manageable steps and commit to taking the first step within the next twenty-four hours. Document your progress and reflect on how taking action moves you closer to your vision.

7

MINDSET AS A CATALYST

Paving the Way to Peak Performance

Performance mastery is not the product of natural talent alone; it is forged through the intentional cultivation of mindset—the bedrock of tenacity, agility, and exceptional achievement. In a world that demands excellence at every turn, the true differentiator lies in how we train our minds to confront challenges, embrace growth, and transcend perceived limitations. This chapter explores the art and science of mindset as the driving force behind peak performance. Mindset determines our outcomes and expands our capacity to redefine what is truly possible.

The concept may seem lofty, but the application is fiercely practical. Neuroscience reminds us that our brain is malleable, capable of rewiring itself in response to experiences and intentional habits. Neuroplasticity isn't just a buzzword; it's a superpower we all have. By leveraging the brain's plasticity, we can replace self-doubt with self-mastery, reframe setbacks as opportunities, and channel adversity into unparalleled growth. This transformation isn't about ignoring fear or pain but about mastering them. Those who unlock this potential become unstoppable, racking up achievements and navigating complexity and uncertainty with clarity and purpose.

Mindset mastery requires active engagement and deliberate practice. You must reject mediocrity absolutely. To harness mindset as an engine for performance, you must embrace discomfort, push boundaries, and redefine your perceived limits. This chapter draws on the extraordinary science behind Navy SEAL training and a few intriguing, quirky insights into the fascinating inner workings of the human mind. Whether you're conquering physical summits or corporate milestones, the principles of peak performance are universal: adaptability, resilience, and belief in your capacity to grow. Let's delve into the tools and strategies that drive greatness.

FORGED IN ADVERSITY: CHOOSING THE PAIN OF DISCIPLINE OVER THE STING OF REGRET

I will never quit. I persevere and thrive in adversity.
—NAVY SEAL ETHOS

Becoming a Navy SEAL isn't just a matter of training but an extreme transformation of both body and mind. It's one thing to take an ordinary person with no experience in special operations tactics and shape them into someone who can handle physically grueling tasks. But to transform that same person into one of the most feared and sophisticated warriors in modern history? That requires a complete shift in mindset and identity. This is where Navy SEAL training stands apart, not just as a physical crucible but as a journey into the psychology and neuroscience of human potential.

Ordinary People, Extraordinary Goals

To the untrained eye, those who begin the first portion of Navy SEAL training—officially known as Basic Underwater Demolition / SEAL training (BUD/S)—might appear no different from the rest of us. They hail from diverse backgrounds: some are collegiate athletes, others are ordinary high school graduates, a few are young professionals transitioning from the corporate world, and many have prior military experience. Yet, they all share one defining trait: an unrelenting drive to accomplish something extraordinary, almost unfathomable. However, sheer determination alone is not enough to ensure success. BUD/S, with its grueling demands, has the highest attrition rate among special operations training programs, with approximately 85 percent of candidates failing to complete it. This figure doesn't even account for the thousands who apply each year but who are turned away. Remarkably, we cannot attribute the success of the elite few who make it through simply to natural athleticism or raw physical toughness. They undergo an immense transformation during training, one that reshapes their mindset and, in many ways, the essence of who they are.

So, what separates those who succeed from those who don't? To understand this, we need to look at the *neuroscience* and *psychology* behind mindset transformation and how SEAL training forges an evolved identity in those who endure it.

Breaking Down the Mindset: Growth in the Face of Failure

One of the most critical elements that BUD/S instructors are looking for in students isn't sheer physical ability—it's the capacity to endure failure. The physical demands of the program are designed to break you down to your very core, but the real test is psychological. Each task, whether it's a long and brutal underwater swim or running for miles with heavy boats on your head, is a test of mental fortitude. SEAL candidates are expected to fall short again and again—and still come back for more. As the training progresses, those who remain begin to realize something crucial: Failure is not an endpoint but a tool for growth. Failure is not final unless we allow it to be. Microfailures are necessary while en route to extraordinary outcomes. This mindset is imperative for going *all in*.

This aligns with the *growth mindset* theory developed by psychologist Carol Dweck. In her research, Dweck found that individuals who view challenges as opportunities for growth, rather than as insurmountable barriers, are far more likely to succeed. The growth mindset is embedded in SEAL training. The instructors are interested in seeing who can complete the tasks, sure, but more, they want to see who can push past failure and adapt. This is where a SEAL candidate's first major identity shift happens. Instead of identifying with success or physical prowess, those who make it through BUD/S learn to identify with their ability to grow through adversity.

At the heart of this transformation is the concept known as—you guessed it—*neuroplasticity*, the brain's ability to rewire itself in response to experiences. SEAL training is an ongoing process of rewiring the brain for resilience. In BUD/S, the candidates' brains are constantly adapting to new levels of stress. Studies have shown that prolonged exposure to stress can actually enhance the brain's ability to adapt and recover—provided the individual does not succumb to the stress. The brain becomes more efficient at managing cortisol (the stress hormone), allowing SEALs to remain calm and focused even under extreme pressure. This is a gradual, often painful process that requires the SEAL candidate to redefine their relationship with fear and discomfort. As this happens, their identity begins to shift from someone who fears failure to someone who seeks it out as a way to grow stronger. Over time, the repeated exposure to hardship fundamentally changes how the brain processes fear, stress, and uncertainty.

Let's not be naive—mental toughness isn't forged solely during the training process; those who prevail have an undeniable intrinsic quality. SEAL candidates who are successful come into training with a baseline level of resilience that was shaped by their upbringing, life experiences, or passionate connection to the mission. This raw material is then forged in the crucible of BUD/S. However, what's fascinating is that many students enter the program without any special hardship in their background. Although some may have experienced a tough childhood, others come from upper-middle-class families and even extreme wealth. Most are simply average people who, when faced with the choice to quit or continue, discover an untapped well of mental toughness they never knew existed.

Is this toughness a natural gift? Or is it the result of years of subtle conditioning? The truth lies somewhere in between. Studies on grit, led by psychologist Angela Duckworth, show that perseverance and passion for long-term goals are the strongest predictors of success in high-stress environments—often exerting a stronger influence than natural talent or even preexisting "toughness." Instead, these individuals have a deep internal commitment to see something through, no matter how painful or difficult the process, thereby paving the way to peak performance.

This is where the identity shift becomes even more apparent. Those who make it through SEAL training don't just see themselves as survivors or warriors; they see themselves as *finishers*. They become the kind of people who finish what they start, who endure what others cannot, and who thrive in environments designed to break lesser people.

Identity Shift: Becoming More Than Human

SEAL training—more than developing world-class expertise in shooting, land and undersea warfare, and demolition—transcends the limits of physical prowess. A SEAL develops into the kind of person who thrives where others falter—a transformation so unique that by the time a candidate graduates, their identity has irrevocably been reshaped. They emerge as individuals capable of feats of unimaginable perseverance and valor yet infused with humility and a willingness to continually learn and evolve. What makes this transformation remarkable is that it hinges on physical conditioning and, more crucially, mental fortitude. The body, no matter how well conditioned, merely follows the mind's lead.

SEALs master the art of silencing fear, compartmentalizing pain, and making critical decisions with unparalleled clarity and precision—especially in life-or-death scenarios. Let me emphasize that these are ordinary individuals in many ways—husbands, fathers, and people who do yardwork on the weekends. Yet, when duty calls, they tap into an intentionally created identity—a reservoir of unwavering discipline, tactical excellence, and unfulfillable thirst for victory. This identity, rooted in grit and an unshakable commitment to protect those fighting alongside them, transforms them into warriors of unmatched capability and resolve.

These attributes that define the world's finest warriors are undeniably crucial, but one often-overlooked quality stands out: *adaptability*. Though I've touched on this before, it warrants a deeper exploration. SEALs are meticulously trained to embrace change, pivot seamlessly when circumstances demand, and devise innovative solutions to complex problems that have no clear answers.

In psychological terms, this adaptability is known as *cognitive flexibility*. It's the ability to switch between different modes of thinking and to adjust quickly to new situations. SEALs are masters of this skill. Whether we're operating in the desert, an urban setting, or the ocean, we can adapt our tactics to fit the environment. This cognitive flexibility is critical in high-stress environments, where sticking rigidly to a plan can mean the difference between mission success and mission failure. The ability to adapt, to remain mentally agile, is what enables SEALs to succeed where others fail.

This exploration of the Navy SEAL "manufacturing" process reveals powerful insights into achieving peak performance that can be applied far beyond the military sphere. Embracing well-designed routines, intentional habit formation, and a growth-oriented mindset paves the way for anyone to attain extraordinary achievements.

The importance of

- rewiring the mind for emotional endurance,
- redefining failure as an opportunity for growth, and
- cultivating mental elasticity to thrive in ever-changing circumstances

are among the foundational pillars of living *all in*.

These principles empower us to think differently about our goals—not just in terms of what we want to achieve but also in terms of who we must become to achieve them. When these superhero qualities converge, they facilitate unparalleled success, proving that greatness is not a gift but a practice available to all who commit passionately.

KEEP MOVING FORWARD, EVEN WITH A HOLE IN YOUR HEAD

If knocked down, I will get back up, every time.
—NAVY SEAL ETHOS

The human brain, as miraculous as it is maddeningly delicate, holds the blueprint for peak performance—whether in moments of intentional self-improvement or in the chaos of unforeseen adversity. Few arenas illustrate this truth better than Navy SEAL training, where recruits are molded into paragons of mental toughness, where they rewire their minds to endure, adapt, and excel. Yet, for all the cutting-edge methods of modern warriors, one of the most peculiar and illuminating insights into the brain's resilience hails from an unlikely nineteenth-century railroad foreman with a knack for survival—and a flair for dramatic life changes.

Meet Phineas Gage—railroad foreman, nineteenth-century trailblazer, and reluctant neuroscience legend. Not to mention the obvious fact of having an epic name. It's not every day you wake up thinking, *Today, I'm going to make history by having a three-foot iron rod rocket through my skull.* But life's funny like that. Some days, you get promoted at work. Other days, you get a taste of impromptu brain surgery courtesy of an industrial accident. Phineas got the latter, and boy, did it change things.

In the summer of 1848, Phineas, a twenty-five-year-old dynamo who managed railroad construction crews, was living his best life. He was a foreman—*the* foreman—on the Rutland & Burlington Railroad in Vermont. At the time, Phineas was known for his sharp mind and solid work ethic. He could organize a chaotic crew of grumbling workers and blast rock better than anyone in the business. By all accounts, his identity was deeply intertwined with being a competent, reliable leader.

But then came that fateful September day when the routine—quite literally—blew up in his face. Gage and his crew were laying tracks, which involved drilling holes into large rocks, filling them with gunpowder, and using a long iron tamping rod to pack it all in nice and tight. You know, your typical 1840s job with high explosives and minimal safety protocols. They liked to keep it simple back then. No OSHA, no problem. What could possibly go wrong?

Well, Phineas was packing the powder, minding his own business when—BOOM—an unexpected spark ignited the powder before sand could cover it. The result? The tamping rod shot through the air at breakneck speed, entered Phineas's left cheek, rocketed behind his left eye, and exploded out the top of his skull to land several yards away. And here's the kicker: Gage didn't die. He didn't even pass out. No, he sat up, dusted himself off, and allegedly said to the doctor who came to help, "Here's business enough for you." Although Gage survived, the man who got up from that accident was not the same man who had started the day. Pre-accident Phineas was the very picture of industriousness, respected for his discipline and social acumen. Post-accident Phineas, however, had undergone a bit of a personality reboot—one that would make even the most patient HR manager pull their hair out.

The rod had destroyed a significant chunk of his frontal lobe, the part of the brain that's in charge of decision-making, impulse control, and personality—basically, the part of the brain that keeps us from flipping out over minor inconveniences. Gage, who once had a stable, even temperament, became irritable, reckless, and prone to outbursts. His friends and colleagues said he was "no longer Gage." The guy who once embodied leadership was now, to put it mildly, a bit of an asshole.

The change in Gage's behavior wasn't just a curious quirk—it demonstrated neuroscience in action. His injury had fundamentally altered the pathways in his brain that regulated his personality. The frontal lobe is where executive functions happen, cognitive processes including planning, making decisions, controlling impulses, and maintaining social norms. It's the part of the brain that says, "Hey, maybe don't scream at your coworker for borrowing your stapler." Without the full functioning of this critical area, Gage was unable to regulate his emotions and social behavior. Neuroscientists would eventually marvel at this case because it offered the first real insight into how specific brain regions control different aspects of personality. But poor Phineas? He just knew he wasn't the same. His peak performance mindset had been disrupted, literally, and the man who once thrived on routine now struggled to piece together a sense of identity. It's as if life played a cosmic joke on him, saying, "You think you've got it all figured out? Watch this."

But here's the other kicker: Despite his dramatic transformation, Phineas didn't give up on life. Sure, his days as a railroad foreman were over, but after wandering a bit—working as a sideshow curiosity (because, of course, 1800s America couldn't resist a good freak of nature)—he found a second career as a stagecoach driver in Chile. Why Chile? Who knows. Anyway, stagecoach driving required planning, adaptability, and resilience, which means that even though Phineas's brain had been literally rearranged, he still managed to reconfigure himself and find a new purpose, albeit a vastly different one.

So, what does Phineas Gage's story teach us about identity transformation? Well, for one, it's a reminder that not all transformations are voluntary. Sometimes, life slams you with a metaphorical iron rod, and suddenly, everything changes. Phineas didn't choose to have his frontal lobe destroyed, just like we don't always choose the unexpected upheavals that force us to reconsider who we are.

But even after life's most shocking disruptions, there's still the opportunity for reinvention. Phineas's brain was damaged, yes, but the remaining parts adapted. They found new ways to connect, new routines to follow, new goals to pursue. His transformation wasn't the one he wanted, but it was one he had to accept. The underlying science that shows us the brain is remarkably plastic applies to all of us: With intention, effort, and time, we can rewire our thinking and behavior to shape new identities.

Sure, most of us won't have a metal rod shot through our brains (thankfully), but life has a way of throwing other curveballs our way—ones that force us to rethink how we show up in the world. The key is realizing that our identity is not fixed. Just like Gage's brain adapted, so too can we intentionally design routines, habits, and mindsets that lead us to the person, the leader, or the visionary we aim to become.

And let's face it, there's a bit of dark humor in this whole mess. If Phineas, with half his brain literally out of commission, could find a way to keep going, to carve out a new sense of self, what excuse do the rest of us have? His story is a wild, bizarre reminder that we don't always get to choose the circumstances of our transformation, but we do get to choose how we move forward.

At the end of the day, Phineas Gage didn't let his injury define him. He may not have been the same man after the accident, but he adapted and found a way to keep working, keep living, and, most importantly, keep moving. And in a strange way, his story gives us all a bit of hope: No matter what life throws at us, there's always room for reinvention.

SAVED BY THE BELL: IF YOU'RE NOT DEAD YET, PLEASE LET US KNOW

I'm not afraid of death;
I just don't want to be there when it happens.
—WOODY ALLEN

In Navy SEAL training, you never ever want to ring the bell. The notorious bell is a symbol of both challenge and choice. It is prominently displayed in the training compound and serves as a visible and ever-present reminder of the mental and physical toll of the program. The formal act of ringing the bell signifies to the instructors that you are voluntarily Dropping on Request. Quitting. But, sometimes, ringing the bell is in fact a matter of life and almost death.

Let's stick to Phineas Gage's time period for a moment, because, well, it's fun. Imagine, for a moment, you're living in the nineteenth century. You're wearing a tight corset or a top hat, and—if you're really lucky—a bell has been installed on your coffin. Because, well, life was weirdly unpredictable back then. Remember what happened to Phineas? In an era when the line between dead and *almost dead* was pretty blurry, a strange fear gripped people's imaginations: the fear of being buried alive. The result? A surge of radical innovation brought about the *safety coffin*, a high-tech contraption complete with a string and a bell that a buried-but-not-quite-dead person could use to ring for help. Yes, you read that right: a bell…for your coffin. Welcome to the world of nineteenth-century "posthumous precautions."

But let's back up a little. Why, you might ask, were people so obsessed with avoiding the great faux pas of premature burial? Well, medical science at the time wasn't exactly the beacon of precision it is today. Doctors had a nasty habit of declaring people dead when they were, in fact, very much still alive but temporarily unconscious, in a coma, or suffering from what we'd now call catalepsy (a condition where the body becomes unresponsive). These near-death experiences were often misinterpreted as actual death. And so, with horror stories swirling, inventive minds stepped in with a variety of safety coffins designed to give the not-quite-dead a fighting chance at clawing back to life—or at least ringing a bell to alert the cemetery staff that they were still hanging on. Whether or not anyone came to your aid most likely depended on how well you were liked, I suppose.

One of the most famous stories involved a particularly anxious German aristocrat, who, terrified of being buried alive, requested that her coffin be equipped with a feeding tube and an air supply system. The coffin also featured a bell connected to a string that would allow her to signal from below should the Grim Reaper's visit turn out to be premature. Whether or not she ever needed to use it is lost to history, but the story is enough to make you question how comfortable you'd feel living in a time when death wasn't exactly a permanent condition—at least not right away.

But it gets even weirder. The German physician Christoph Wilhelm Hufeland, in 1791, advocated for creating "waiting mortuaries," where the recently deceased were laid out in full view and monitored by attendants for signs of life. Only after a certain period of "no-movement certification" would the body be considered eligible for burial. Imagine visiting the "mortuary" and seeing Aunt Mabel lying there, just in case she decided to stir back to life. As unsettling as it sounds today, it was a necessary precaution back when coffins with bells were considered another layer of insurance against an existential mix-up.

Now, here's where it gets entertaining—or horrifying, depending on your point of view. Although it's hard to track down definitive records of people actually being saved by a coffin bell, stories certainly abound. One tale tells of a young woman in nineteenth-century France who was buried after being pronounced dead from cholera. Shortly after her interment, the bell attached to her coffin started ringing furiously. Graveyard workers, likely not expecting an actual resurrection, were jolted into action. They dug her up to find her alive but in a delirious state. While this is one of those "it could've happened" stories, it speaks to the paranoia of the time—and the chilling fact that people *might* have been saved, all thanks to a little bell ringing from six feet under.

I realize you are probably wondering why we are talking about coffin bells and how this unusual bit of history relates to forming our identity and goals. In life, we often find ourselves metaphorically buried by the expectations of others, by the weight of our responsibilities, or by the limitations we impose on ourselves. We feel trapped—just as a person mistakenly buried alive might feel—and the real question is, Do we have the courage to ring the bell? Do we have the presence of mind to pull the proverbial string and signal that we're still here, that we've still got fight left in us? Sometimes, life buries us under the weight of unmet goals or crushed dreams, but it's how we respond to those moments that defines our identity moving forward. Do we panic, or do we start ringing the bell for all we're worth?

Just like in the nineteenth century, life can throw unexpected curveballs that leave us feeling entombed in situations we never chose. But it's in those moments of entrapment that we have a choice: We can give up, accept the burial as inevitable, or we can take control, ring the bell, and fight our way back to the surface. The coffin bell, though a quirky relic of a more morbid time, serves as a potent metaphor for resilience. It reminds us that even when the world has figuratively buried us alive—whether in our careers, our relationships, or our personal struggles—there's always a bell string to pull, a way to signal that we're not done yet.

It also speaks to the power of self-awareness. The people who equipped their coffins with bells were preparing for the worst-case scenario, but they were also acknowledging that life is unpredictable. Much like any modern contingency plans we may devise, these nineteenth-century solutions for premature burial were built on the idea that *things go wrong*. All the time. Safety coffins are a testament to human tenacity, our stubborn refusal to let life bury us before we've finished writing our story. And that's where identity comes into play. Just as Phineas Gage didn't choose to have a tamping rod rocket through his skull, none of us get to choose all the circumstances that shape our identities. We do, however, have a choice in how we adapt.

So, as you sit there, envisioning the absurdity of bells attached to coffins in the nineteenth century, consider this: Those bells were symbols of hope. They were placed there as a last line of defense against the ultimate misidentification. But today, we don't need literal bells—we need the mental and emotional tools to recognize when we're feeling crushed by life's challenges. We must not always attempt to avoid adversity; we must cultivate the awareness to pull ourselves out when we find ourselves six feet deep in doubt, fear, or failure. And remember, asking for help shows courage, not weakness.

Even in the nineteenth century, people understood that life rarely unfolds as planned. You may think you're on the fast track to a promotion or financial windfall, only for life to hand you a shovel and whisper, "Start digging." In such moments, you face a choice: keep digging blindly, or pause, reassess, and ring the proverbial bell to signal readiness for a new path. Just as burial practices evolved to prevent untimely interment, our approach to identity must also adapt to life's unpredictability. We must focus not on holding onto who we were yesterday or conforming to others' expectations for tomorrow but on developing the flexibility to adapt swiftly when life takes unexpected turns. Part of going all in means recognizing when to seek support, when to reassess your path, and when to summon your inner strength to push forward with determination. Then you are ready to pave your way to peak performance and remarkable results.

GOING *ALL IN*

TO ACCESS YOUR ALL IN WORKSPACE, VISIT APP.EXLR8.AI/ALL-IN

HOW DO I HANDLE FAILURE OR SETBACKS IN MY PERSONAL OR PROFESSIONAL LIFE?

Reflection

Navy SEAL training reveals that failure is not an endpoint but a tool for growth. SEAL candidates who succeed aren't the ones who avoid failure but those who use it to build resilience and adaptability. The ability to view setbacks as opportunities rather than as roadblocks is a cornerstone of peak performance.

Action

Reflect on a recent failure. Identify one lesson it taught you and outline one specific way you can use that insight to improve your approach in the future.

WHEN WAS THE LAST TIME I CONSCIOUSLY REFRAMED MY RESPONSE TO STRESS OR ADVERSITY?

Reflection

Phineas Gage's story highlights the brain's neuroplasticity, its ability to rewire and adapt in the face of adversity. Gage's journey, though involuntary, demonstrates that even after life-altering events, the brain can forge new pathways and possibilities.

Action

Identify a stressful situation you're currently facing. Write down one way you can reframe the challenge to see it as an opportunity for growth or learning. Take one action today to reinforce this new perspective.

AM I CULTIVATING THE ADAPTABILITY NEEDED TO THRIVE IN UNPREDICTABLE SITUATIONS?

Reflection

The adaptability of Navy SEALs, built through practicing cognitive flexibility and deliberate mental conditioning, enables them to navigate chaos with clarity and precision. This skill is not innate but developed through consistent exposure to challenges and intentional practice.

Action
Challenge yourself to step outside your comfort zone this week. Take on an unfamiliar task or experience that requires you to think creatively and adapt quickly. Reflect on how this experience strengthens your mental agility.

8

VISIONARY MINDSET

When Going All In,
You Gotta Know Where You're Headed

If someone had told me years ago that I'd be writing about "manifestation" one day, I would have rolled my eyes so hard they'd still be stuck pointing backward. Manifestation? Really? I once affectionately called my incredible wife a "little California hippie" after she scolded me for using one of her sound bowls to toss a salad. How was I supposed to know it wasn't kitchenware? The word *manifestation* conjures images of crystal-wielding gurus sitting in the lotus position humming, not exactly the crowd I typically roll with. Navy SEALs from Texas aren't exactly known for chanting in circles while polishing grenades.

But here's the thing about reality: It's an uncompromising teacher that doesn't care about your preconceived notions. The deeper I ventured into the realms of neuroscience and psychology, the more I realized that manifestation isn't so much about cosmic wish lists as it is, at its core, a framework for setting intentions, focusing energy, and, most importantly, taking action. When combined with a vision—a genuine, clear, actionable vision—manifesting becomes not only plausible but also profoundly practical. It turns out, the universe is far more intricate—and fascinating—than my initial skepticism allowed.

So, let's set aside the eye-rolling (but hold onto the sarcasm—it's essential) and dive into how we can develop a compelling vision for what we want to accomplish, maintain it through inevitable challenges, and make it a reality.

Because whether you're manifesting a personal goal, a career milestone, or your next great idea, vision is the starting point. And when paired with deliberate effort and a sprinkle of audacity, it just might work some magic.

A BRIEF EXPLORATION IN MANIFESTATION

As you think, so shall you become.

—HINDU PROVERB

The concept of manifestation—the age-old belief that our thoughts, desires, and intentions hold the power to shape reality—has roots in Hinduism. Christians hold diverse views on manifestation and often emphasize trust in God's will over self-reliance. Although aligning desires with faith and prayer agrees with biblical teachings (Mark 11:24), Christians caution against modern interpretations of manifestation that marginalize God's role or emphasize materialism, which may conflict with seeking God's kingdom first (Matthew 6:33). Some see manifestation as cocreation with God, combining prayer and action (James 2:17), whereas others critique its overlap with New Age practices that focus on self-power rather than divine dependence. Ultimately, Christians prioritize surrender to God's will (Luke 22:42), trust in His plan, and aligning aspirations with His purposes.

Unlike today's "manifestation" trends, which promise prosperity through affirmations and "good vibes," the original concept was wrapped in philosophical wisdom, rigorous introspection, and a cosmology that viewed the universe as the playground of consciousness. So, if you've ever considered "manifesting" a new career path or a healthier marriage by imagining it hard enough, you're about to take a journey back to where it all began—long before vision boards made with magazine cutouts became popular the ancient sacred scriptures of Hinduism were calling us to go far beyond the mundane and shallow to explore the very nature of reality, consciousness, and human potential.

The principles of manifestation rooted in the Vedas and the Upanishads provide a profound framework for aligning vision, thought, and action with desired outcomes. The Vedas, ancient sacred texts composed in Sanskrit between 1500 BC and 500 BC, introduced the concept of Brahman, the universal consciousness that connects all existence. Human consciousness, seen as a reflection of Brahman, has the potential to influence reality through disciplined intention and alignment. The Upanishads, a subset of scriptures, expanded on this foundation by emphasizing the unity of Atman (individual self) and Brahman. Manifestation, in this context, is not a casual wish but a disciplined process requiring alignment of values, actions, and purpose.

Key to this practice is *sankalpa*, setting a focused and meaningful intention. Unlike modern "wish for it" philosophies, *sankalpa* demands inner commitment and self-transformation, as seen in mythological figures such as Sage Vishwamitra, one of the most revered sages in ancient Indian mythology who attained extraordinary power through focus. Similarly, modern innovators like Elon Musk illustrate this principle by aligning their lives fully with their visionary goals and transforming ambition into reality through resolute dedication. Manifestation is further understood through concepts like karma (cause and effect) and dharma (duty) that emphasize that success comes not from fleeting desires but from ethical, purpose-driven actions.

Practical applications include mantras, prayer, and meditation, which serve as tools to harmonize mind, body, and spirit with higher aspirations. However, the ancients warned against "spiritual materialism," stressing that true manifestation is not an exercise in fulfilling fleeting desires but a cultivation of alignment with universal truth. Contemporary mindfulness practices, such as those embraced by former Twitter CEO Jack Dorsey—known for his unconventional lifestyle and focus on mindfulness and wellness—echo this sentiment and focus on creating resilience, clarity, and purpose over material gains.

These teachings remain relevant in modern times, offering a counterpoint to our instant-gratification culture. Manifestation in the Hindu tradition is a journey of self-discipline and transformation that invites individuals to align their lives with higher truths. Far from conjuring desires out of thin air, we can reshape our inner world to influence the outer world in a meaningful way—a timeless reminder that achieving greatness begins with alignment and intention.

THE FIVE PILLARS OF CULTIVATING A VISIONARY MINDSET

The only thing worse than being blind
is having sight but no vision.
—HELEN KELLER

To achieve greatness—whether in the boardroom, at the home office, or on the battlefield—one must begin with a vision. Not just a fleeting idea or a vague ambition but a vision so compelling it becomes the gravitational force pulling everything else into its orbit. Any goal not tethered to a grander vision is merely a daydream, a fleeting wisp of hope destined to dissipate without action. And vision, no matter how lofty, without execution, is little more than a mirage of greatness that evaporates under the harsh light of reality.

True visionaries—those who turn their dreams into reality—understand that vision is not a passive act of imagination. It is the cornerstone of deliberate strategy, the North Star guiding purposeful action, and the catalyst for transformative change. They know that a vision gains power only when paired with persistent execution that transforms intangible aspirations into concrete achievements. This is not the work of dreamers but the work of doers, those who see the gap between what is and what could be and commit to bridging it using discipline, focus, and action.

Five pillars are essential for cultivating a visionary mindset that doesn't just dream but also executes, a mindset that turns impossibilities into inevitabilities. We aren't talking about wishing upon a star or manifesting in the abstract but rather harnessing the incredible power of your mind, aligning it with intentional effort, and unlocking extraordinary outcomes. Together, these pillars lay the foundation for turning bold ideas into tangible results. Your vision is a road map to remarkable success.

Pillar 1: Embrace the Power of Visualization

As an entrepreneur, I often wrestle with the elusive concept of vision. Is it about generating profit, creating shareholder value, or building an exceptional team? Whereas all these elements are undeniably important, none fully capture the deeper essence of the question: What is the driving force that transforms potential into achievement, that converts fleeting opportunities into enduring success? What is the aspirational foundation that defines our very purpose and reason for existence? To truly grasp what vision is, we must distill it down to its fundamental components. At its heart lies visualization—the cornerstone of every great achievement, the granddaddy of manifestation techniques.

Visualization, when practiced with purpose, is a dynamic and disciplined mental exercise: vividly imagining your goals, rehearsing success in your mind, and priming your brain to seize opportunities with precision and clarity. It's not fluff; it's the mental architecture that bridges the gap between where you are and where you dare to go.

Think of your brain as the world's most sophisticated simulator. When you imagine performing an action, you're firing up the same neural pathways you'd use if you were actually doing it. It's like a dress rehearsal for your mind. Neuroscience calls this "mental imagery" or "motor imagery," and its effectiveness is backed by solid research. We talked about Michael Phelps in Chapter 4, and I will use him as an example again. To become the most decorated Olympian in history, Phelps didn't just practice in the pool; he spent countless hours visualizing every stroke, every turn, every possible scenario—including his goggles filling with water. So when that exact mishap happened during the Beijing Olympics, he didn't panic. He'd already "been there, done that" in his mind. He swam blind and still won gold, setting a world record. Coincidence? Hardly.

Navy SEALs, who set the gold standard for mental and physical toughness, don't just rely on brute strength; we also harness the power of visualization to survive and thrive. I've already described the punishing gauntlet of constant physical training, freezing water, and virtually no sleep. In these moments, visualization is a lifeline. And, no, students who succeed are not imagining themselves snuggled in a warm bed with a cup of cocoa. That's a slippery slope to ringing the bell and calling it quits. Instead, they fixate on the long game—the ultimate result, the triumph beyond the pain. They see the outcome with clarity, understanding that the deep suffering they endure is not a barrier but an essential element of the forging process. And so, with resolute determination, they lean in, embracing the hardship as the crucible that will shape their greatness.

Why does visualization work so well? Enter neuroscience—the ultimate buzzkill for all our excuses. A study in the *Journal of Neurophysiology* reveals that simply imagining doing exercise can increase muscle strength by up to 22 percent. Yes, you read that correctly: Your brain is out there doing reps without so much as breaking a sweat. This phenomenon occurs because the brain sends signals to the muscles that reinforce neural pathways as if you were actually moving. Apparently, the brain isn't great at distinguishing between real and imagined experiences—it processes them almost identically. While Navy SEALs are visualizing their survival under extreme duress, this research suggests you could sculpt your biceps from the comfort of your couch. Tempting, right? But let's not get carried away. Visualization is a powerful tool, but it's no replacement for actual effort. So, before you trade your workout gear for Netflix marathons, let me just say: Keep up the fitness regime. Your future self—and your real-life gains—will thank you.

So, how do you harness the power of visualization without feeling like you're engaging in wishful thinking? Here are some practical steps:

- **BE SPECIFIC.** Don't just visualize "success." What does success look like to you, specifically? Is it launching a new product? Delivering a flawless presentation? Picture the scene in high definition. If your goal is to build a tech start-up, what does the business look like in five years? What kind of leader will you be? How will the company culture affect results? What is the valuation of the business at that time?
- **ENGAGE ALL SENSES.** What do you see, hear, smell, feel? The more sensory details you include, the more real it becomes to your brain. What will the energy feel like at your annual sales kick-offs? What will the Las Vegas casino hotel venue smell like? (We know the answer to that one.) Who will attend?
- **INCLUDE OBSTACLES.** Life isn't a smooth ride, and neither should your visualization be. Anticipate challenges and visualize yourself overcoming them. This prepares you mentally for setbacks. What if it takes longer to reach product-market fit than you thought? How will you adapt? What if customer success isn't coming together the way you envisioned? All special operators do this before each mission, visualizing the "what ifs" and the contingencies alike.

- **BE CONSISTENT.** Make visualization a daily practice. Like any skill, it improves with regular exercise. So, get your reps in.

In essence, visualization is like sharpening your tools before you start building. It doesn't do the work for you, but it sure makes the work more efficient.

Pillar 2: Build a Mindfulness Practice to Hone Awareness

Having tuned up your mental simulator, it's time to ground yourself in the here and now. Enter *mindfulness*, a term that's been co-opted by wellness blogs and influencers, often stripped of its profound potential. But at its core, mindfulness is the act of cultivating a deep awareness of the present moment without judgment.

"Great," you might say, "but how does sitting cross-legged and focusing on my breath help me dominate my battlefield?" Fair question. Again, crisscross-applesauce grenade polishing alone doesn't defeat the enemy.

Mindfulness enhances your ability to focus, reduces stress, and improves decision-making—skills crucial for anyone aiming to achieve lofty goals. It's not emptying your mind but honing it. Neuroscientists have found that mindfulness practices increase the density of gray matter in brain regions associated with learning, memory, emotion regulation, and empathy. A study in *Proceedings of the National Academy of Sciences* shows that meditation can reduce the brain's fight-or-flight response and allow for more thoughtful reactions under stress.

In everyday life, mindfulness equips you with the composure to navigate challenges with grace. Imagine you're in a high-stakes meeting and asked an unexpected, difficult question. A mind trained in mindfulness can sidestep the spiral of panic, remain grounded in the present moment, and deliver a thoughtful, measured response.

Here's a breakdown of four approachable steps to cultivate mindfulness without the need to abandon your daily life:

1. **START SMALL.** You don't need to commit to long, intensive mindfulness sessions to see the benefits. Start with just five minutes a day and focus on the present moment by tuning in to your breath, the sensations in your body, or your surroundings. This small, intentional

practice removes the pressure of a significant time investment and makes it easier to build a lasting habit of mindfulness that can gradually expand over time. As you get comfortable, you can gradually increase the time, but remember, the real power of mindfulness isn't in the duration of the practice but in the quality of your presence.

2. **BE CONSISTENT.** As with building any skill, mindfulness requires regular practice to show lasting results. Pick a time each day—maybe right after waking up or during a lunch break—and dedicate it to mindfulness. Consistency helps reinforce the habit and retrains your mind to be more naturally present. You'll find that over time, this consistency creates a foundation of calm and focus that you carry into all areas of your life.

3. **APPLY BROADLY.** Mindfulness isn't confined to formal meditation; it's a way of fully engaging with your everyday experiences. Start by practicing mindfulness during simple routines, such as when you are eating: notice the flavors, textures, and colors of your food; when walking, pay attention to each step; when listening, focus on the other person's words without planning your response. Bringing mindfulness to everyday activities turns ordinary moments into opportunities for presence and enjoyment.

4. **PRACTICE NONJUDGMENTAL AWARENESS.** One of the core aspects of mindfulness is observing your thoughts and feelings without assigning them labels like "good" or "bad." When a thought or emotion arises, notice it as if you're watching it from a distance. Rather than reacting or pushing it away, acknowledge its presence and let it pass naturally. This nonjudgmental approach allows you to experience life without experiencing the emotional roller coaster of constant self-critique and leads to greater clarity and inner peace.

By integrating these steps into your daily routine, mindfulness becomes a practical practice, one that doesn't require drastic lifestyle changes but does gradually transform how you experience each moment. Mindfulness bridges the gap between your vision and your actions. It ensures that you're not lost in the future but are taking deliberate steps in the present to get there.

Pillar 3: Align Vision with Values

Now that you've primed your mind and grounded yourself in the present, it's time to delve into what is the driving force behind all your decisions: your core values. Without them, your vision is like a ship without a compass—adrift and vulnerable to every changing wind.

Philosophers have long emphasized the importance of values. Aristotle spoke of *eudaimonia*, often translated as "flourishing" or "the good life," which could be achieved by living virtuously in accordance with reason. In modern terms, your values are your why—the motive power behind your goals.

Consider the Navy SEAL Ethos, which includes values like *tactical proficiency* and *attention to detail*. These aren't just words; they're measurable principles that guide every decision and action. When special operators are faced with impossible odds, it's our commitment to these values that pushes us forward. As stated in the ethos, "The execution of my duties will be swift and violent when required, yet guided by the very principles I serve to uphold." Meaning that we will do everything within our power to win, but we will never sacrifice our values to do so.

In the business world, companies such as Patagonia align their operations with values of environmental stewardship and social responsibility. This isn't just marketing fluff; it's integrated into their business model, influencing everything from supply chain decisions to employee benefits. At EXCELR8, we have embedded a feature in our software that allows leaders and organizations to more specifically action their core values and integrate them into every area of the organization, especially performance management. Values must come with a set of specific standards and defined behaviors. Those standards and behaviors must then be assigned qualitative or quantitative metrics for measuring actions and performance. Then, and only then, are values actionable.

Identifying your core values is an essential process for aligning your actions with what truly matters to you. Here's a more detailed exploration of the steps involved:

- **REFLECT ON PEAK EXPERIENCES.** One of the most revealing ways to understand your core values is to reflect on the moments in your life when you felt the most happiness, pride, or fulfillment. These experiences often happen when we're acting in alignment with our deepest values, even if we didn't consciously realize it at the time. Ask yourself: When did I feel truly alive or proud of myself? What was happening in those moments? Did you experience a sense of accomplishment, connection, or creativity? The emotions tied to these experiences—whether it was a sense of achievement, love, freedom, or service—can point to the underlying values that drove them. By reflecting on these high points, you can uncover the values that give your life meaning and direction.

- **IDENTIFY WHAT ANGERS YOU.** Often, our reactions of frustration or anger can be just as telling as our feelings of joy. When something triggers strong negative emotions, it can be an indicator of a value being violated. For instance, if you feel a deep sense of anger or injustice when you see inequality, it may signal that fairness or social justice is a core value for you. Similarly, feeling upset by dishonesty could reveal a strong value of integrity or authenticity. By exploring what angers you and why, you gain insight into the values you hold dear, and this will help you understand where your boundaries lie and what you stand for.

- **PRIORITIZE YOUR VALUES.** Once you've identified your values, it's time to evaluate which ones are most important to you. Not all values are created equal, and some may be situational or flexible, while others are nonnegotiable. Take time to rank your values according to what matters most in your life. For example, you might value both success and family, but if family is nonnegotiable, it needs to take precedence when you're making major decisions. Prioritizing values ensures that you are clear on which principles will guide your choices so that you can make difficult decisions when faced with competing interests. You must understand which values you're willing to stand firm on and which ones can adapt based on context.

- **ALIGN GOALS WITH VALUES.** Setting goals that are out of alignment with your core values can lead to dissatisfaction, burnout, or a sense of disconnection. And ultimately, mission failure. To ensure that your actions are aligned with your values, take a step back and assess whether your current goals honor them. Ask yourself: Do the goals I've set reflect the things I care about most? For example, if work-life balance is a top value, setting a goal that requires neglecting time with family would conflict with that value. Aligning your vision and actions with your values ensures that your journey is fulfilling and sustainable, rooted in purpose and integrity, and your resilience sees you through challenges.

Following these steps will help you gain clarity on your most significant guiding principles, which empowers you to make intentional choices aligned with your authentic self, ultimately fostering a life of greater fulfillment and purpose.

Pillar 4: Harness the Energy of Intentional Language and Self-Talk

Words have power. It's a psychological fact. The language you use shapes your thoughts, which in turn influence your actions. Cognitive psychologists have long studied the concept of "self-talk"—the internal dialogue that runs through our minds. Negative self-talk can undermine confidence and performance, whereas positive self-talk can enhance them.

In a study published in the *Journal of Sports Sciences*, athletes who engaged in positive self-talk improved their performance in tasks requiring greater perseverance. They reported feeling less exertion, which enabled them to push harder. Muhammad Ali famously declared, "I am the greatest," long before the world recognized him as such. Was it arrogance? Perhaps. But it was also an affirmation that reinforced his belief in himself and drove him to train harder and fight smarter.

Here's an in-depth look at each key element of cultivating meaningful self-talk:

- **POSITIVE AND AFFIRMING:** The language you use in self-talk has a direct impact on your confidence, motivation, and resilience. Aim for phrases that reinforce your strengths, abilities, and determination, even in challenging times. For example, instead of saying, "I hope I can do this," shift to "I am capable and ready to handle this." Positive, affirming language shifts your focus from doubts to possibilities and strengthens your belief in yourself. This supportive self-talk acts as an internal cheerleader, helping you feel empowered and prepared to face whatever comes your way.

- **PRESENT TENSE:** Framing your self-talk in the present tense creates a sense of immediacy and confidence. Instead of seeing success as a future achievement, statements like "I am succeeding" or "I am resilient and resourceful" reinforce the idea that you're embodying these qualities right now. Using the present tense signals to your brain that these traits are already part of who you are, which makes it easier for you to act in alignment with them. This shift from "I will" to "I am" not only enhances motivation but also builds a sense of identity around positive qualities and goals.

- **PERSONALIZED:** To ensure your affirmations and goals truly come to fruition, specificity is key. Vague, generic phrases like "I am strong" can often feel hollow and lack the power to inspire action. Instead, tailor your self-talk to resonate deeply by being precise and intentional; craft language that aligns with your values, experiences, and unique aspirations. For example, replace a broad statement with something more specific, like "I overcome challenges with strength and resilience, staying focused on solutions." When your affirmations are clear and detailed, they become more tangible and emotionally meaningful, which creates a stronger connection to your goals and reinforces the mindset needed to achieve them.

- **CONSISTENT:** Like any habit, effective self-talk requires regular practice and attentiveness. Make it a daily routine to monitor your internal dialogue, and be proactive about shifting any negative or doubtful thoughts toward positive affirmations. The consistency of this practice helps rewire your mind to default to a more supportive and encouraging tone, especially when you are facing obstacles. You might start each morning with a few affirmations or use them as a mental reset throughout the day. By consistently nurturing positive self-talk, you build a mental environment that supports growth, confidence, and resilience.

By incorporating these principles—positive language, present tense, personalization, and consistency—you transform your self-talk into a dynamic tool for self-support and can approach each day with confidence. Effective communication extends beyond self-talk; it also encompasses how you engage with others. The words you choose have the power to inspire, motivate, and influence those around you. Leaders, for example, Martin Luther King Jr., exemplify the transformative impact of intentional language when they use it not merely for eloquence but as a tool to galvanize action toward a shared vision.

Pillar 5: Take Consistent, Aligned Action and Activate Feedback Loops

At this point, you've built a solid mental framework. But without action, it's all just a well-constructed castle in the sky. Manifestation requires movement, but not just any movement—consistent, aligned action informed by feedback loops.

As we know, the concept of neuroplasticity tells us that the brain changes in response to repeated behavior. The more you perform an action, the stronger the neural pathways facilitating that action become, making the behavior more automatic.

This is where the methodology of deliberate practice comes into play. Deliberate practice is a concept popularized by psychologist K. Anders Ericsson that emphasizes purposeful, structured, and consistent efforts to improve performance. Unlike mindless repetition, deliberate practice involves setting specific, measurable goals, breaking down skills into smaller, manageable components, and consistently pushing beyond one's comfort zone to achieve incremental progress. It requires focused attention, immediate feedback, and the ability to identify and correct mistakes along the way. Deliberate practice isn't about merely putting in the hours—it's about ensuring those hours are intentional, productive, and aligned with the ultimate outcome you're striving for. By committing to this methodology, individuals can systematically build expertise and turn raw potential into exceptional performance.

In special operations, formal feedback loops are initiated through after-action reviews (AARs), or debriefs. After every mission or training exercise, we systematically evaluate what went well, what didn't, and what can be improved. Although the process is far more detailed than completing a simple checklist, the core idea remains: Consistent reflection and refinement elevate performance to the highest level. However, learning without immediate implementation—putting that new knowledge into action—is a wasted opportunity. Let me be clear: Ideation without execution is nothing more than an illusion of progress.

The after-action review process—whether conducted individually or within a group—fosters behavioral shifts and promotes transparency, psychological safety, attention to detail, and a relentless commitment to continuous improvement. Performance assessment is most effective when it is integrated iteratively throughout the lifecycle of a project, rather than waiting until the project's conclusion, the end of a quarter, or the close of the year. Regularly scheduled (structured) check-ins allow teams and individuals to evaluate progress, make adjustments, and ensure their actions align with objectives in real time.

For individuals, this means:

- SET CLEAR, MEASURABLE GOALS. Define which actions you need to take and what success looks like.
- CREATE A STRATEGIC PLAN. Outline the steps required to achieve your goals.
- TAKE ACTION. Execute the plan consistently.
- GATHER FEEDBACK ALONG THE WAY. Reflect on what's working and what's not.
- ADJUST ACCORDINGLY. Be willing to pivot and adapt your approach.

Consistency is key. Small actions compounded over time lead to significant results. It's like compounding interest—not flashy but meaningful over the long term.

MANIFESTATION AS A PRACTICAL STRATEGY

So, there you have it—a road map to cultivating a visionary mindset that's grounded in science, philosophy, and practical action. No crystals, no chanting (unless you're into that), just a systematic approach to turning vision into reality. The universe may indeed be made up of energy particles vibrating at different frequencies. But sitting around hoping they'll rearrange themselves in your favor without any effort on your part is, well, delusional.

Instead, harness the incredible power of your mind—visualize with intent, ground yourself in the present, align with your core values, speak to yourself with purpose, and take consistent action informed by feedback. Identity transformation in this sense isn't about becoming someone else; it's about becoming the best version of yourself. It's about going all in on your life and work, armed with tools that have propelled Navy SEALs through impossible missions, athletes to world records, start-ups to incredible initial public offerings, and ordinary people to extraordinary achievements.

So, the next time someone mentions manifestation, maybe—just maybe—you'll think twice before dismissing it. You might even smile, knowing that when you align this philosophy with your core beliefs, you've peeked behind the curtain and found something real, something actionable, something powerful.

And let us not forget the profound power of prayer. Your higher power will answer—not always in the way you might expect but with blessings that far surpass our limited human understanding. These gifts, woven into the greater design, remind us of the infinite wisdom at work beyond our comprehension.

THE TOWER THAT ALMOST WAS

If you want to find the secrets of the universe,
think in terms of energy, frequency, and vibration.
—NIKOLA TESLA

Nikola Tesla, the eccentric genius whose name has become synonymous with innovation, was born in 1856 in Smiljan, a small village in present-day Croatia. From an early age, Tesla displayed a unique brilliance. He often spoke of intense flashes of light accompanied by vivid visions—spontaneous ideas for inventions that seemed to come from a source beyond himself. When most would have been overwhelmed, Tesla found clarity in these moments and used them as a conduit for extraordinary ideas. In many ways, he was a human lightning rod, capturing insights others couldn't imagine.

Tesla's gifts were apparent early on. Despite his father's wish for him to become an Eastern Orthodox priest, Tesla was irresistibly drawn to science and engineering. After studying in Europe, he moved to the United States in 1884 with little more than his clothes and a letter of introduction to Thomas Edison. Though Tesla initially worked for Edison, their contrasting approaches quickly led to a split. Edison valued practicality and profit, whereas Tesla was driven by vision and possibility. A notorious story claims Edison offered Tesla $50,000 to improve one of his inventions, only to laugh off the payment as a joke after Tesla delivered. Disillusioned, Tesla struck out on his own, beginning a journey that would lead to one of the most ambitious projects in modern history: Wardenclyffe Tower.

Wardenclyffe: Tesla's Tower of Dreams

Tesla didn't only want to revolutionize electricity; he envisioned transforming humanity's relationship with energy itself. His dream was a world in which power could be transmitted wirelessly across continents. "He's insane and probably a warlock of some kind," many might have said as they placed orders for their safety coffins. Imagine illuminating homes, powering factories, and communicating across oceans without a single wire. To most, this was a fantasy; to Tesla, it was an inevitable reality. By the late 1890s, after pioneering alternating current (AC) systems, Tesla focused on his magnum opus: the Wardenclyffe Tower.

Tesla envisioned Wardenclyffe as the first in a global network of towers that would transmit energy through the earth and the atmosphere. He believed humanity could harness the planet's energy as easily as tuning a radio. Securing funding from industrialist J. P. Morgan in 1901, Tesla began the tower's construction on Long Island. The tower rose nearly two hundred feet and was topped with a fifty-five-ton metal dome. For Tesla, it was a symbol of cosmic ambition. To skeptics, it seemed like an outlandish—and quite phallic—experiment. Look it up.

However, as Tesla's ambitions expanded—to controlling weather, transmitting images, and even influencing minds—Morgan grew wary. Tesla's utopian vision of free energy for all horrified the financier, who saw no profit in a world without energy meters. Morgan quickly withdrew funding, leaving Tesla scrambling for resources. Pleas to other investors failed, and by 1906, Wardenclyffe was abandoned. In 1917, the tower was demolished for scrap to pay Tesla's mounting debts.

Tesla's Legacy and the Power of Vision

Despite Wardenclyffe's failure, Tesla's vision was far from misguided. Today, concepts like wireless energy transfer are actively researched and applied in technologies such as wireless chargers and telecommunications. Tesla's belief that humanity could tap into unseen forces now forms the foundation of modern advancements. His life is a reminder that visionary ideas are often rejected in their time, yet their influence can echo for generations.

Tesla wasn't motivated by wealth or fame but by the limitless possibilities of the human mind. His relentless pursuit of a world interconnected by energy illustrates the audacity required to push boundaries. Though he died penniless and dismissed as a madman (by the same people who were taking postmortem family photos with their dead relatives—at this point in the book you shouldn't be shocked by this), Tesla's legacy as a pioneer of visionary thinking endures, proving that the greatest achievements often require risking failure and embracing the impossible.

Tesla's story underscores an important truth: Manifestation is not about passively waiting for dreams to materialize. It's an active process of aligning vision, thought, and action. Like Tesla, we must dare to dream big and commit to the work required to bring those dreams to life. Manifestation paired with clarity and determination becomes a tool for turning aspirations into reality. Tesla's journey teaches us that even when the immediate rewards are unclear, pursuing a bold vision can leave a lasting legacy and inspire others to see beyond the limits of the present.

GOING *ALL IN*

TO ACCESS YOUR ALL IN WORKSPACE,
VISIT APP.EXLR8.AI/ALL-IN

ARE MY GOALS ANCHORED IN A COMPELLING AND CLEAR VISION?

Reflection

This chapter emphasizes that a strong vision is the foundation for any meaningful pursuit. Without it, goals risk becoming fleeting ambitions rather than purposeful endeavors. Clarity in your vision ensures every action aligns with your ultimate destination.

Action
Dedicate fifteen minutes daily to visualize your goals with vivid detail. Engage all your senses and include potential challenges to prepare yourself for the journey ahead.

HOW ALIGNED ARE MY THOUGHTS, ACTIONS, AND HABITS WITH MY VISION?

Reflection
Manifestation requires more than intention—it demands consistent, deliberate effort and alignment. As Tesla demonstrated, vision must be paired with focused execution and resilience, even in the face of doubt.

Action
Audit your daily routines (yes, again) to identify habits that support—or detract from—your vision. Replace one unaligned habit with a purposeful action starting today.

DO I VIEW OBSTACLES AS BARRIERS OR ESSENTIAL COMPONENTS OF MY JOURNEY?

Reflection
Challenges are not roadblocks; they are the crucibles that refine us. Like Tesla's struggle to realize Wardenclyffe Tower, obstacles often push us to innovate and deepen our commitment.

Action
Reframe one current challenge as an opportunity to grow. Write down how overcoming it will contribute to achieving your vision, and take one actionable step toward addressing it.

9

SELF-DISCIPLINE

Transforming Vision into Consistent Action

When going all in, one foundational trait stands as the bridge between wishful thinking and tangible achievement: self-discipline. Big surprise, right? It is the engine that doesn't merely ignite ambition but also sustains it, transforming lofty aspirations into steady, deliberate action. True discipline, however, is not unfocused hustle or doing more for the sake of doing more—it's having the wisdom to identify and commit to an intentional pathway to personal growth and professional excellence. This is where the Remarkable Results Pyramid begins to take form, guiding us to channel our energy, time, and talent into the foundational elements that drive mission success. Self-discipline is the force that sharpens our focus so that we can shed distractions and devote ourselves to the critical few over the trivial many. It is the quiet commitment to consistency that transforms effort into excellence, one deliberate choice at a time.

Throughout history, from the ancient Spartans and Stoics to the modern-day impact makers, discipline has been revered as the backbone of strength and resilience. Marcus Aurelius, the Roman emperor who embodied Stoic philosophy, didn't sit in luxury contemplating life's meaning; he woke up early, led armies, and governed with steadfast purpose—all while documenting the importance of controlling one's mind to master one's life. His disciplined approach wasn't solely focused on self-restraint but also aligning every action with his higher purpose. The power of discipline, ancient wisdom tells us, is that it clears a path through the noise, giving us the ability to act on what matters and ignore the rest.

In today's world, extreme discipline manifests in countless ways, from the grueling preparation of Olympic athletes striving for gold to the commitment of Navy SEALs mastering life-or-death skills. It's seen in the entrepreneur burning the midnight oil to turn an idea into a thriving business, the single parent juggling work and school to create a better future for their family, and the artist perfecting their craft through years of unnoticed effort. It's present in the teacher who tirelessly shapes young minds, the healthcare worker or firefighter pulling double shifts to save lives, and even the volunteer sacrificing personal time to serve a greater cause. Across all walks of life, discipline is the driving force that transforms vision into reality.

Modern champions of self-discipline—consider fellow SEAL Jocko Willink's mantra "discipline equals freedom"—have resurrected this age-old wisdom for a new era. They remind us that it's not motivation but disciplined action that creates real change. By narrowing our focus, we unlock the freedom to invest deeply in our most meaningful goals. In this chapter, we delve into self-discipline—not as a rigid constraint but as a gateway to intentional prioritization. It serves as the cornerstone of turning vision into reality, enabling us to go all in on the pursuits that genuinely drive success in our lives, careers, and relationships.

SO, YOU WANT TO BE AN ASTRONAUT?

The creation of a thousand forests is in one acorn.
—RALPH WALDO EMERSON

Let's take a moment to marvel at the life and mind-bending accomplishments of a fellow Navy SEAL—a man whose existence feels less like reality and more like the fever dream of an overzealous screenwriter. His story doesn't just defy the limits of ambition but takes those limits, shreds them, and uses the scraps to build a rocket ship to the moon. Frankly, it's the kind of tale that makes the rest of us question whether our biggest accomplishment—like finally organizing the garage—even deserves a participation trophy. I'm fairly convinced this person was placed on earth solely to make the rest of us feel like we've been treading water while he's out there in the stratosphere—literally. Johnny Kim's life story is almost supernatural. Let me paint the scene: an inner-city kid from Los Angeles, raised in a family that didn't have much in terms of material wealth but had something money can't buy—a strict, unrelenting belief in hard work and discipline. Fast-forward to today, and Kim's résumé boasts three impressive titles that most of us would consider life goals on their own: decorated Navy SEAL, Harvard-trained medical doctor, and NASA astronaut. No need to adjust your reading glasses, you read that correctly. Johnny Kim didn't pick one path; he went full throttle on three, each more demanding than the last.

Born in 1984 to Korean immigrants, Johnny's upbringing was, as he describes it, humble. His family ran a small liquor store in Los Angeles, the kind of job that requires patience, grit, and late nights, not unlike the environments Kim would later find himself in. Though his early years were tough, Kim's story took a definitive turn after the September 11 attacks. He was a sixteen-year-old high school student when those events shook the world. For Kim, 9/11 was a call to action. The allure of a life of service took hold, and by 2002, he had enlisted in the Navy, signing on for a journey that would push him to the very limits of human perseverance.

Act One: Becoming a Navy SEAL

Let's start with a foundational principle of Johnny's journey: discipline. In 2002, he entered the Navy and set his sights on something few dare to attempt—becoming a Navy SEAL—a perfect finishing school to polish his perseverance. As we have covered, SEAL training isn't for the faint of heart. He had that rare mix of grit and dedication that allowed him to not just survive but also thrive in the brutal world of special operations. BUD/S training is known for its generous "welcoming committee" of freezing water, endless hauling of heavy boats and logs, and instructors who make you question every choice you've ever made. In spite of all this, Kim's internal drive and tenacity saw him through, and, graduating with Class 247, he earned the privilege to wear the Trident pin.

As a SEAL, Kim deployed twice to the Middle East and saw the harshest realities of combat firsthand. He earned a Silver Star and a Bronze Star with Valor, awards that symbolize immense courage under fire. But more than that, these accolades represent profound steadfastness in the face of overwhelming odds. Still, even as he excelled, he was searching for something more. In the midst of war, surrounded by chaos, he found himself fascinated by the human condition, particularly in moments of extreme trauma. While most of us would have been solely focused on dodging the deadly whistle of 7.62 rounds, Johnny's mind was dissecting the deeper intricacies of life, death, and the boundless possibilities of medicine.

Act Two: From Battlefield to Harvard Medical School

One could forgive Johnny Kim if he decided, after his combat deployments, that he'd accomplished enough for a lifetime. But that's the thing about Kim: Enough is never enough. He wanted to heal others, to understand the science behind saving lives—a purpose forged in the intense fires of his combat experiences. So, after his deployments to Iraq, he did what any highly decorated Navy SEAL with no formal biology background would do: He applied to Harvard Medical School. Obviously.

Getting into Harvard Medical School is notoriously difficult; doing so with nothing but combat experience and no traditional pre-med education? That's the kind of plot twist that makes even the most ambitious overachievers feel like they're slacking. But Johnny Kim isn't your average mortal. Displaying the same determination that propelled him through SEAL training, Kim embarked on an academic journey as audacious as his military feats. He began with an undergraduate degree in mathematics at the University of San Diego—a field not exactly known for handing out easy A's. For most, this alone would be an impressive accomplishment.

With a freshly minted bachelor's degree and the figurative blood and dust of the battlefield still clinging to him, he set his sights on Harvard Medical School—arguably the Mount Everest of academia. And, true to form, he didn't just knock on the doors of this prestigious institution; he marched in, armed with an iron will and a vision as clear as his surgical precision would soon become. It wasn't just an acceptance—it was a victory lap for a man redefining what's possible.

Medical school, for most, is a four-year marathon. For Kim, it was a place where his battlefield skills translated to life-or-death decisions in a clinical setting. Medicine, after all, is a different kind of mission. But where other students might have been daunted by the academic rigors, Kim had something invaluable: perspective. After seeing the most extreme sides of human nature in combat, he could approach the intense pressures of medicine with a sense of calm. He specialized in emergency medicine and became a trauma surgeon, areas that aligned well with his SEAL background. For Kim, helping to mend the bodies of the broken was just another way to serve—an extension of the purpose that had led him to the military in the first place.

Act Three: The Astronaut Roster

So, Johnny Kim, Navy SEAL and Harvard-trained doctor. Surely that's enough for one lifetime, right? Not quite. In 2017, NASA put out a call for astronaut applicants, and out of more than eighteen thousand hopefuls, only twelve made the cut. Among them? You guessed it—Johnny Kim. Again, thanks a lot for making the rest of us feel utterly inadequate, Johnny. I did a fairly good job of cutting my toenails this morning if anyone is interested and wants to hear more.

Let's pause for a moment. Picture yourself in a room filled with the most accomplished individuals you've ever encountered—PhDs, fighter pilots, engineers—and you realize that the "new kid on the block" is not only a highly decorated combat veteran from the world's most elite special operations unit but also a Harvard-trained physician. Johnny Kim isn't just qualified; he's in a league of his own. It wasn't a stroke of luck that landed him there. NASA saw in Kim a unique blend of skills, resilience, and intellect—the kind of person who can thrive in the isolating, high-stakes environment of space.

As an astronaut, Johnny Kim is preparing to go farther than most of us can even dream of, with NASA's Artemis mission aiming to take him to the moon. If that sounds like a sci-fi movie waiting to happen, it's because Kim's real-life story practically reads like one. And yet, to hear him speak about it, it's as if each step—SEAL, doctor, astronaut—was simply a logical progression, each role leading seamlessly to the next. Add extreme humility to his résumé. Unreal.

The Unrelenting Drive: Why Kim Continues to Push

One might wonder: What drives someone to take on so much? For Johnny, it's purpose. Each stage of his life is built on a foundation of passionate commitment to serve and improve himself. He has often said that he doesn't see himself as extraordinary; he's simply someone who has committed himself to fulfilling his potential. But that's where the paradox lies: Kim's humility is precisely what makes him extraordinary. For him, achievements are not end goals; they are steps toward the broader vision he has of serving humanity.

Johnny's perspective is what makes him truly remarkable. He has lived a life most people can't imagine, and yet he is consistently focused on what's next, not on what he's already achieved. Kim, valuing progress over praise, embodies a form of quiet leadership and challenges himself in ways that most of us wouldn't even dare to attempt.

In a world where attention spans are short and true dedication is hard to find, Johnny is a testament to what's possible when someone is committed to pushing the limits of human potential. From the battlefields of Iraq to the operating rooms of Harvard-affiliated hospitals and then the outer reaches of space, Kim has taken the road less traveled. He has chosen paths that require sacrifice, grit, and an unshakable sense of duty to others.

Kim's story serves as a beacon of possibility. He shows us that we're only limited by our beliefs about what we can achieve. Although most of us may not have his level of discipline and drive, his life stands as a reminder that we are capable of much more than we might think. The next time you find yourself wondering what's possible, remember Johnny Kim. Whenever you feel daunted by your own goals and responsibilities, consider this: Somewhere out there, a Navy SEAL turned doctor turned astronaut is probably working harder, pushing further, and reminding us all what it means to truly go *all in*. So, get up and get after it.

BUILDING LASTING CHANGE
ONE STEP AT A TIME

Self-discipline begins with the mastery of your thoughts. If you
don't control what you think, you can't control what you do.
Simply, self-discipline enables you to think first and act afterward.
—NAPOLEON HILL

In the pursuit of self-discipline, mastery is achieved not in sudden, monumental leaps but through the quiet power of consistency—small, deliberate steps that, when compounded over time, forge an unshakable foundation of self-discipline built on three pillars. The first of the three pillars is mastering micro-habits. These incremental actions may seem deceptively simple, even trivial, but their impact will change your life. A single push-up, one page of reading, or a five-minute walk may feel insignificant in isolation, yet dedication to such small behaviors bypasses the brain's resistance to change, strengthens novel neural pathways, and gradually embeds new habits into the fabric of daily life. Over time, micro-habits shift from intentional efforts to ingrained behaviors, signaling that discipline has resulted in a seamless progression of growth: Hundreds of push-ups a day. An hour of focused reading. Predawn workouts every morning. It's this transformative power of habits that inspired me to dedicate the opening chapters of this book to the art and science of habit formation—a discipline that leads to lasting success.

Micro-habits are only the beginning. True self-discipline requires embracing delayed gratification, the second pillar. This timeless practice teaches us to resist fleeting temptations in favor of pursuing lasting rewards. We train the mind to prioritize the meaningful over the immediate. If you've read my previous book *Embrace the Suck*, you'll recall the character I call Taming Temptation Tiger. Delayed gratification is the quiet architect of success that teaches patience and reinforces long-term vision. It shifts focus from instant pleasures—the Temptation Tiger—to purposeful pursuits. It reveals a mindset where temporary sacrifices pave the way for extraordinary outcomes.

As discussed previously, our inner dialogue holds immense power, either as a catalyst for growth or a barrier to progress, which is where the third pillar, positive self-talk, fits in. Again, this is not about staring yourself down in the mirror and repeating, "You got this." It's about weaving positive, present-tense self-talk into your growing habit of self-discipline. By consciously shifting the narrative we tell ourselves, we replace doubt with determination and fear with focus. Positive self-talk doesn't ignore challenges; it reframes them and turns setbacks into opportunities and failures into feedback. When combined with micro-habits and delayed gratification, positive self-talk creates a virtuous cycle of resilience, intentionality, and growth.

Together, these three pillars create a science-backed framework for self-discipline, proving that mastery in any area of life begins with intentionality. By embedding small actions, delaying immediate rewards, and fostering a constructive inner voice, self-discipline ceases to be a battle of willpower and becomes a natural way of being—a path not of struggle but of sustained achievement and meaningful transformation.

Pillar 1: Mastering Micro-Habits—Because No One Becomes a Ninja Overnight

Except for Johnny Kim. He might actually become a real ninja after he is done being an astronaut. So, here's the truth: Extreme self-discipline doesn't involve diving in headfirst and immediately becoming a productivity powerhouse. Instead, it's built on the unsung hero of behavioral psychology: the micro-habit. We're once again talking about tiny daily actions—actions so seemingly insignificant that your brain barely registers them as changes. But therein lies the magic. Neuroscience tells us that micro-habits create incremental shifts in behavior by activating and strengthening neural pathways until the new behaviors become routine. Essentially, by starting small, you're perpetrating a sneak attack on your brain, rewiring it to adopt these behaviors automatically.

Let's say your grand vision is to become fit and active—a noble and transformative goal, but one that might feel utterly unattainable if your current idea of exercise is the arduous trek from the couch to the fridge. Let's be honest, it's also not the most measurable vision. Instead of diving headfirst into an ultra-marathon training plan, start with something seemingly laughable, like walking half a mile a day. Yes, it might sound absurdly simple—almost too easy—but the idea isn't to transform into David Goggins overnight. It took me years of painstaking mentorship to mold David into the beast he is today. Okay, maybe that last part isn't true. But the real objective is to initiate the act of showing up, no matter how small the step.

Psychologist B. J. Fogg, founder of the Behavior Design Lab at Stanford, emphasizes the power of these "tiny habits." They act as psychological anchors, creating momentum that paves the way for larger habits to follow. By starting small, you sidestep the daunting inertia that often derails ambitious plans and build a foundation of consistency. Over time, these micro-actions compound, turning your initial shuffle into a full-fledged sprint toward a healthier, more active life. It matters not how or where you begin—the magic lies in setting the stage for where you're determined to go.

Each time you hit that single push-up, your brain gets a burst of dopamine, our little neurochemical friend responsible for pleasure and reward. Over time, you'll find yourself adding a second push-up, then a third. Before you know it, you're knocking out a mini workout, and the act of moving daily becomes second nature. In fact, studies show that habits formed in this gradual, manageable way are far more likely to stick, because we're giving our brains time to adjust and build on the initial steps. I recall one beautiful day in Coronado, California, during the first phase of SEAL training, an instructor ordered me to "drop" and bust out fifty push-ups. I said, "Actually, I will begin with one push-up today, Mr. Instructor. I am trying to build micro-habits." Okay, fine... that's not true either.

But it does remind me of the day my parents shipped my mom's champagne-colored Toyota Avalon—complete with gleaming gold trim—straight to the Naval Special Warfare Training Center. Yes, right to BUD/S. And, no, I didn't say "badass Toyota Raptor." I said champagne-colored Toyota Avalon. Nothing screams "ready for elite special operations training" like your mommy and daddy shipping you a hand-me-down sedan during the first phase of the program.

I distinctly remember the instructors calling my name over the megaphone during a particularly savage beatdown session on the beach. They didn't miss the opportunity to turn the Avalon's dramatic entrance into prime fodder for public ridicule. "Gleeson! You have a delivery. You've got to be kidding me?!" yelled an instructor in a quite sinister and foreboding manner, straining not to crack a smile. "Is that your mommy's car out there, Gleeson?" Knowing that honesty and integrity are core values in Naval Special Warfare, my only answer had to be, "Yes, instructor!" Let's just say the rest of this day did not go well for me. Thanks, Mom and Dad. But I digress.

Remember, according to habit formation studies, a new simple behavior takes approximately twenty-one days to form a neural connection, and more complex habits may take up to sixty-six days. Each time we repeat an action, we're laying down more myelin (insulation for nerve fibers) around that pathway in our brain. This increases the efficiency and speed of that behavior. What starts as a five-minute journaling session gradually builds into a robust neural network that makes the behavior automatic. Micro-habits act as Trojan horses, sneaking discipline into your life until, eventually, these actions require no conscious effort.

Pillar 2: Embracing the Power of Delayed Gratification

Let's use entrepreneurship as the lens through which we explore this wildly important pillar. Since transitioning from the SEAL Teams, I've embraced the role of "founder," an entrepreneur who builds companies. Officially, a founder is someone who establishes or initiates the creation of an organization, business, or venture. Founders are tasked with shaping the core idea, laying the operational groundwork, and driving the entity's initial strategy, culture, and vision. In the world of start-ups, they are the risk-takers—the ones who launch businesses and navigate them through their formative, often chaotic, stages. That's the polished, textbook definition. But here's my version:

> A **founder** is someone audacious (or unhinged) enough to turn a wild idea into reality, shoulder every conceivable risk, and bet it all on a vision that often seems more like a fever dream than a practical plan. Founders are the gladiators of delayed gratification (even though they crave immediate results), who trade sleep, stability, and sometimes sanity for the hope of a bigger win down the road. They're the ones who cling to their vision with stubborn foresight, even when everyone else is whispering, "Maybe it's time to let it go." Founding something isn't just a job—it's a relentless roller coaster of breakthroughs, breakdowns, and betting on yourself when the odds aren't great. And somehow, a founder wouldn't have it any other way.

In entrepreneurship, balancing urgency with discipline is the ultimate challenge. Entrepreneurs must navigate rapid decisions—when to launch, hire, or scale—while resisting the pull of short-term gains that could derail long-term goals. This delicate dance requires emotional discipline, analytical precision, and the humility to seek and heed wise counsel.

The key differentiator of successful leaders is their ability to master delayed gratification. In a culture that glorifies instant results, disciplined entrepreneurs understand that sustainable growth comes from sacrificing immediate wins for lasting impact. The Stanford marshmallow experiment—where children were offered one immediate treat or double the number of treats after waiting fifteen minutes without touching the first—famously showed that those who resist instant rewards achieve better outcomes, a principle that holds true in business. Saying no to distractions or premature opportunities creates space for decisions that align with a larger vision. I suggest that anyone start by making a "Stop Doing" list. The outcome of checking items off this list is often far more powerful than accomplishing your "Start Doing" list.

Entrepreneurs face constant temptations—shiny objects, rushed launches, overhiring, funding without scrutiny of the source. Yet, success lies in pausing, analyzing, and ensuring every move serves the long-term mission. Neuroscience supports this: Resisting instant gratification strengthens the brain's decision-making center and reinforces disciplined choices until they become second nature. Such techniques as *mental contrasting*—envisioning success while acknowledging obstacles—help entrepreneurs balance ambition with clarity and focus on the bigger picture.

Delayed gratification means mastering the skill of aligning timing and intention to magnify success. Entrepreneurs who embrace this mindset don't just build businesses—they become impact makers. By exercising restraint, staying true to their vision, and making disciplined decisions, they transform fleeting rewards into lasting fulfillment, paving the way for meaningful and enduring success.

Pillar 3: Confronting Self-Doubt Sam

The overlooked cornerstone of self-discipline is not silencing the inner voices that tempt you to quit but engaging them in a deliberate, controlled dialogue. When the voice whispers, "Stop, this is too much," you don't suppress it or ignore it but instead acknowledge it, understand it, and choose a different path. Unless you're doing something harmful to yourself or others. Then, please listen. We're not talking about blind positivity or clichéd pep talks; this is having the mental discipline to confront discomfort and still step forward.

Imagine waking and rising before dawn even as the warmth of your bed begs you to stay. The voice of comfort pipes up: "You need rest. One day off won't hurt." But instead of blindly following or suppressing that voice, you respond: "Rest is important, but growth requires showing up. This is who I am—someone who thrives in discomfort." By engaging with the voice, you're not fighting yourself but redirecting your energy toward disciplined action.

This practice transforms discipline from a rigid rule into a deliberate choice. Neuroscience backs this up by showing that acknowledging and reframing internal resistance activates the brain's reward pathways, boosts motivation, and rewires your mind for resilience. Don't banish self-doubt—build a relationship with it. Give it a name, perhaps something like "Self-Doubt Sam." Become Sam's mentor. Acknowledge him, address his concerns, and offer him all the practical wisdom you can muster. Then, when you've patiently guided Sam to his limits, it's time to place him in a permanent "time-out" or, better yet, send him to the "naughty corner" indefinitely. He's served his purpose; now it's time for you to move forward without him.

True discipline lies in mastering this internal conversation, not ignoring temptation but engaging with it, dismantling its power, and choosing the harder, more rewarding path. Over time, this mental conditioning strengthens not only your resolve but also your identity: You forge a self-image of someone who consistently shows up, even when it's hard.

Tying It All Together: Putting the Pillars to Work

Cultivating self-discipline using these three pillars does not require Herculean willpower but does require hacking your brain to work for you, not against you. By starting with micro-habits, you're laying the foundation without overwhelming yourself. Delayed gratification strengthens your ability to stay committed over the long haul, even when temptation is screaming in your ear. And, finally, confronting Self-Doubt Sam turns your internal monologue into a tool of reinforcement that consistently pushes you toward your goals.

In the end, extreme self-discipline is a continuous cycle. You start with a small step, resist the urge to give up halfway, and coach yourself to the finish line—all while building a new identity as someone who *can*.

DISCIPLINE DOES ACTUALLY EQUAL FREEDOM

Discipline equals freedom.

—JOCKO WILLINK

One of the most profound yet lesser-known stories of self-discipline and survival comes from the experience of US Air Force colonel George "Bud" Day, who was captured during the Vietnam War and endured brutal treatment as a prisoner of war (POW). After being shot down in 1967, Day was captured and taken to a North Vietnamese prison camp, where he faced torture, malnutrition, and isolation. One of the most remarkable aspects of his story lies in his approach to survival through self-discipline and mental fortitude.

Despite his grave injuries, Day used self-discipline to stay mentally sharp. He set daily routines that included mental exercises, such as rehearsing his military training, and visualized the steps necessary to return to freedom. At one point, after a failed escape attempt, Day suffered a broken arm and blindness in one eye but continued to hold himself to a mental regimen. Day also recited prayers, poetry, and the Pledge of Allegiance daily—symbols of his identity and fortitude that he held onto fiercely. By maintaining this routine, Day kept his spirit intact and refused to give his captors the satisfaction of seeing him broken.

Day's inner discipline was so strong that he even resisted the impulse to reveal information under extreme duress, which earned him the respect and admiration of fellow POWs and made him a symbol of leadership and patriotism. His self-discipline not only helped him survive but also empowered him to support others until his release in 1973. His story illustrates that survival isn't always about physical strength; sometimes, it's the quiet, unbreakable discipline of the mind that sustains us through the darkest times. But let's dive deeper.

Self-Discipline as the Foundation of Survival

Colonel George "Bud" Day's extraordinary survival during years of brutal captivity illustrates the profound power of self-discipline. Despite facing torture, starvation, and solitary confinement designed to shatter his will, Day recognized that, although his body was imprisoned, his mind could remain free. He crafted strict mental routines, clinging to daily recitations of poetry and structured exercises to shield himself from despair. This discipline became his lifeline, ensuring his resolve never wavered.

Day's resilience inspired his fellow POWs and encouraged them to adopt similar practices. By demonstrating the power of mental routines, he gave his comrades a shared strength that helped them resist the psychological torment by their captors. Through self-discipline, Day safeguarded his own spirit while fostering unity among his fellow prisoners.

Visualization as a Tool for Hope

In solitary confinement, Day relied on visualization to sustain his hope. (See, I'm not making this stuff up.) He vividly imagined his life outside the prison walls and replayed cherished memories of his family, his Iowa hometown, and the freedoms he was fighting for. These mental escapes were more than a coping mechanism—they reinforced his belief in a future beyond captivity and strengthened his commitment to survival.

Day's ability to mentally construct a brighter reality not only fueled his perseverance but also inspired other POWs to do the same. By visualizing loved ones and the lives they wanted to return to, the prisoners' determination was renewed, proving that even in the darkest circumstances, the mind can be a source of light that guides you through to better times.

Identity as a Beacon of Strength

Day's unyielding commitment to his identity as an American soldier became a source of immense strength. Viewing his captivity as an extension of his duty, he refused to betray his principles, even when faced with unbearable torture. For Day, surrendering his loyalty or compromising his values was not an option.

His quiet defiance, from refusing to bow to guards to enduring the physical cost of resistance, inspired his fellow POWs and reinforced their collective resilience. These acts of noncompliance became powerful reminders of the dignity and purpose that could not be stripped away, even in the harshest conditions.

Rituals and Mental Fortitude

Day's daily rituals grounded him in purpose. Simple acts, such as reciting the Pledge of Allegiance or performing limited physical exercises despite his injuries, maintained his sense of control and determination. These routines, serving as anchors of continuity amid chaos, connected him to a life beyond captivity.

Small but intentional practices reinforced his refusal to succumb to helplessness. They symbolized a mental strength that defied the physical constraints of his environment, enabling him to endure and inspire others through these acts.

Triumph Through Discipline

Day's mental conditioning transformed unimaginable suffering into a testament of loyalty and strength. He viewed each session of torture as a challenge to overcome, using his mind as a weapon against his captors' attempts to break him. His strength not only ensured his survival but also earned the reluctant respect of his enemies.

When Day was released in 1973, he returned to the States not broken but triumphant. Through visualization, discipline, and adherence to his values, Day exemplified how the human spirit can prevail even in the direst circumstances.

The Discipline to Thrive

Day's journey illustrates that self-discipline is more than a tool for survival—it is the bridge between vision and reality. By cultivating daily habits rooted in values and purpose, we can transform fleeting intentions into consistent action. Whether in personal growth, professional endeavors, or overcoming adversity, self-discipline empowers us to endure, adapt, and ultimately thrive.

The commitment to discipline is not a singular effort but a way of life. It enables us to face challenges with clarity, pursue goals with tenacity, and turn dreams into reality. Like Day, we all have the capacity to transform the trials of today into the triumphs of tomorrow.

GOING *ALL IN*

TO ACCESS YOUR ALL IN WORKSPACE, VISIT APP.EXLR8.AI/ALL-IN

AM I BUILDING THE RIGHT MICRO-HABITS?

Reflection

Johnny Kim's journey from Navy SEAL to doctor to astronaut began with disciplined, incremental steps. Each accomplishment, no matter how extraordinary, was built on the foundation of daily, intentional effort. Kim's story highlights the way transformative achievements often start with small, manageable actions.

Action

Identify one ambitious goal you want to achieve and break it into micro-habits. If it's fitness, commit to one simple activity a day. If it's professional growth, read one article or book chapter daily. These small actions will snowball into major progress over time as your brain is rewired for consistency and success.

AM I DELAYING GRATIFICATION FOR LONG-TERM IMPACT?

Reflection

The example of entrepreneurs making tough decisions—such as resisting the urge to launch a product prematurely and declining immediate but misaligned funding—illustrates the power of delayed gratification. This practice requires saying no to tempting short-term gains as a way to preserve the integrity of long-term goals.

Action

Think of one decision you're facing that tempts you with immediate rewards but that might derail your broader vision. Use mental contrasting: Vividly imagine the benefits of achieving your ultimate goal and overcoming the obstacles you will inevitably encounter to get there. Commit to making the choice that aligns with your long-term priorities, not fleeting desires.

HOW IS MY INNER DIALOGUE SHAPING MY BEHAVIOR?

Reflection

Colonel Bud Day's ability to endure unimaginable suffering as a POW was rooted in the discipline of his inner dialogue. By reciting the Pledge of Allegiance daily and visualizing his freedom, Day turned his internal narrative into a source of strength, resilience, and purpose.

Action

Begin practicing *distanced* self-talk. When faced with a challenge, speak to yourself as you would a trusted friend. Instead of saying, "I can't handle this," tell yourself, "You've got this. It's part of the journey. This is just one step toward [specific goal]." Incorporate specific, actionable language to reframe your mindset and approach obstacles with clarity and resolve.

By reflecting on these questions and implementing these actions, you'll strengthen the self-discipline needed to transform vision into reality. Whether you're cultivating micro-habits, resisting immediate gratification, or reshaping your inner dialogue, the power to achieve lies in your ability to consistently align daily actions with your greater purpose.

10

GROWTH MINDSET

For Shattering Limits and Battlefield Domination

As we conclude Part 2, we immerse our journey in the transformative work of Dr. Carol Dweck—a psychologist whose groundbreaking research on mindset has reshaped our understanding of growth and the true essence of achievement. Her insights transcend academia and serve as a practical compass for anyone striving to unlock their full potential. At EXCELR8, we hold Dr. Dweck's work in the highest regard, and her expertise has influenced how our software products empower continuous improvement in people and teams. Her principles of fostering a growth mindset aren't just theories—they're tools we actively integrate to empower leaders and teams to go beyond perceived limitations and achieve remarkable results.

Dweck, a professor at Stanford University, introduced the concept of "growth mindset" in the 1990s and expanded on it in her landmark book *Mindset: The New Psychology of Success*, published in 2006. Through her research, Dweck explores the dichotomy between *fixed mindset*—where individuals view their talents and intelligence as predetermined, unchangeable traits—and *growth mindset*, where they view these qualities as flexible and improvable through effort, learning, and resilience. What she has found is nothing short of astonishing: Individuals with a growth mindset don't merely achieve more; they actively pursue challenges, view failure as fuel, and use setbacks as stepping stones that set them apart from the rest. Her work redefined our understanding of achievement, making the concept of a growth mindset a foundational principle in discussions of personal development, education, business, and psychology.

A growth mindset represents a radical shift in the way we approach learning, failure, and transformation. You cannot go all in without it. In this chapter, we dive deeper into what it takes to transition from a fixed to a growth mindset. This process, often uncomfortable and challenging, goes far beyond blind optimism and surface-level affirmations. It demands intense self-reflection, a willingness to confront limiting beliefs, and a commitment to rewiring our very sense of self. Using Dweck's research as our foundation, we'll explore the resonant stories of those who have faced adversity, reframed setbacks as possibilities, and turned their challenges into transformative journeys toward mastery. A growth mindset isn't merely a building block for commitment and personal growth—it's the architecture of a life lived in pursuit of heroic potential and meteoric transformation.

EMBRACING GROWTH THROUGH CHALLENGE AND CHANGE

A gem cannot be polished without friction,
nor a man perfected without trials.
—ANCIENT CHINESE PROVERB

Growth mindset is often misunderstood. Many believe it's simply about positive thinking—if you "believe" you can do something, you will. But, according to Dweck's work, a growth mindset cultivates actionable grit; this mindset requires hard work, a tolerance for discomfort, and a willingness to learn from mistakes.

Jim Abbott, a one-handed baseball pitcher, is a stunning example of someone with a growth mindset. Jim Abbott's journey is nothing short of extraordinary. Born in Flint, Michigan, in 1967, Abbott faced what most would consider an insurmountable barrier to a career in baseball: He was born without a right hand. Why did he choose baseball? Why not soccer, or "football" as our friends across the pond call it? From the beginning, Abbott had two choices: to accept this limitation as a permanent obstacle, or to see it as a challenge to be overcome. Fortunately, he chose the latter. His story reveals the true power of a growth mindset, where limitations are not roadblocks but catalysts for development and mastery.

Growing up, Abbott was no stranger to the frustration of feeling "different." He focused on what he *could* control instead of yielding to the whims of Self-Doubt Sam, an acquaintance who visited often. Determined to participate fully in sports—specifically, baseball—he developed a unique way of fielding and throwing with his left hand. He would cradle the baseball glove on his right forearm, quickly switch the glove to his left hand after pitching, and be ready to field any ball that came his way. Achieving this fluidity required years of focused, disciplined practice, a willingness to adapt, and a deep commitment to skill building. Each time Abbott practiced this technique, he reinforced his belief in his potential. Abbott's commitment to improvement paid off. By high school, he had not only joined the baseball team but excelled, capturing the attention of scouts and fans alike. He went on to play college baseball at the University of Michigan, where his talent and determination earned him the Golden Spikes Award, which recognized him as the best amateur baseball player in the United States. Despite what many saw as a disadvantage, Abbott refused to be boxed in by expectations and instead leaned into the belief that he could continuously improve and perform at the highest levels.

Abbott's journey didn't stop there. In 1989, he was drafted by the California Angels and made history by reaching Major League Baseball without ever spending a day in the minor leagues—an impressive feat even for players with both hands. One of the most iconic moments in Abbott's career came on September 4, 1993, when he pitched a no-hitter for the New York Yankees against the Cleveland Indians. In that game, Abbott's years of perseverance and adaptability and his unbreakable growth mindset were on full display. His performance was a testament not only to his skill but also to his belief that with enough dedication, anything was possible.

Jim Abbott's life exemplifies the growth mindset that Carol Dweck describes. He chose to see his physical difference as an opportunity to grow, adapt, and redefine what was possible. His success speaks to the belief that, with diligent effort, we can push past boundaries and become more than even we imagined.

Confronting the Fixed Mindset Within:
Superb Self-Awareness

Moving from a fixed to a growth mindset requires radical self-awareness. Dweck's research suggests that nearly everyone harbors fixed-mindset tendencies, which often remain hidden until challenges arise. When someone avoids trying a new skill for fear of failure, resists feedback, or dismisses challenges as insurmountable, these are signs of a fixed mindset at play. Growth mindset, in contrast, embraces failure and views it as a necessary component of learning.

A perfect example of this is Sylvester Stallone. Long before he became a household name, Stallone faced obstacle after obstacle, any one of which could have easily led him to abandon his dreams. Born in 1946 to a working-class family in Hell's Kitchen, New York, Stallone had a challenging start. A complicated birth left him with partial facial paralysis, which resulted in his distinctive slurred speech and drooping smile—characteristics that would later become iconic but, at the time, made him the target of mockery and rejection. From an early age, Stallone was painfully aware of his differences, but he refused to let them define him.

As he pursued his dream of becoming an actor, Stallone found that his unique voice and appearance made casting directors hesitate. He auditioned for countless roles but was met with little more than polite dismissals or outright refusals. He was told repeatedly that he didn't have the "look" or the "sound" of a leading man, and he was even advised to consider another profession. A fixed mindset might have led him to believe these judgments were final, that he "just wasn't cut out for this." But Stallone didn't see it that way; he viewed every rejection as one step closer to eventual success. Driven by his vision, he decided to take matters into his own hands.

With few opportunities and facing financial struggles, Stallone began writing. Fueled by his passion and the determination to prove himself, he wrote the screenplay for *Rocky* in a frenzy of inspiration, reportedly finishing it in three days. The story of a down-and-out boxer fighting against the odds was deeply personal to him, a reflection of his own life, struggles, and indomitable spirit. Stallone poured his heart and soul into the script, and he was determined not only to sell it but to star in it. This was an audacious move for an actor with little experience and no reputation, but it was also the growth mindset at work. Stallone understood that to realize his vision, he couldn't just sit back and hope;

he had to confront the industry's resistance head-on. His steadfast belief in his dream was a form of manifestation in action—an alignment of his vision, his work, and his deep faith that the universe would meet him halfway.

When he began shopping the screenplay, studios were interested but balked at the idea of casting Stallone as the lead. Some offered substantial amounts of money—up to $360,000—on the condition that he relinquish the role to a more established actor. For Stallone, who was nearly broke at the time, this was an agonizing decision. He was living in poverty, even selling his dog because he couldn't afford to feed it, and struggling to pay his bills. Still, Stallone refused to let his circumstances dictate his dreams. Despite the financial hardships, he turned down lucrative offers to protect his vision, knowing that selling out meant betraying his belief in himself.

Eventually, his persistence paid off, and a studio agreed to let him star in *Rocky*—albeit on a very modest budget. What followed was nothing short of extraordinary. Of course, *Rocky* became a massive success, earning ten Academy Award nominations and winning three, including Best Picture. Stallone's performance catapulted him into the limelight, and the film's underdog story resonated worldwide. Stallone's willingness to confront setbacks, insist on his vision, and continue pushing forward despite countless rejections exemplified resilience in its purest form.

Stallone's journey aligns seamlessly with Carol Dweck's findings on the growth mindset. Rather than allowing himself to be limited by industry standards or financial adversity, Stallone saw every challenge as an opportunity to grow. His decision to write *Rocky* and his insistence on playing the lead role were acts of radical self-belief and grit. Self-Doubt Sam auditioned but was not given a role in this movie. At every setback, Stallone chose to see possibility rather than limitation, demonstrating the mindset that had not only shaped his career but also inspired millions. His story reminds us that growth is indeed a choice made in moments of challenge, as Dweck teaches—a decision to persist, adapt, and continue striving, even when success seems impossible.

Intentional Identity Shift: Go to War with Yourself

Dweck's research highlights a crucial but often-overlooked element of growth mindset: *identity transformation*. Adopting a growth mindset isn't just about taking action; it's about changing how you see yourself. A fixed mindset says, "I can't do this," whereas a growth mindset says, "I can become the person who can do this." This shift is transformative and requires that we redefine our self-concept and choose a new identity.

My BUD/S classmate and SEAL Team 5 teammate David Goggins, a former Navy SEAL and extreme endurance athlete, exemplifies this. In his youth, Goggins faced extreme hardship and abuse, and by his own account, he was plagued by self-doubt. He transformed himself through mental and physical challenges and built a new identity based on unbreakable resolve. In alignment with Dweck's research, Goggins didn't just try to become resilient; he built a self-image around mental toughness that redefined who he was. His story underscores Dweck's point that a growth mindset requires identity transformation—it's about becoming a person who values growth and embraces challenge as a way of life.

Intentional identity transformation is the deliberate process of reshaping your self-concept and identity to align with your desired goals, values, and aspirations. Unlike passive changes that might occur over time because of circumstances, this transformation is actively pursued by a person who wants to fundamentally redefine who they are. It's a commitment to intentionally reframing beliefs, behaviors, and habits that no longer serve you, in favor of building an identity that reflects the person you wish to become. Which is why we have spent significant time on this topic.

To pursue intentional identity transformation, a person must first gain self-awareness, an understanding of the beliefs and patterns that are holding them back. They then clearly envision the identity they want to embody, followed by consistently taking action and reinforcing the behaviors that align with this new identity. For example, Carol Dweck's concept of a growth mindset illustrates a form of identity transformation when individuals shift from seeing themselves as "fixed" to believing in their ability to grow through effort. This process requires discipline, self-reflection, and often the courage to step outside one's comfort zone to reinforce this new sense of self. Ultimately, intentional identity transformation is about freedom from self-imposed or societal constraints so that a person can fully express their potential and shape a life that resonates with their highest aspirations.

TRANSFORMING OBSTACLES INTO OPPORTUNITY

The obstacle is the path.

—ZEN PROVERB

The ultimate test of a growth mindset lies in how we respond under extreme pressure. In the philosophy of Stoicism, Marcus Aurelius famously wrote, "The impediment to action advances action. What stands in the way becomes the way." This ancient wisdom teaches us that obstacles are not roadblocks but the very path to enlightenment and achievement. Similarly, Carol Dweck's work reveals that those with a growth mindset not only accept challenges but embrace them as catalysts for transformation. They see adversity not as a barrier but as an opportunity to grow stronger, wiser, and more capable.

So, What Did You Fail at Today?

Dweck's studies consistently show that those with a growth mindset embrace failure as a beginning, not an ending. Failure, as she discovered, is an integral part of growth because it teaches us valuable lessons that success often cannot. Sara Blakely, founder of Spanx, exemplifies this lesson. Her story is one of those rare entrepreneurial fairy tales that reveals the truth lurking behind the glitzy facade of success: It's not the wins that shape us but rather the merciless, bruising encounters with failure. Today, Blakely is known as the billionaire founder that revolutionized women's shapewear, but her journey began far from the boardrooms and luxury branding empires of fashion. Her early career was less a steady climb than a bumpy road, marked by a series of bold pitches, creative pivots, and, of course, plenty of "no, thank you"'s and "not interested"'s. Each rejection only fueled her resolve. If the story of Spanx tells us anything, it's that Blakely's career was built less on success and more on what she did when success seemed elusive.

Growing up in Clearwater, Florida, Blakely was primed for resilience by her father, who had an unorthodox approach to dinnertime conversation. Rather than asking his kids what they succeeded at that day, he would ask, "What did you fail at today?" For Blakely, failure wasn't a source of shame; it was a daily rite of passage. Under this familial ethos, she developed a comfort with failure that would later serve as the backbone of her growth mindset. After graduating from Florida State University, Blakely set her sights on law school but quickly pivoted when she didn't pass the LSAT—probably not the kind of failure her father was envisioning, but an apt one nonetheless. She took a job selling fax machines door-to-door instead, a position that most would consider less "career move" and more "form of punishment." For seven years, she trudged from office to office in the Florida heat, enduring rejection after rejection.

It was during these days as a reluctant fax machine salesperson that Blakely stumbled upon her golden idea. Frustrated with her wardrobe's inability to deliver the "flawless look" under white pants, she took a pair of scissors to her pantyhose and created a makeshift version of what would later become her flagship product. The notion was absurdly simple but potentially revolutionary. With a flicker of entrepreneurial insight, Blakely decided that women everywhere might need this product—but first, she would have to figure out how to actually make it. Lacking any background in fashion, design, or manufacturing, Blakely faced a steep learning curve, but she didn't allow her inexperience to deter her. Instead, she rolled up her sleeves and began researching everything she could about textiles, manufacturing, and patents, teaching herself as she went.

Of course, genius ideas don't always translate into immediate support, and the road to success for Spanx was paved with ample skepticism and polite rejections. When Blakely approached manufacturers, she was met with a familiar chorus of no's and sidelong glances. The hosiery industry was dominated by men, many of whom simply couldn't grasp the appeal of her "footless pantyhose" concept. Undeterred, she continued to pitch her idea, refining her approach after each setback. Her willingness to embrace these rejections is emblematic of Carol Dweck's growth mindset; Blakely saw every no as a chance to reassess and improve.

One day, after months of rejection, Blakely finally caught a break. A manufacturer in North Carolina agreed to produce her product—thanks in part to the manufacturer's daughters, who understood the appeal of the design and persuaded their father to take a chance on Blakely's idea. With a prototype in hand, she faced the next monumental task: convincing major retailers to carry Spanx. Using her now finely honed pitching skills, Blakely managed to secure a meeting with a buyer at Neiman Marcus. Here, she employed a now legendary tactic: Rather than delivering a standard business pitch, Blakely took the buyer to the bathroom and demonstrated the product herself. Seeing the transformation firsthand, the buyer was sold, and Spanx hit the shelves at Neiman Marcus.

Spanx quickly gained traction, but Blakely's journey was far from over. With no advertising budget, she relied on unconventional marketing tactics, which included sending free samples to talk show hosts, hoping they might mention the product. In an unexpected twist of fate, one of those samples found its way to Oprah Winfrey, who named Spanx one of her "favorite things" in 2000. Sales skyrocketed, and Spanx went from a niche product to a household name almost overnight.

Blakely's story is a masterclass in ferocious determination. Every rejection, every failure, was treated as feedback, an opportunity to tweak, refine, and move forward. Her success wasn't a single stroke of luck or a smooth ascent but rather a series of informed decisions built on the lessons of repeated failure. As Carol Dweck's research illuminates, a growth mindset doesn't eliminate failure; it simply redefines it. For Blakely, each no was part of the process of going from door-to-door fax machine saleswoman to billionaire entrepreneur. In the end, Sara Blakely's career wasn't built by avoiding failure but by diving straight into it, scissors in hand, ready to cut her own path.

Dweck's research reminds us that a fixed mindset would view all the rejections Blakely endured as proof of her incompetence—imperfections in the individual or the product that would lead to a halt in effort. Instead, Blakely's willingness to embrace setbacks reflects growth-mindset thinking: Failure isn't a stop sign but a launching pad. Her journey from rejection to building a billion-dollar brand exemplifies the transformative power of turning setbacks into fuel for your rocket ship to relentlessness.

That Time Colin O'Brady Walked Across Antarctica

Endurance athlete Colin O'Brady's journey exemplifies the importance of stepping out, stretching ourselves, and actively confronting resistance. Colin O'Brady's story reads like something an author of epic adventure novels dreamed up—a modern-day Odysseus armed only with sheer willpower and, perhaps, a remarkable tolerance for discomfort. In 2018, O'Brady carved his name into the annals of exploration by becoming the first person to traverse Antarctica solo, unsupported, and unaided, a feat of unparalleled endurance and determination. It was a journey fraught with punishing cold, mental isolation, and seemingly endless physical strain. Carol Dweck's research on growth mindset suggests that real growth blooms in discomfort; O'Brady's trek across the desolate Antarctic expanse is the fullest embodiment of that principle.

O'Brady's story, however, doesn't begin on the frozen plains of Antarctica; it begins with a moment of devastating adversity. In his early twenties, he suffered severe burns over 25 percent of his body during an accident in Thailand, after which doctors suggested he might never walk normally again, let alone run or pursue any dreams requiring athleticism. Most people might have taken that diagnosis as a lifetime prescription for "recommended mediocrity." But O'Brady had other plans. With the gritty resolve of someone who refuses to let circumstances define him, he set about proving the doctors wrong by undertaking a grueling recovery that defied the medical expectations for him.

Overcoming physical limitation and injury became the foundation of a growth mindset that would guide O'Brady through some of the most harrowing perseverance challenges in the world. From completing triathlons to setting records in mountaineering, he was determined to test the boundaries of human capacity. But none of these feats could prepare him fully for the Antarctic, a place not known for its warmth or welcome—qualities shared by O'Brady's competition, a British Army captain named Louis Rudd, who was racing him to complete the solo journey first. The conditions were extreme, with temperatures plummeting below –60°F, winds capable of driving a person backward, and the endlessly daunting solitude of the ice-covered landscape.

For fifty-four days, O'Brady faced a grueling daily reality as he dragged a sled packed with supplies across the barren continent. His progress was painfully slow, each step a battle against the elements and fatigue. The monotony, coupled with the biting cold, would have been enough to make even the most resilient mind question its sanity. And yet, every morning, he emerged from his tent, fortified by a growth mindset that embraced discomfort as an opportunity to expand the limits of what he thought possible. As Goggins might say, "Growth doesn't happen in a soft [insert expletive] environment!" Antarctica was the perfect test tube for proving that theory.

In addition to the physical torment, there was the isolation. Out there, with nothing but the expanse of ice for miles and the sound of wind for company, the mind has a tendency to play tricks. O'Brady found himself confronting a kind of existential loneliness that few people will ever experience. He became his only source of encouragement, his only competition, and his only support system. It was a mental feat as much as a physical one, a battle between his ambition and the stark reality that surrounded him. Having a growth mindset became more than a strategy; it became survival as O'Brady learned to frame each torturous mile as a step toward proving what could be accomplished with enough determination.

On Christmas Day, still far from his goal, O'Brady decided to push himself to a level of discomfort that would later become the defining moment of his journey. With seventy-seven miles left, he resolved to finish the trek in a single, continuous push—a feat that required thirty-two straight hours of exertion. When he finally reached the edge of Antarctica, he had completed the crossing in fifty-four days, setting a world record and defying every reasonable limit of human perseverance.

Colin O'Brady's journey across Antarctica is a testament to Dweck's principle that true growth results from stretching oneself to the brink, facing down resistance, and finding the resolve to carry on. O'Brady's story is a reminder that we are capable of far more than we believe; discomfort isn't an inconvenience but a gateway to discovering our own strength. O'Brady's crossing of Antarctica exemplifies growth mindset in its purest, most authentic form. O'Brady chose to see each day as an opportunity to prove his perseverance. Dweck's findings underscore that real transformation results when we actively seek resistance, with the understanding that discomfort is the gateway to progress.

How to Become Rejection Proof in a Hundred Days

For an unconventional example, we turn to Jia Jiang, who practiced "rejection therapy" for one hundred days by intentionally seeking out rejection to desensitize himself to the fear of it. Born in Beijing, China, Jiang moved to the United States at the age of sixteen, carrying with him the familiar dream of achieving greatness and fulfilling a life of purpose. He pursued a degree in computer science, launched a successful career in the corporate world, and appeared to be on track for a stable, comfortable life. Yet Jiang had a calling beyond corporate comfort; driven by an ambition to bring his own ideas to life, he wanted to be an entrepreneur. But he soon discovered that the path to entrepreneurial success was paved with what he feared most: *rejection*. This revelation sent him down a path that would become a most unexpected—and strangely inspiring—story of personal growth in recent years.

In 2012, after a particularly crushing rejection from an investor, Jiang found himself at a crossroads. The experience didn't just bruise his ego; it left him questioning his capacity to handle setbacks—an essential quality in the entrepreneurial world he longed to be a part of. Like many people, Jiang realized he had been playing it safe for years, subconsciously avoiding situations where rejection might rear its ugly head. But rather than let fear dictate his life, he took a page from the growth mindset playbook. Jiang made an unusual choice: Instead of dodging rejection, he decided to seek it out, to confront his fear head-on through a project he called "100 Days of Rejection Therapy."

Armed with a camera, a notebook, and an admittedly unusual list of requests, Jiang embarked on a journey of calculated absurdity. Each day, he set out with a goal to be rejected by someone new in increasingly creative (and at times cringeworthy) ways. It was a social experiment with a very personal goal: to desensitize himself to the sting of rejection so that he could build resilience through repeated exposure. To observers, Jiang's journey appeared to be a blend of performance art, social psychology, and absurdist humor.

His rejection therapy unfolded in a series of memorable encounters. One day, he approached a stranger and asked for $100—a bold, if not financially effective, request. Another day, he ventured into a Krispy Kreme and asked for donuts shaped like the Olympic rings, a request so specific and seemingly impossible that it would have led most people to politely show him the door. But to his surprise, the manager of the Krispy Kreme actually accepted the challenge and created the donut masterpiece free of charge. That moment was a turning point for Jiang because it proved his assumption—that "no" was inevitable—was incorrect and revealed a world of surprising possibilities. Instead of letting the fear of rejection keep him from making audacious requests, Jiang learned that a growth mindset could transform these encounters into opportunities.

As Jiang's experiment continued, he looked forward to each day's rejection not as a mark of failure but as a springboard to self-discovery and mental badassery. He came to see rejection as a teacher—sometimes a harsh one, but always instructive. He learned that rejection wasn't about personal inadequacy; often, it was just a situational response with little to do with his worth or potential. Each no taught him something new: the importance of persistence, the art of negotiation, and the surprising generosity that sometimes emerged in unexpected places. As my father-in-law used to say, "You don't ask, you don't get."

By the time Jiang completed his hundredth day of rejection, his entire perspective on failure had shifted. He had become rejection proof in the truest sense, and this had built a mental platform that would empower him to pursue his goals with newfound freedom and confidence. His journey became a viral sensation, with people around the world drawn to the humor, humanity, and bravery of his experiment. In 2015, he published his experiences in a book, *Rejection Proof,* which quickly became a bestseller. The book, along with his subsequent TED Talk, resonated globally: People saw in Jiang's story a blueprint for overcoming the fears that hold us back from reaching our full potential.

Jia Jiang's story, a testament to his own innovative approach to character building, is a vivid, unconventional example of how embracing a growth mindset can transform our relationship with failure. By leaning into rejection instead of running from it, Jiang demonstrated that discomfort is not only a necessary part of growth but also the gateway to it. Rejection doesn't have to be a roadblock; with the right mindset, it can lead to courage, confidence, and a life without limits.

Growth Mindset as a Pathway to Radical Transformation

Carol Dweck's research has changed the way we understand human potential. At its core, a growth mindset is about embracing change, confronting fears, and taking action despite uncertainty. This chapter has explored what Dweck herself revealed: Growth mindset is about adopting emotional elasticity and mental durability as a way of life. When we commit to growth, we make discomfort our ally, failure our teacher, and transformation our reward. A gift that keeps on giving.

Growth mindset is a powerful pathway, but it requires work, daily dedication, and a willingness to redefine ourselves. So, here's the challenge: Move beyond comfort, embrace your setbacks, and choose growth. A true growth mindset doesn't happen by accident—it's an intentional, ongoing pilgrimage toward becoming the unbreakable, ever-evolving everyday hero you were meant to be.

GOING *ALL IN*

TO ACCESS YOUR ALL IN WORKSPACE, VISIT APP.EXLR8.AI/ALL-IN

AM I EMBRACING CHALLENGES OR AVOIDING THEM?

Reflection
Consider Jim Abbott's story from this chapter. Born without a right hand, he didn't avoid the challenges his physical limitation presented but instead redefined his path to success by mastering techniques that led to a no-hitter in Major League Baseball. His ability to embrace and adapt to challenges exemplifies a growth mindset.

Action
Identify one challenge you've been avoiding because it seems insurmountable. Write down one small, actionable step you can take to face it head-on. For example, if public speaking feels overwhelming, start by practicing a short presentation in front of a trusted friend or colleague.

DO I VIEW FAILURE AS A DEAD END OR AN OPPORTUNITY?

Reflection
Reflect on Sara Blakely's journey. She was rejected repeatedly when pitching Spanx, but instead of internalizing those rejections, she used each no as a tool to refine her product and her pitch. Her resilience turned rejection into a billion-dollar empire.

Action
Think about a recent failure or rejection. Instead of dismissing it, analyze what went wrong and what you can learn from it. Write down one adjustment you'll make to approach a similar situation differently in the future.

AM I STEPPING OUTSIDE MY COMFORT ZONE TO GROW?

Reflection

Colin O'Brady's grueling fifty-four-day solo trek across Antarctica pushed him to the edge of his physical and mental limits. His story reminds us that real growth doesn't happen in comfort; it happens when we deliberately stretch ourselves beyond what feels safe or easy.

Action

Choose one area of your life—personal, professional, or physical—where you've been staying in your comfort zone. Commit to one action that will stretch you, such as volunteering for a project outside your expertise, tackling a fitness goal, or learning a new skill. Set a clear timeline to hold yourself accountable.

These questions and actions are designed to inspire reflection and drive meaningful growth in your growth journey. Remember, as this chapter has shown, cultivating a growth mindset requires embracing discomfort, reframing failure, and constantly challenging the boundaries of what you think is possible. Your next step forward could be the one that transforms everything.

PART 3

COMMITMENT AND PURPOSE

THE REMARKABLE RESULTS PYRAMID (RRP)

11

THE PURPOSE COMPASS

Discovering and Activating Your Why

Friedrich Nietzsche, the German philosopher, introduced the concept of the *will to power* as a fundamental human drive—not merely for survival or pleasure but for self-overcoming, growth, and creation. This intrinsic force, Nietzsche argued, embodies humanity's potential to rise above limitations and achieve greatness. When aligned with purpose, the will to power transforms from an abstract energy into focused, intentional action, turning challenges into opportunities for growth and mastery. Much like Nietzsche's Übermensch— an idealized figure who transcends societal norms—those driven by purpose channel the will to power to embrace obstacles as integral steps toward self-actualization.

Purpose, then, is more than a vague sense of direction; it is the guiding channel through which the will to power flows so that you can shape a life of meaning, commitment, and transformation. Individuals with a distinct purpose, embodying Nietzsche's philosophy in their pursuit of a life well lived, do not shy away from difficulties but leverage them as tools for evolution. This chapter explores how purpose enhances adaptability, focus, and satisfaction and offers practical insights and stories to help you crystallize your own sense of purpose as the foundation of both personal and professional fulfillment.

PIRATES OF THE INDIAN OCEAN

When the roots are deep, there is no reason to fear the wind.
—AFRICAN PROVERB

The dhow creaks like an old man's bones, swaying beneath us as the sea carves patterns against its hull. One mile off the coast of East Africa, the air swells with the pungent fragrance of diesel and brine, and there's an eerie quiet here that fills the spaces where waves slosh against weathered wood. The boat is large but rough around the edges, the kind of vessel that's seen enough years to earn the wily respect of its crew but not enough upkeep to be anywhere close to seaworthy by any American standard. In another life, it could pass for a pirate ship. Perhaps, on occasion, that is its function. The crew of nine men move with a loose, practiced familiarity, their bare feet sure on the uneven wood. They're as ragtag as the vessel, some strong and competent, others weary or barely capable, but all equally ready to turn a blind eye in the pursuit of a decent payout.

They don't know why we're here, other than the simple, well-paid directive: two Americans, a supply run, no questions. It's as straightforward as it is dubious, and the less we interact with them, the easier it is for everyone to mind their own business. We are dressed to blend in, at least as much as possible, given the circumstances—shorts and worn T-shirts that smell faintly of spices and sweat from the vendor stalls where we bought them. Our waterproof black trunk is the only thing that speaks of military precision amid the otherwise ramshackle environment. It stands as a silent sentinel in the corner of the deck, holding weapons, night-vision goggles, and our SOTVS platform (special operations tactical video system) like secrets waiting to be told. The crew hasn't shown much interest in it, but they keep a certain distance as if they can sense the weight of what's inside.

The engine hums with a steady, low grumble that vibrates up through the floorboards and into our bones, a constant reminder of the ship's age and its stubborn refusal to die. The last few days have seen two engine-room fires, a common occurrence according to the crew. The wind tears through the tarp above us, woven together in a makeshift pocket of shade on the upper deck. It rips and flutters, snapping with sharp, irregular bursts that remind me of small-arms fire—quick, startling, then fading into silence. There is no hot tub, chef, or chief stew pouring cocktails aboard this nautical nightmare. But there is plenty of drama.

The nights are different, quieter, often filled with the steady lull of darkness, leaving our minds to wander. The sky is vast and starless on many nights, with the clouds hanging low, and they cast a silver hue across the water that's both beautiful and unsettling. Sometimes the rain pours down in sheets, turning the deck into a slick battlefield of puddles and slippery wood. The crew doesn't flinch but moves through the storms as naturally as breathing, accustomed to the uncertainty of the sea.

There's a crude toilet on the aft bottom deck—a hole in the floor that offers little privacy and no dignity, but the crew and our small team have learned to adapt. The smell of diesel mingles with the faint, ever-present stench of saltwater and sweat. It clings to us, creeping into our clothes and settling like a second skin. Our diet, too, is far from ideal. We've subsisted on a week's worth of tepid overly sweet tea and pancakes that are more akin to rubbery flatbreads. Each bite is a reminder that this isn't a place of comfort. It's a place of purpose, a place to keep moving, a place to simply make do and get the job done.

As we pass each night, stopping at small ports that dot the coast, the routine becomes surreal. The ship drops anchor in the dark, and my teammate and I, blending with the shadows, leave the vessel and slip into the silence and obscurity of the night. Our movements are deliberate, precise, each step an echo of countless hours of training. When we return before dawn, soaked or sweating, depending on the whims of the weather and the evening's activities, we find the dhow waiting like a silent conspirator. The crew barely stirs, save for the occasional curious glance or nod of acknowledgment.

The sun, as it ascends, casts a golden light over the weathered decks, revealing every scarred plank and frayed rope, each a testament to battles endured and obstacles overcome. Shadows dance with the rhythm of the boat's steady roll, a quiet reminder of the ceaseless interplay of beauty and uncertainty. Yet, amid the stark illumination of hard-earned wear, there is a profound sense of relief and triumph—a silent acknowledgment of accomplishment. In our world, the "rewards and recognition" program consists of only two prizes: the satisfaction of mission completion and the unspoken gratitude of survival. For those who embrace the grind, no medal or accolade can rival the quiet, enduring pride of a job well done.

By day, the dhow is an almost picturesque sight, lumbering through the deep blue of the water sparkling beneath a vast sky. The heat is intense, searing, baking us as we settle into the rhythms of this strange, self-contained world. I find myself struck by the incongruity of it all—this floating microcosm of lives, ours intertwined temporarily with the lives of men who understand nothing of our mission, of our language, of our purpose. But we are careful to not think them naive.

Our interpreter, who somehow manages to bridge the gulf between us and the crew with weary patience, has his hands full. The crew speaks no English, so the interpreter becomes our lifeline to understanding, translating fragmented exchanges as we pick up bits of Swahili that allow us to get by in brief interactions. There's a mutual respect here, a tacit understanding that we're all bound to this vessel, each with our own motives and secrets.

As the days stretch on, I find myself acutely attuned to the subtle, unspoken signals that ripple through the crew—the flicker of unease in their glances, the captain's contemplative tilt of the head as he scans the horizon, the darting eyes of a younger crewman when his gaze lingers too long on our weathered black trunk. Our tattered, hastily purchased clothing does little to obscure the stark contrast of our tattooed, athletic frames—etched with stories these sailors will never hear. We keep our distance, understanding that curiosity is inevitable but trusting in the quiet leverage of money and the heavy weight of silence. Yet, beneath the surface, there is an undeniable tension, an undercurrent that hums like the strained timbers of the ship—a sense that our presence is a riddle they are unsure they want to solve.

The boat's motor coughs and sputters at times, a reminder of the thin line we tread between purpose and peril. The rhythmic hum that fills the air is oddly comforting, a steady beat that underscores each day's passage. I listen to it as I stand on the deck at night, gazing out at the dark expanse of water, feeling the weight of the silence pressing in. The sea is an inky black void, stretching out to the edge of the world, interrupted only by the faint glow of distant lights from shore. It's both beautiful and deeply unsettling—a reminder that we are far from home, surrounded by unfamiliar faces, with only our purpose to ground us.

And as we push forward, night after night, small port after small port, I feel a strange sense of peace amid the discomfort. It's a hard, gritty kind of peace, born from knowing that this mission, whatever it may demand, is the reason we're here. It's the reason we endure the bad tea, the strange looks, the isolation, and the endless miles of open sea. This is commitment stripped bare—no glory, no fanfare, just a quiet, unyielding dedication to the task at hand.

But one night, we faced a special kind of unforeseen obstacle.

Can I Call My Lawyer?

Scotty and I are perched on the top deck, watching the faint shoreline lights blink and shimmer in the distance. The night air is cool against our faces, but there's a humid weight to it that presses down as we approach another nameless port along the coast. Out here, technology is practically nonexistent—the vessel has no GPS, no radar, no lights but a few weak beams from our ship's ancient deck lanterns among those that pinprick the shore. We're left with our senses, feeling the subtle shifts in the sea's rhythm, reading every dark shadow and faint sound that rises above the hum of the engine.

Then, out of the blackness, it appears. A smaller dhow, moving with an unmistakable intent, emerges from the darkness and closes in fast on our starboard side. Blinding spotlights snap on and wash over us in an unforgiving glare, stealing away our sight and flooding our minds with a thousand questions. As SEALs, we are typically the aggressor in these scenarios. Not tonight. I shield my eyes, squinting against the beams, but it's impossible to see who's on board or how many. There's no subtlety in their approach—they want us to know they're here, and they want us to know they mean business. My mind races, cycling through possibilities: Are they pirates or local officials? Neither option bodes well.

I lean down, barking to our interpreter, who scrambles over to the captain. A quick exchange of words in low, rapid Swahili, and he returns with a grave expression. "They're either pirates or corrupt local authorities," he mutters, his tone clipped. His face is tight, and for a man who's spent his career bridging gaps between worlds, he looks out of his depth. The implications hang thick in the air. Scotty and I have fake credentials, a flimsy cover story about a supply run, but we hadn't planned on needing to use either. We were meant to stay as invisible as the night that now feels like it's closing in on us.

Voices rise from the other dhow. Rough, guttural commands spill out over the water, demanding that our captain kill the engine. I hear our crew answer back in nervous, hurried tones as they exchange glances that flash between frustration and fear. With a lurch, our ship slows, the engine sputtering as it powers down. The other dhow pulls up alongside with an unsettling ease, and before the reality of it fully sinks in, men are climbing aboard. They move with an air of practiced confidence, their actions smooth and deliberate, as though this is just another day at the office. AK-47s hang casually over their shoulders, their presence commanding but not chaotic. Each man assumes his position with an unspoken rhythm, not the razor-sharp precision of a Navy SEAL boarding operation, but undeniably trained, reasonably disciplined, and familiar. I glance at Scotty; his jaw is locked, his eyes tracking every movement of the intruders with the calculating calm of someone who's weighed risk against reward too many times to panic. You can almost see the gears turning behind his unflinching gaze, the options measured, the risks tallied.

The half-assed search now complete, we're escorted to a small, dimly lit marina, the sound of water lapping against the hull amplified in the eerie silence. My skin prickles as the boat bumps against the dock. Scotty and I are far from the safety of our black trunk now, from the night-vision goggles and weapons we'd packed as contingencies; it all may as well be locked in a safe halfway across the world. We disembark with slow, measured steps, guided by the shadowy figures who now hold control over every move we make. The air is still thick with diesel and salt, a heady mix that feels like a slap in the face after the relative openness of the sea. Under other circumstances, it might smell like freedom; tonight, it smells like something closer to entrapment.

As we step onto the dock, one of the men gives a sharp shove, pushing us toward a cluster of buildings nestled in the dark. The walls are stained and crumbling, barely illuminated by a few dim, flickering lights that cast just enough glow to reveal the expressions of our captors. A lone donkey nibbles on the flaky exterior wall of one of the buildings. I catch a glimpse of a smirk on one man's face, a glint in another's eye, the slight tightening of a hand on a rifle stock. Time stretches, every second measured, as my senses sharpen to a razor's edge. Each detail becomes magnified—the faint creak of the dock under shifting boots, the metallic glint of a weapon catching the sun, the barely audible murmur of exchanged words. I review a mental checklist, assessing every scenario with focused precision. A shakedown? Almost certainly. A robbery? Distinctly possible. Something darker, something my instincts warn me not to name? Chillingly plausible. Yet amid the chaos of potential outcomes, my thoughts remain anchored in focused problem-solving. The fear that hovers at the edges of my awareness is acknowledged, but it doesn't dictate. Instead, it fuels the cold clarity that survival demands.

Our interpreter stays close, visibly straining to pick up fragments of conversation among the men. He murmurs a translation here and there—words about "Americans," about "money"—but none of it adds up, and the unknowns are piling up faster than I can sort through them. It's as though every torture scene from every war movie I've ever seen is flashing through my mind, an uninvited slideshow of grim possibilities. But fear can be a useful tool, sharpening focus, fueling clarity. I take a steadying breath, forcing myself to tune in, analyze each step, each shift in their body language, each fleeting glance they share with one another. *Hell, waterboarding is a great way to stay hydrated, my ribs haven't been cracked in a while, and my fingernails are too long anyway, so...* It's all about reframing!

The sounds around us amplify in the quiet night. The shuffle of boots on worn concrete, the faint rustle of fabric as one of them adjusts his weapon, the creak of a door swinging open as we're ushered into one of the dimly lit buildings. Inside, the smell is sharp, metallic, mingled with the damp mustiness that comes from years of neglect. Shadows pool in the corners and stretch across cracked floors and peeling walls. No donkey in the room though. My eyes sweep the space, cataloging exits, calculating angles, assessing the men around us, reading their faces for any hint of intent. Scotty's posture is calm but alert, every muscle coiled, his gaze shifting from face to face with the intensity of a man sizing up prey—or predators.

The silence stretches, tense and loaded, as one of the men steps forward, his face barely illuminated by the dull light. He says something low and forceful to our interpreter, who stiffens, his jaw tight as he absorbs the words. He leans in close to us, his voice a strained whisper. "They want to know who we are and why you're here. They're asking for...assurances. Payment." His eyes flicker to mine, a silent warning.

Assurances and *payment*—two words that could mean anything, from a simple bribe to a more insidious demand. Silently, I weigh the options and dissect the possible outcomes. We can't simply fight our way out; even if we had our weapons, we're outnumbered and in unknown territory. And without knowing their endgame, any rash move could shift this from tense to lethal. We have to manage the situation carefully. I exchange a glance with Scotty, a quick, silent transfer of thoughts that only years of shared experience can communicate. His eyes are steady, unyielding, but I can see the same calculations turning in his mind.

In the dimness, I catch sight of a figure standing at the back of the room, leaning against the wall with an unsettling calm. He's not like the others; there's a calculating intelligence in his gaze, as though he's studying us with the same intensity we're using to assess him. He looks important. He mutters something to one of his men, who nods in silent acknowledgment, and suddenly, our small group is broken apart. I feel a hand on my arm, firm but not rough, directing me away from Scotty and our interpreter. The air shifts, thickening as they lead us to separate rooms, each with a guard posted outside. I lose sight of Scotty, though I can still feel the tension that links us, taut and electric, through the thin wall that divides us.

My own "cell" is dimly lit, with cracked plaster walls and a small, grated window that lets in slivers of cool night air. A guard stands in the corner, watching me with the detached stare of someone whose job is less about enforcing the rules and more about existing as a silent threat. I settle into a chair, my senses heightened, cataloging every smell—the sharp tang of sweat, faint traces of mold, the ghost of diesel fumes clinging to my clothes. I can hear murmurs drifting in from the adjacent rooms, muffled conversations, and the occasional, quiet scrape of a boot across the floor.

Then, slowly, the man from before—the one with the calculating gaze—makes his way toward me, his steps unhurried. In this place, there's no sense of urgency, no hurry to get to the point. Time, here, seems to stretch, a concept made flexible and sluggish by the night, the isolation, and the strange, lethargic rhythm of our captors. He doesn't introduce himself, doesn't even ask my name; he simply observes me with a faint, unreadable expression before speaking—in English—in a low, almost conversational tone. His questions are few, vague, probing, with the same measured indifference of a cat toying with an almost-deceased mouse, testing reactions rather than expecting answers. Each question hangs in the air like smoke, slowly dissipating, and I answer only as much as I must, choosing my words carefully, knowing that each response is a calculated gamble.

He moves on, leaving the room as slowly as he entered, and I hear him slip into Scotty's room. I'm wondering if Scotty is being asked the same hollow questions, if he's facing the same languid scrutiny. For now, control means staying calm, analyzing, preparing for contingencies I'm not even certain will come to pass. Then, a shift. Two guards step into my room, exchange brief, clipped words, and I sense the air thicken with an unfamiliar edge. They don't ask questions; they're not here to talk. The largest one of them steps forward, closing the distance with a sudden shift in weight—sharp, dismissive, like swatting away a fly. A white flash cuts through my vision, pressure blooming along my jaw. I steady myself, locking my face into stillness. This isn't about destruction; it's a signal, a probe. I know this language.

Something else follows—heavier, deeper. My ribs tighten as the air thins. The room blurs at the edges for a beat, but my focus sharpens, anchoring to the details: the flicker of amusement in one face, the cool detachment in the other's eyes. Everything slows. Every nerve is awake. They want to see fear, to see weakness, to confirm that they hold the power here. I give them nothing, even as I feel the adrenaline spike through my veins, every muscle taut and coiled.

When they finish, the man with the calculating gaze returns, glancing at me with a faintly approving expression. It's as if this rough treatment was a necessary formality, a rite of passage that we both understand without words. His eyes linger on mine for a fraction longer, as though weighing my reaction, and I hold his gaze, allowing just enough defiance to show that I'm still very much present, very much aware.

He moves on, and I'm left alone in the dimness, with only the faint sounds of Scotty and our interpreter shifting in their rooms to remind me that I'm not entirely alone. My mind races, assessing, planning, calculating each possible scenario that might unfold. Somewhere beyond the walls, I hear the low hum of the boat's engine, a faint reminder of the mission, of why we're here, and it grounds me, pulls me back from the brink of uncertainty. We're here for a reason.

We're here with a purpose, and I cling to that purpose now, finding strength in it, finding clarity in the knowledge that no matter what, I am prepared.

Let's Get the Hell Out of Here

The hours stretched on as we waited in our separate rooms. Every second felt like it might be the one that would break the standoff, send a signal, reveal the answer to the questions my mind kept turning over. But each second remained painfully quiet, filled only with the faint hum of tension and the slow, rhythmic clink of metal from somewhere out of sight. My guard barely moved, his eyes flickering toward me now and then, like a man watching a caged animal, curious but cautious. I stayed still, eyes sharp, every sense on high alert, waiting for whatever came next.

Finally, footsteps approached, heavy and deliberate, and the door creaked open. The calculating man stepped inside, his gaze steady, lips curling into something between a smirk and a grimace. He didn't waste any more time with questions. Instead, his words fell flatly into the space between us, like a demand that had been brewing from the start: money. He wanted money—a lot of it, judging by the quiet menace in his voice and the way his eyes narrowed, sizing me up as though he could already count the dollars.

We had cash stowed away, tucked into the depths of that heavy black box back on our vessel—about ten thousand, American. Enough to get us out of a tight spot, we'd reasoned back then. This qualified. After a few more tense exchanges, a little haggling, and a lot of side-eyes from both of us, we settled on a deal. His dissatisfaction was evident in the tight line of his mouth, the small flares of anger beneath his calm, but ultimately, the lure of US dollars in hand was enough to make him reconsider whatever darker plans might have lurked in his mind.

The man's eyes bored into mine, and in that silent, heavy moment, an understanding seemed to pass between us. He wasn't buying our story; that much was clear. There was a glint of something else in his gaze, a flicker of suspicion. Perhaps he sensed, in the way we carried ourselves or the quiet readiness in our eyes, that we weren't simply supply runners out for a night on the sea. He seemed to know there was more to us than we'd let on. He most likely suspected we were military, though the reality of just two of us—a couple of strangers in tattered shirts, bargaining their way out of a mess in the dark hours of the night—seemed to leave him confused.

The exchange completed, we were escorted back to our vessel. As we stepped back on board, the creaking of the old wood and the steady hum of the engine felt like a long-lost friend, a lifeline to something solid in this haze of distrust and danger. Scotty and I made quick work of casting off, the crew's silence thick with a mix of fear and resentment as they watched us, wary but relieved. Our interpreter kept close, his eyes flickering with a shared tension that needed no translation.

Within minutes, we were pulling away, the small port fading into a dark speck on the horizon as we moved swiftly into open waters. Only when the shoreline dissolved into the distance did the knot in my chest finally loosen. The weight of the night hung heavy around us, the sharp tang of diesel mingling with the salt as the wind picked up, and for a moment, everything was still. We'd made it out. By the skin of our teeth, perhaps, but we'd made it.

Scotty gave me a nod, his expression a mixture of exhaustion and triumph, and I returned it with a grim smile. This wasn't exactly what we'd signed up for, but we'd done what we came to do and slipped out without any lives lost—a quiet success in a place where quiet successes are the best kind. As the waves rolled beneath us, the night vast and empty once more, I took a deep breath, letting the tension finally drain away. There was still work ahead, miles of uncertain seas, but for now, we were free. And in this world, sometimes that's all you need.

MAYBE THAT NIETZSCHE GUY WAS ON TO SOMETHING

Efforts and courage are not enough
without purpose and direction.
—JOHN F. KENNEDY

I must preface this part by saying Scotty Wirtz is gone now. I write this knowing that we both had lived, at least for a time, with the reckless conviction that death was an abstract notion, something that existed in other timelines but that would always pass us by. Scotty was one of my closest friends at SEAL Team 5, a brother forged in the fire of missions, training, and time. A true warrior in every sense of the word. We both knew our job was a dangerous one, but that knowledge didn't make it easier. Scotty was killed along with several other Americans in a suicide bombing on January 16, 2019, in Manbij, Syria, in a café targeted by ISIS. He was over there working as a CIA contractor—a continuation of the work we believed in, in a way only Scotty could. He is missed by many every day.

Now, let's go back to one of the last missions we ran together off the coast of East Africa. I remember the following day after the close call—we were back on the dhow, the ocean stretching endlessly around us, dark and reflective as glass. Scotty sat across from me on the upper deck aft, his face cast in shadow as he thumbed through a worn copy of *Beyond Good and Evil* by Friedrich Nietzsche, of all things. I looked at him, amused and curious as ever. Scotty, a Navy SEAL with a Nietzschean obsession—it was so like him. He was one of the most interesting people I knew in the Teams. And utterly wild at heart.

"You still on that Nietzsche kick?" I asked, struggling to pronounce the name, as usual, but settling back against the rail, feeling the quiet lapping of the waves beneath us.

He looked up, smiling slightly, and closed the book but kept his finger marking the page. "Yeah, there's something about the guy," he said, shrugging. "He doesn't exactly pull his punches, you know?"

"Right," I nodded, watching him. "So, what's the takeaway this time?"

He glanced down at the book, and I could see he was trying to condense it, pull out something concise for my benefit. "Well, *Beyond Good and Evil*—he's challenging the whole idea of conventional morality. Nietzsche thought people cling to these black-and-white ideas of right and wrong because it's comfortable, because it makes life feel manageable. But he saw reality as more complex, something that goes beyond what we'd call 'good' or 'evil.'"

"So, he's saying we make our own rules?" I asked. "Now I get why you like his work."

"More or less," Scotty replied, scratching his chin. "He talks about the Übermensch as someone who creates his own values, lives by his own purpose. Nietzsche thought that was the way to true power, real freedom. He believed people could transcend their limitations by accepting that life is chaotic and pushing through anyway. We can't rely on any universal, external set of rules to tell us what matters."

I leaned back, letting his words settle over me. "And you think that's what we're doing out here?" I asked, half joking, half serious. "Living beyond good and evil?"

Scotty laughed, a deep, easy laugh that sounded as natural as the waves breaking against the hull. "Well, we're not exactly running a morality clinic out here," he said, smiling. "But we're definitely doing something unconventional, and you could argue we're creating our own rules as we go."

I sat with that for a moment, letting the sea breeze cut through the heaviness of the previous night's events. "You know," I said, my voice quieter now, "last night…there were moments I was holding onto purpose like a lifeline. Reminding myself of the mission, what we're here to do. That's what kept me steady. It's like…purpose became the only thing that mattered, you know? Gunfights in Iraq are one thing. But being out here with very limited support, practically making it up as we go, that is something very different."

Scotty nodded, his gaze shifting to the open horizon. "Purpose," he repeated, almost to himself. "It's what drives us forward, especially in situations like this. Nietzsche called it the 'will to power.' He thought it's what makes people push through fear, chaos…even death. He believed the most powerful thing a person can have is a reason to keep going, something bigger than himself."

I nodded, feeling a strange comfort in the notion. "It's funny," I said. "As SEALs, our purpose is pretty cut and dry. Serve, protect, crush evil, complete the mission. But in moments like last night, it's not so clear-cut. It's one thing to understand our purpose, another thing to live it when every instinct is screaming at you to do something else."

Scotty looked at me, his face reflecting the mixture of conviction and acceptance he wore so well. "Yeah, purpose isn't always a warm, fuzzy thing. It's more like an anchor. It's what keeps you grounded when things get chaotic. And sometimes it's the only thing standing between you and…I don't know…giving in to whatever easier path there might be. Nietzsche would say it's what separates people who drift from those who steer their own ship, regardless of the storm."

He paused, looking down at the book in his hands. "I think Nietzsche was onto something. The idea of creating our own purpose, not relying on what the world says we should value but instead deciding for ourselves. Purpose doesn't remove the fear, the doubts—but it gives us a reason to face them."

I let his words sink in, feeling the weight of them. We both knew the stakes of what we did, what it meant to live by a purpose that went beyond ourselves. "But that's the challenge, isn't it?" I said, "To keep holding on to that purpose, even when everything around you threatens to tear it away. I guess that's what Nietzsche meant by power—having something worth fighting for, no matter what."

Scotty nodded, a faint smile tugging at his lips. "Exactly. It's not about strength alone. It's about resilience, the kind that goes deeper than muscle or bravado. It's mental, it's spiritual…it's whatever it takes to keep going when the odds are stacked against you. That's purpose. And maybe that's what Nietzsche was getting at."

We sat in silence after that, each of us turning over the profundity of those words, the gravity of what it meant to live a life defined by purpose, by that will to push forward. Scotty's words stayed with me, carving out a space in my mind that would remain long after we returned from this mission, long after we'd left the waves and the distant shorelines of Africa.

Looking back now, that conversation feels like a farewell, even if we didn't know it at the time. Scotty left this world as he lived—driven by a purpose he believed in, a will that wouldn't be shaken. He died in the service of something greater than himself, and perhaps Nietzsche would say he'd found the essence of the Übermensch, was a man who lived by his own values and created meaning in a world often devoid of it.

And as I remember him there, sitting across from me on that creaking old dhow with Nietzsche in hand, I can't help but smile. Because, in a way, he is still with me, reminding me to stay anchored when necessary, to take risks when inspired, and to navigate the dark seas with purpose in my heart.

Purpose is not merely a guiding star—it is the anchor that holds us steady in the storm, the fire that drives us forward when every force seems determined to push us back. As I hope this chapter has shown, purpose transforms the chaos of life into a meaningful voyage, where obstacles are turned into opportunities and challenges into catalysts for growth. Whether navigating the treacherous waters off the East African coast or grappling with the trials of everyday life, purpose provides clarity and inner courage, shapes our decisions, and strengthens our resolve.

In the end, purpose is not something granted or bestowed; it is something we define, refine, and hold onto. It is what separates those who drift aimlessly from those who steer their own course, regardless of the storms they face. As Nietzsche suggests, purpose is the embodiment of our will to power—a force that not only drives us to overcome but also allows us to create meaning in a world of volatility and ambiguity. It is the essence of living fully, deliberately, and with a steadfast commitment to something greater than ourselves.

GOING *ALL IN*

TO ACCESS YOUR ALL IN WORKSPACE, VISIT APP.EXLR8.AI/ALL-IN

HOW DOES PURPOSE SHAPE MY RESILIENCE IN DIFFICULT SITUATIONS?

Reflection
Consider the story of Scotty Wirtz reflecting on Nietzsche's philosophy while on the dhow, acknowledging purpose as an anchor in the face of chaos. Purpose grounded Scotty even in the midst of danger, giving him a reason to face fear and uncertainty head-on.

Action
Identify one challenge in your life that feels overwhelming and connect it to your greater purpose. Write down how overcoming this obstacle aligns with your broader goals and values.

AM I DEFINING MY PURPOSE, OR IS IT BEING DEFINED FOR ME?

Reflection
Nietzsche's concept of the Übermensch challenges us to create our own values and live by them, rather than adopting those imposed by the world. Scotty's life exemplifies this idea because he lived by his own code, grounded in service and commitment to something greater than himself.

Action

Take fifteen minutes to reflect on your current goals. Ask yourself: "Are these goals truly mine? Do they align with my values and vision, or are they shaped by external expectations?" Make adjustments as needed to align with your authentic purpose.

HOW DO I MAINTAIN PURPOSE WHEN CIRCUMSTANCES THREATEN TO DERAIL ME?

Reflection

During our tense moments with the captors, purpose became a lifeline—focusing my mind and driving disciplined decision-making under pressure. Purpose did not eliminate fear but provided the clarity to navigate it.

Action

Develop a personal "purpose mantra"—a short statement that encapsulates your core mission and values. Use this mantra as a mental anchor during moments of stress or uncertainty to remind yourself why you persevere.

12

EMOTIONAL FUEL

Fusing Passion and Purpose

In the journey of personal transformation, few forces rival the power of a connection between our emotions and our purpose. At the core of every meaningful goal lies a reservoir of emotional energy, a magnificent pool that fuels our determination to overcome challenges and sustain commitment over time. This emotional force transcends mere motivation; it acts as a compass that guides us through setbacks and recalibrates our course when progress feels slow or obstacles seem insurmountable. Without this vital connection, even the most well-crafted plans and routines risk becoming empty activities that lack the essential spark for achieving extraordinary outcomes.

Tapping into our emotional connection to purpose means embracing our principles, passions, and causes that inspire us to rise above mediocrity. This emotional energy transforms routines and rituals from ordinary tasks into intentional practices rich with meaning. By grounding our goals in a crystallized sense of purpose, a clear vision of our true selves—all guided by a definitive road map—we unlock the capacity to achieve feats that verge on the mythological.

Purpose, when fused with passion, becomes the emotional engine driving us toward meaningful success. It bridges the gap between where we are and where we want to be and turns even ordinary effort into extraordinary results.

A TALE OF SURVIVAL, REVENGE, AND DOWNRIGHT STUBBORN REFUSAL TO DIE

I ain't afraid to die anymore. I done it already.

—HUGH GLASS, *THE REVENANT*

The air was sharp and clean, carrying the scent of pine needles and damp earth, a soothing contrast to the feral stench of blood and metallic tang of desperation that clung to Hugh Glass like an uninvited specter. For those unfamiliar, Hugh Glass (1783–1833) was the quintessential American frontiersman, a man whose name would echo through the annals of history, inspiring *The Revenant*, the film that finally earned Leonardo DiCaprio his long-overdue Oscar. Glass was the real-life embodiment of grit. His tale unfolds not in the grandeur of Hollywood but in the unforgiving wilderness near the Grand River, in what is now Perkins County, South Dakota.

It was there, in late 1823, during an expedition under General William Henry Ashley of the Rocky Mountain Fur Company, that nature itself seemed to orchestrate a brutal symphony of survival. The attack was as sudden as it was merciless, a blur of fur and fury as a grizzly bear, driven by the raw instincts of a mother protecting her cubs, descended on Glass. Her claws sliced through his flesh with horrifying ease, each stroke a grim reminder of nature's indifference. Bones cracked under the bear's immense weight, the sound like brittle branches snapping in the stillness. The wilderness, usually alive with the harmonious chatter of birds and the rustling of leaves, fell eerily silent, as if the very land had paused to bear witness to this primal collision of life and death. It was a moment suspended in piercing, unfiltered brutality, the kind that strips away all pretense and reveals the raw tenacity of the human spirit.

When it was over, the bear was dead—thanks to Glass's desperate will to fight for life—and Glass, well, he was reconsidering that coffin bell. His flesh was torn open in great, glistening ribbons, his ribs poking through the skin like grotesque tree roots breaking through soil. His face, once ruggedly handsome by the standards of men who measure attractiveness by scars, was unrecognizable, a swollen mask of pain and gore. And yet, as his fellow fur trappers debated the logistics of his burial, he blinked. The man was not dead, despite the enthusiastic efforts of the grizzly and, it seemed, the wilderness herself.

The decision to leave Hugh Glass behind was not made lightly—or so his companions might have argued if ever pressed. But in truth, altruism was not exactly a cherished commodity among frontiersmen in 1823, especially when survival was a daily negotiation with death. The wilderness was an unforgiving realm where weakness was a liability, and the cost of compassion could easily tip the scales against your own survival. Glass's injuries—gruesome and extensive—were a stark reminder of this harsh reality. Torn flesh, exposed bones, and a body rendered almost unrecognizable by the bear's assault left no doubt in their minds: He would not recover.

Initially, a pretense of duty prevailed. Two men—John Fitzgerald, a hardened and pragmatic trapper, and Jim Bridger, a young and inexperienced frontiersman—volunteered to stay behind. Their mission was ostensibly to "tend" to Glass until his inevitable death and provide him the dignity of a shallow grave. But "tending" in this context was a grim euphemism. There would be no comforting words or gentle ministrations. The reality was more akin to a death watch, an exercise in waiting for the inevitable while trying to ignore the moans of a man too stubborn to die on schedule.

Days stretched into nights, and Glass's refusal to succumb became a source of growing frustration. His labored breaths, the pitiful gurgles that emerged from his mangled throat, and his uncanny will to cling to life began to feel less like a testament to human perseverance and more like a maddening delay. For Fitzgerald and Bridger, every moment spent with the dying man was a moment spent exposed in hostile territory, vulnerable to attacks from Native tribes and territorial animals. The weight of Glass's survival—or lack thereof—was not only moral but increasingly logistical. The longer they waited, the thinner their patience wore, like leather left too long in the sun.

Fitzgerald, the more seasoned of the two, was the first to break. The pragmatism of the frontier demanded ruthless efficiency, and in his eyes, hauling a dying man's dead weight through the wilderness was neither efficient nor survivable. Bridger, though wracked with guilt, was young, impressionable, and ultimately swayed by Fitzgerald's hard-nosed logic. Together, they made their decision.

Leaving was one thing, but taking Glass's tools—the rifle, the knife, and the flint—was another. These were not just items of utility; they were lifelines, the bare essentials for survival in an unforgiving land. Fitzgerald likely rationalized the theft as a matter of necessity; after all, the dead would have no use for such things. Bridger, his conscience gnawed raw, perhaps hesitated longer before giving in. And so, they left him: Stripped of his weapons, his fire-starting tools, and even the illusion of companionship, Glass was abandoned to the elements. His shredded dignity was his only possession, along with the bitter realization that betrayal stung as deeply as any claw or tooth.

But Hugh Glass, with the grit of ten men and perhaps the worst streak of luck imaginable, did not die. The wilderness Glass faced was as merciless as the grizzly that had tried to end him. The winds across the vast expanse of the Great Plains howled like wolves, whipping through the prairie grass that stretched endlessly in every direction. The ground was a patchwork quilt of dirt, mud, and jagged stones. He moved inch by agonizing inch, using his elbows to pull his mangled body forward, the ground beneath him slick with blood and pus that oozed from his wounds. His body screaming in agony with every movement. Every breath.

The smells emanating from his own body were enough to drive a lesser man mad. The sharp, acrid odor of his own infected flesh mingled with the earthy aroma of the natural terrain, creating a nauseating cocktail that clogged his nostrils. The faint tang of smoke occasionally teased his senses, a reminder of the distant camps of Native tribes or fellow trappers, any of whom might prove as dangerous as the wilderness itself.

Flies swarmed his wounds, a living cloud of torment that added insult to injury. He slapped at them feebly, his strength barely enough to scatter the buzzing pests before they returned, drawn to the rotting banquet of his flesh. The taste of bile mixed with the metallic flavor of blood lingered in his mouth, a constant reminder of his fragile mortality. And then, like a hallucination conjured by fever, pain, and the slim hope that the universe might offer a brief reprieve from its cruelty, a figure emerged on the horizon.

At first, Glass squinted through swollen eyelids, half expecting a mountain lion to stride closer and expedite his own slow shuffle toward the grave. But no, this figure moved upright, with a peculiar bounce in their step, far too confident for any self-respecting scavenger. As the shape came into focus, he saw that it was a woman—neatly dressed in clothing so absurdly pristine it practically screamed "misplaced." Her clean, tailored attire stood in comical contrast to the blood-soaked, pus-streaked wreckage of his own existence. The very sight of her crisp blouse and spotless boots made him suspect she was either a ghost with a taste for theatrical entrances or an emissary from some particularly judgmental afterlife, here to scold him for his poor life choices. There is some debate among historians as to the details of this part of the story, or if it even happened at all. But let's continue.

"Who's there?" he rasped, his throat ravaged from the bear attack, the words barely escaping his lips in a series of gurgling croaks.

"Oh, hello!" the woman replied brightly, crouching close with alarming cheer. Her boots, impossibly polished, barely crunched the dirt as she settled beside him. "I don't mean to disturb you, but you appear to be in quite...uh, well, a rather precarious situation."

Glass blinked at her, half convinced he was hallucinating. Her face was serene, her expression one of polite concern, as though he'd been caught in an awkward social faux pas rather than lying half dead in a field. "Who...who the hell are you?" he managed to growl.

"My apologies. I'm Angela Duckworth!" she exclaimed with a smile, brushing a stray wisp of hair from her face, acting as if this was all completely normal. "Author of *Grit: The Power of Passion and Perseverance*. I was just passing through, conducting research for my next book. And, oh my goodness, you are exactly what I've been looking for!"

Glass stared at her, his blood-caked lashes barely holding up under the weight of his incredulity. "Lady, I don't care who you are or what damn book you're writin'. As you can see, I'm in a bit of a jam here. If you ain't got medicine, food, or a rifle, you're about as useful as a gnat on a buffalo's ass."

Unfazed, Duckworth pulled a pristine leather notebook from her satchel and flipped it open with an air of academic determination. The scratch of her pencil on paper seemed wildly out of place against the backdrop of wilderness and rotting flesh.

"Fascinating," she murmured, glancing at Glass, who was clearly trying to decide whether she was real or a very peculiar fever dream. "Your resilience is extraordinary—textbook grit, really. Tell me, Mr. Glass, what's fueling your survival instinct right now? Is it the thought of returning home to your family? Or perhaps a deeper, existential sense of purpose? Wait—could it be revenge? Oh, revenge is always such a compelling driver of human behavior!" Her tone was as bright and curious as if she was discussing the mating habits of migratory birds, not the blood-soaked remains of a man hell-bent on avenging himself.

Glass blinked at her, the sheer absurdity of her presence momentarily outweighing his pain. "Lady," he rasped, his voice like rusted metal dragged over gravel, "if you don't start making sense, I'm gonna assume you're some kind of witch."

She cocked her head, a slight grin emerging.

"But, yes, you nailed it. Revenge," he snarled. "Plain and simple. Now get lost before the vultures take you too."

But she didn't leave. In fact, she made herself surprisingly at home, trailing behind him as he continued his grueling crawl across the prairie. For all her enthusiasm, Duckworth was spectacularly unhelpful. She had no medical skills, no wilderness knowledge, and couldn't even identify which plants weren't poisonous. Zero hunting skills. The one thing she *did* offer was an endless stream of motivational observations. Or at least she thought so.

"You know," she chirped one evening as they camped by a trickling stream—though "camped" might be too generous a word. Glass lay prone in the mud, half covered by a makeshift blanket of moss and branches, while she perched on a nearby rock, cocooned in some kind of shiny, puffy blue contraption. It shimmered in the firelight like fish scales, and he couldn't make heads or tails of it. Was it armor? Some kind of sorcery? It made an odd crinkling noise every time she shifted, and he found himself staring at it with the same suspicion one might reserve for a rattlesnake in one's boot.

"Your ability to persist despite overwhelming odds is remarkable," she continued, utterly oblivious to his bewilderment. She hugged the strange sack tighter, its absurd fluffiness a stark, almost mocking contrast to the grim reality of his shredded, mud-caked existence. "It's exactly what I mean by aligning emotional fuel with purpose. Fascinating, really."

Glass narrowed his gaze and picked at a wound on his hand that oozed with pus. "What in the hell are you wearing?" he grunted, the words barely escaping his cracked lips. "Looks like a blue possum swallowed you whole and gave up halfway through."

She blinked, then glanced down at her sleeping bag. "Oh, this? It's a sleeping bag. Lightweight, waterproof, and rated for subzero temperatures. Quite practical, really."

Glass painfully rolled his eyes, then stared at her in silence for a moment before muttering, "Practical for what? Annoying bears to death?" Glass, gnawing on a raw fish he'd managed to club to death with a stick, spat a bone onto the ground. "My emotional fuel is hate, lady. Pure and simple."

She beamed. "And that's perfectly valid! Emotional fuel takes many forms. Though I would encourage you to consider reframing this episode as a pursuit of justice rather than mere vengeance. It's healthier."

"Healthier?" he barked, which quickly turned into a coughing fit that left blood speckling his chin. "You think I give a damn about healthy? I've got one purpose: Find the bastards who left me for dead and make 'em pay. Now, get lost!"

Duckworth nodded sagely as she jotted down more notes. "Classic purpose-driven grit. But what happens after the revenge? Have you considered how you'll channel your perseverance once this mission is complete? And what about your identity? It seems pretty wrapped up in all this hate right now."

Glass's glare could have melted iron. "You think I'm planning my retirement? I'm busy tryin' not to die, woman. Beat it!"

And yet, she stayed. Through the endless days of agony, the blistering sun, the icy nights, and the constant threat of coyotes, Duckworth remained a focused observer, only occasionally offering advice he didn't ask for. She even attempted to coach him through some deep breathing exercises once, though he quickly shut that down with a string of curses that would've made a sailor blush.

As weeks turned into months, Glass's survival took on an almost mythical quality. He fashioned crude tools from bone and stone and used them to hunt small game and protect the two of them from predators. In his astute observation, Duckworth seemed like more of an indoor girl. His wounds began to heal, leaving behind scars that would be the envy of any horror movie enthusiast. But it wasn't just survival that drove him—it was revenge.

The thought of the men who had left him to die, of their cowardice and betrayal, burned in his mind like a fever. Each inch he dragged himself forward, each mile he hobbled on a makeshift crutch, was fueled by a singular desire to confront those who had wronged him. Glass wasn't just surviving; he was clawing his way back to life to settle the score.

Hugh Glass's pursuit of revenge, forged in the crucible of his suffering and driven by the rage-fueled need to confront those who had abandoned him, culminated in a scene that was as poignant as it was haunting. Months of survival against impossible odds had stripped him down to the essence of raw human willpower.

When this unlikely duo finally reached Fort Kiowa—Glass little more than a walking corpse and Duckworth somehow as pristine as the day they'd met—she watched in awe as he confronted his betrayers.

The fort itself, bustling with the chaotic energy of traders, trappers, and soldiers, fell silent at his arrival. Conversations stopped midsentence, and all eyes turned toward the spectral figure that limped through the gates. Whispers of disbelief spread like wildfire—rumors of the man mauled by a grizzly, left for dead, and swallowed whole by the wilderness had reached the fort long before Glass himself. And now here he stood, a living legend carved from sinew, scar tissue, and sheer force of will.

His hollow eyes scanned the crowd with a sharpness that belied his frail form, searching for the faces of those who had betrayed him. And there they were: John Fitzgerald, the seasoned trapper who had chosen self-preservation over loyalty, and Jim Bridger, the younger man, whose wide-eyed panic had condemned him to complicity.

Fitzgerald's reaction was a mix of disbelief and dawning dread. The blood drained from his face as he realized the nightmare he had convinced himself was impossible now stood before him real as day. Bridger, just a boy by frontier standards, looked as though he might collapse under the weight of his guilt. His youthful face, already weathered by the harshness of life in the wilderness, crumpled as he realized the consequences of his choices had finally come calling.

Glass approached them with a gait that was more measured than menacing, his every step punctuated by the silence of those watching, holding their breath. He made no grand speech, no fiery proclamations of vengeance—just limped along with the chilling calm of a man who had endured too much to waste energy on theatrics.

"Now this," Duckworth whispered to him, "is emotional fuel in action. You've got this. Just stay calm and express how this betrayal made you feel. Use your words. No violence, like we discussed."

Glass ignored her completely. He closed in on Fitzgerald, the man who had not only abandoned him but also robbed him of his weapons and possessions—tools that could have been the difference between life and death. Glass unleashed his fury, driven by the pent-up anguish of months spent crawling, starving, and bleeding across an unforgiving landscape. The specifics of what happened next remain shrouded in frontier legend, but one thing is clear: Glass dealt out his vengeance with the quiet precision of a man who had honed his survival instincts to a razor's edge.

And when it was over—when Fitzgerald lay crumpled and bloodied, his pride as shattered as his bones, and Bridger stood trembling like a leaf in a storm—Duckworth approached Glass with her ever-present notebook in hand, her expression unwaveringly earnest. "You know," she began, flipping to a fresh page, "there's a fascinating psychological component to forgiveness. Some say it's liberating, but I imagine it pairs quite well with a thorough beating." Legend has it Glass may have found it in himself to forgive Fitzgerald—though, let's be honest, likely only after ensuring the man's dignity was left somewhere back in the dirt. Who knows?

"You've truly redefined grit, Mr. Glass," she said, her voice tinged with a bit of horror and a mild degree of admiration. "This journey, your perseverance—it's the stuff of legend. Would you consider writing the foreword for my new book? I think I'll call it *Grit Revisited: A Frontiersman's Guide to Purpose-Driven Revenge*."

Glass didn't respond. He simply walked past her, his eyes fixed on the horizon, his battered frame silhouetted against the setting sun. The faintest growl escaped his lips: "Sure thing, lady. Contact my agent."

"Okay, Mr. Glass. Great to spend this time with you. I'll be in touch!" she called out cheerfully.

In the end, Glass did what the frontier demanded: He survived, he avenged, and he moved on. Revenge, as it turns out, is not just a dish best served cold—it's a full-course meal capable of sustaining a man through two hundred miles of hell. But the scars he bore—on his body and in his soul—served as

204 | ALL IN

a constant reminder that vengeance, while satisfying in the moment, could never truly restore what had been lost.

Hugh Glass's journey, whether it included his uninvited life coach Angela Duckworth or not, is far more than a gritty tale of survival; it is an ode to the human spirit's unyielding capacity to endure when fueled by purpose and a flair for holding epic grudges that would make Justinian II blush. Glass's odyssey proves that even when you're dragging a body so battered it doubles as a cautionary tale, a fire forged from raw determination and emotional connection to purpose can light the way through the darkest wilderness.

Duckworth's timely appearance on this wild frontier—draped in modern absurdities and preaching the gospel of grit—may be improbable, but her message holds true. The immense power of aligning emotional fuel with purpose is not confined to textbooks or lectures; it is carved into the scars of men like Glass, etched into history by sheer force of will. Whether it's a relentless pursuit of vengeance or the drive to live for something greater, it reminds us that purpose, however unlikely or unconventional, can be the ultimate survival tool.

✪

Emotional fuel is the unseen force that drives purpose beyond mere intention—it is the why that transforms effort into endurance and turns commitment into something sacred and powerful. It is the fire that keeps us moving forward when the odds seem insurmountable, when the path ahead is fraught with discomfort, and when logic might suggest we turn back. This fuel, though intangible, is potent; it makes purpose nonnegotiable, something worth fighting for no matter the cost.

What makes emotional fuel so extraordinary is its ability to be cultivated even when it doesn't seem to exist naturally. By identifying the personal stakes in a mission, by connecting deeply and authentically to a cause, we can generate this vital energy and sustain it. Purpose fueled by emotion transcends mere duty—it becomes a wellspring of resilience. It empowers us to persist through adversity, to rise after every fall, and, in extraordinary cases, to hold fast for decades, as we have learned from the inspiring lives of the legendary trailblazers in this book.

This reminds me of yet another eternal truth: With a strong emotional connection to our purpose, we can endure far more than we ever believed ourselves capable of. It empowers us to find strength in moments of doubt, clarity amid chaos, and meaning in the midst of struggle. I challenge you to let this emotional connection serve as an invitation to cultivate and deepen your attachment to your purpose, to ignite it with authenticity and passion, and to carry it steadfastly through the inevitable challenges life will place in your path. With emotional fuel, purpose becomes not merely a direction but a lifeline, guiding us to achievements once thought impossible.

THE UNSEEN POWER
OF SERVICE-DRIVEN COMMITMENT

Let no one ever come to you without leaving better and happier.

—MOTHER TERESA

As I continue writing this manuscript on Veterans Day, November 11, 2024, I am deeply moved by the profound connection between service and purpose—an inseparable duo that has defined my journey as a Navy SEAL and now shapes my reflections as my wife and I nurture our children along their own paths. My time in the Teams taught me that true purpose is rooted in something larger than self, a cause that transcends individual ambition and echoes into something enduring. Though I often wish I had stayed in the fight longer to give more, the clarity I now hold is undeniable: Purpose and fulfillment are found in service. Without it—without reaching beyond our own needs to meaningfully affect the lives of others—purpose becomes hollow, and life itself loses its richness. Let us now delve deeper into the concept of "emotional fuel" and its capacity to drive us to fully commit to our purpose through the lens of service.

We've explored how altruism seemed to be in short supply on the American frontier, where survival often eclipsed the luxury of generosity. But let's bring this discussion into the present, making it relevant and applicable to our lives today. To go all in—whether in pursuit of happiness, wealth, meaningful relationships, or however we define success—we must embrace a life centered on giving. Research increasingly shows that going all in isn't sustainable if it's driven solely by personal gain. This isn't just philosophical musing; it's grounded in behavioral science and psychology. Studies have consistently found that tying our purpose to serving others—whether through acts of kindness, being a servant leader at work and at home, choosing a service-oriented career, mentoring and uplifting our colleagues, or contributing to our communities—activates the brain's reward centers and delivers fulfillment far beyond the transient satisfaction of individual accomplishments. Here, we'll explore three foundational principles for strengthening our connection to purpose, each grounded in the transformative power of service to others.

Principle 1: Purpose Rooted in Service to Others

Purpose becomes genuinely transformative when it transcends self-interest and connects to the broader goal of having an impact and serving others. This principle is supported by research that highlights the psychological and physiological benefits of altruism. Behavioral scientists have found that people who engage in service-oriented activities experience what's known as the "helper's high," a rush of endorphins and dopamine that promotes feelings of happiness, reduces stress, and increases their sense of meaning. Researchers from the University of Michigan found that individuals who regularly engage in acts of service—whether through organized volunteer work or simple everyday gestures—report significantly higher levels of life satisfaction and overall well-being.

Consider professions devoted to service—teachers, healthcare providers, first responders, and firefighters—where the demands are high, the stress constant, and yet the sense of purpose runs deep. These individuals, driven by a connection to their work that transcends personal gain, exemplify resilience. As I finished writing this book, devastating wildfires ravaged Los Angeles County. The devotion and strength of the first responders during the crisis are truly commendable. My oldest son, Tyler, embarked on the next chapter of his fire service journey by starting at the Fire Academy here in San Diego in January 2025—a milestone he has pursued with determination and heartfelt passion over the past four years.

His calling is not just a career choice; it's a commitment to embody courage, selflessness, and grit in the face of challenges that will require him to serve something far greater than himself. It's a reminder that true purpose often arises when you dedicate yourself to the well-being of others, which transforms your effort into fulfillment and sacrifice into meaning.

Research supports what we intuitively understand about these vocations: Those who devote their lives to serving others consistently report higher job satisfaction, remarkable longevity in their field, and a profound sense of purpose. For them, purpose is not an abstract ideal but a tangible, deeply rooted calling, a connection to humanity itself that transcends personal achievement. When our purpose is tied to the well-being of others, it generates a resilience in us that is unmatched by goals centered solely on individual success. Service acts as an anchor, grounding purpose in something enduring and unshakable, even in the face of adversity. It's this grounding of purpose that allows us to thrive and weather the inevitable storms of life with grace.

Opportunities to serve others present themselves daily; we need only to seize them. Consider a manager leading a customer service team facing high-pressure demands who often absorb the frustrations and emotions of customers while striving to deliver them a positive experience. A thoughtful manager recognizes the need to connect the team's daily efforts to the broader purpose of improving customers' lives, beyond mere transactions. Instead of focusing solely on productivity metrics, this manager regularly shares stories of how their work has directly solved problems for customers, such as the time the team's quick action restored a family's access to critical utilities or helped a small business get back on its feet.

The manager also ensures team members feel personally valued by acknowledging their unique contributions and aligning their roles with individual strengths. By framing the work as not just a task but a service that genuinely affects others, the manager fosters an environment where team members feel emotionally invested in their purpose. As a result, the team becomes more resilient during challenging times, collaborates more effectively, and feels a deeper sense of fulfillment in their work. Commonly referred to as *employee engagement*, this emotional connection doesn't just make the team stronger but also transforms their purpose into something dynamic, enduring, and profoundly meaningful.

Principle 2: Service as a Pathway to Joy and Fulfillment

Dr. Martin Seligman, a pioneer in positive psychology, identifies altruism and social connection as critical components of well-being. Seligman's work reveals that people who consistently contribute to the happiness of others experience a heightened sense of life satisfaction and joy that goes beyond the transient pleasures of personal gain.

In modern workplace settings, this principle is increasingly evident. Organizations that weave social responsibility into their missions, such as Patagonia and Salesforce, report higher levels of employee engagement, retention, and overall job satisfaction. Patagonia, renowned for its commitment to environmental stewardship, exemplifies this by connecting employees to a cause far greater than profit. Its mission fosters a culture where purpose transcends a corporate statement and becomes a shared experience that unites employees in a collective sense of responsibility. Similarly, Salesforce's philanthropic initiatives inspire employees to see their roles as contributors to a larger societal impact, which creates an environment where emotional engagement is a natural extension of day-to-day work.

However, organizations don't need to orchestrate large-scale corporate social responsibility campaigns to cultivate this sense of purpose. Leaders at every level can nurture a culture of fulfillment and engagement by grounding their teams in clearly defined values and guiding principles. At my last company, which I founded and ran for eleven years before selling it, we embraced both approaches: a strong emphasis on culture, supported by annual acts of social responsibility. By establishing a core set of shared values and intertwining them with meaningful acts of giving back, we created an environment where employees felt connected to a mission that mattered. This dual approach—values-driven leadership and tangible contributions—demonstrates that fostering purpose doesn't require grand gestures; it starts with intentionality and a genuine commitment to aligning everyday work with a greater sense of meaning.

But service as a pathway to joy and fulfillment is not limited to grand gestures and high-profile causes. The science of micro-interactions—consistent positive exchanges—reveals that these moments of service or kindness have a compounding effect on well-being. Studies by Barbara Fredrickson at the University of North Carolina suggest that even brief social interactions, when infused with kindness and empathy, enhance feelings of happiness and emotional resilience. Whether in the form of a helping hand or a supportive conversation, these small acts add up and build a sense of joy and purpose that connects us to our larger community while providing a steady, fulfilling sense of direction.

Principle 3: The Transformative Power of Small Acts of Service

As mentioned, service doesn't always demand monumental sacrifices; often, small, consistent acts of kindness have the greatest impact on both the giver and the receiver. Behavioral science underscores the significance of these micro acts of service with evidence that even the smallest gestures activate the brain's "bonding hormone," oxytocin. Oxytocin release strengthens social bonds, boosts feelings of trust, and creates a sense of security and well-being. This hormonal response, though subtle, builds up over time to foster deeper relationships and create an emotional foundation that bolsters our sense of purpose.

Consider how this plays out in a community. When people engage in micro acts of service—simple gestures such as greeting neighbors, offering help, or expressing gratitude—they create an atmosphere of trust and connectedness. Research from UC Berkeley's Greater Good Science Center shows that these small gestures significantly increase individuals' sense of purpose and community. In one study, individuals who performed "random acts of kindness" for a week reported a measurable increase in happiness, a reduction in loneliness, and an enhanced sense of purpose.

In the workplace, the same principle holds true. Small acts of acknowledgment and appreciation create a culture where people feel valued and connected, which in turn fosters purpose. Imagine a company where employees consistently recognize each other's contributions, support each other through challenges, and practice empathy. These small acts of service build a culture of mutual respect while translating purpose into a daily, lived experience. It's the difference between working in isolation and feeling part of a mission-driven community. Purpose, based in small, intentional acts, becomes not just a statement but a daily practice that strengthens over time.

✪

Reflecting on these principles, I find myself returning to the core of service. Purpose, when tied to service, takes on a weight that sustains us even when we feel weak, uncertain, or doubtful. Acts of service shine vividly on the battlefield. A young soldier braves the chaos, risking everything to drag a fallen comrade to safety. A corpsman, with unwavering focus, pours their heart into saving lives as bullets slice through the air. Even in the smallest gestures of understanding, service emerges as a lifeline. Amid the chaos of combat and the quiet intensity of moments between battles, strength is found in leaning on one another and selflessly serving those by your side.

In these moments, purpose becomes more than a personal journey—it grows into a shared experience that binds us to each other and to the world. Our purpose in life, our reason for waking each day, becomes most powerful when it reaches beyond us. In large ways or small, through big gestures or quiet acts, service to others is the key that unlocks purpose, offering fulfillment and joy that endure. This, ultimately, is what it means to go all in on life: to commit fully to a purpose rooted in the betterment of those around us.

EIGHT STEPS TO BUILD EMOTIONAL FUEL FOR PURPOSE-DRIVEN PURSUITS

The meaning of life is to find your gift.
The purpose of life is to give it away.
—PABLO PICASSO

Now that we've explored the enduring connection between emotional fuel and purpose, the natural next step is understanding how to cultivate and maintain this connection in our own lives. Purpose is not static; it evolves with time, experiences, and shifting circumstances. Similarly, emotional fuel requires nurturing. Your purpose needs a continuous infusion of emotional connection, actionable habits, and Duckworth-worthy degrees of grit to thrive. In this section, I'll break down actionable strategies to help you develop and sustain the emotional fuel necessary for meaningful, purpose-driven pursuits.

Define Your Values and Passion Points

Emotional fuel begins with clarity. As we have covered, a crucial step in the *all in* journey is taking the time to reflect on your core values—the principles that define who you are and what you stand for. So, here it is one more time. These values are the foundation of your purpose. Ask yourself:

- What makes me feel alive and energized?
- When I am at my best, what principles am I leaning on?
- When I am most resilient, what values guide my mindset?
- What issues, causes, or pursuits stir my emotions deeply?
- What do I want my contributions to the world to reflect?

Your values and mission don't need to be grand or world-changing; they just need to be authentic. What matters most is that they resonate deeply with who you are and what drives you. Start by reflecting on the causes and passions that stir something in you. Is it advancing education, creating game-changing products, protecting the environment, fostering inclusivity in the workplace, or simply creating opportunities for others? These passion points—the unique intersection of your values and what you care about most—become the foundation for your purpose; they will provide an endless reservoir of emotional energy to inspire your actions and sustain you through challenges.

Take it a step further by crafting a personal mission statement that ties your values to your goals. It doesn't have to be elaborate; it just needs to be true to you. For example, "I aim to create a positive work environment, where my team feels valued and supported, and to help them grow while achieving our shared goals." This kind of mission is grounded, relatable, and achievable, yet it carries transcendent meaning. It provides clarity by anchoring your purpose and serving as a compass for decision-making, especially during challenging times. Authenticity, not grandeur, is what makes a mission statement meaningful and impactful.

Create Rituals That Reinforce Purpose

In earlier chapters, we discussed the ways rituals and routines transform abstract ideas into tangible actions. Acting as daily reminders of what matters most, they keep your purpose at the forefront of your mind. Rituals are especially important because they build consistency, even when motivation fluctuates.

Examples of purpose-driven rituals include the following:

- **MORNING REFLECTION:** Spend five minutes each morning reviewing your mission statement or envisioning the impact of your goals. During this time, reflect on how you will lead with purpose that day. What small act will you engage in?
- **GRATITUDE JOURNALING:** Reflect on three ways your work or efforts have positively affected others to reinforce the emotional connection to your purpose.
- **CHECK-INS:** Schedule weekly moments to assess your progress and realign with your goals. This can be done individually or with an accountability partner.

These rituals not only sustain emotional fuel but also create a sense of momentum, helping you push through obstacles with renewed clarity and focus.

Find Your Emotional Anchors

Emotional fuel is stronger when it's tied to meaningful experiences and relationships. Identify the people, memories, or stories that inspire you to keep going, especially when challenges arise.

Examples of how to build emotional anchors include the following:

- **SEEK INSPIRATION.** Surround yourself with narratives of resilience and purpose, whether through books, podcasts, or personal mentors.
- **ENGAGE A SUPPORT NETWORK.** Share your goals with people who uplift and encourage you. Emotional fuel is amplified when others validate and support your purpose.
- **CONNECT TO STORIES.** Reflect on moments when you overcame challenges in pursuit of your goals. These stories become touchstones of perseverance, reminding you of your capacity to endure and succeed.

Keep a "Purpose Journal" where you document inspiring quotes, moments of impact, and personal triumphs. This resource is a reservoir of motivation during tough times.

Embrace Emotional Discipline

Pursuing meaningful goals inevitably comes with setbacks. Emotional discipline requires a combination of mindset shifts and practical strategies.

Examples of strategies for building emotional discipline include the following:

- REFRAME FAILURE. View setbacks as opportunities to learn and grow rather than as endpoints. Ask yourself, "What can this teach me?"
- PRACTICE SELF-COMPASSION. Speak to yourself as you would a close friend. Acknowledge your efforts and forgive yourself for mistakes.
- CELEBRATE SMALL WINS. Break larger goals into smaller milestones and celebrate each step forward to reinforce your progress and commitment. As we say in the SEAL Teams, "Eat the elephant one bite at a time."

The all in mindset transforms challenges from roadblocks to road marks and keeps your emotional fuel burning even during difficult times.

Align Daily Actions with Long-Term Purpose

It's easy to lose sight of the big picture when daily tasks feel disconnected from your larger goals. To maintain emotional fuel, consistently align your actions with your purpose.

Examples of how to align actions with purpose include the following:

- SET INTENTIONAL GOALS. Break your purpose into actionable short-term objectives that lead toward long-term impact.
- PRACTICE THE 1 PERCENT RULE. Commit to small, daily improvements that compound over time toward your larger vision.

214 | ALL IN

- **ASK "WHY?" OFTEN.** Regularly remind yourself why you're pursuing a particular goal. This practice strengthens the emotional connection to your purpose.

Use an accountability system, such as objectives and key results (OKRs), to track how your daily tasks contribute to your overarching mission.

Cultivate Empathy and Service

Purpose becomes most powerful when it transcends self-interest and connects to the well-being of others. Acts of service, both big and small, fuel emotional energy by creating meaningful connections and fostering a sense of fulfillment.

Examples of ways to incorporate service include the following:

- **MENTORSHIP:** Share your knowledge and experiences with others who can benefit from your guidance.
- **COMMUNITY INVOLVEMENT:** Volunteer for causes that align with your values and purpose.
- **TEAM SUPPORT:** Foster collaboration and encouragement in your workplace or community to create an environment where everyone thrives.

Serving others not only reinforces your emotional fuel but also amplifies the impact of your purpose, creating a ripple effect of positivity.

Manage and Replenish Your Energy

Emotional fuel, like any energy resource, needs regular replenishment. Burnout can derail even the most purpose-driven pursuits. To sustain your emotional connection, prioritize self-care and reflection.

Tips for replenishing emotional energy include the following:

- **REST AND RECHARGE.** Ensure you're getting enough sleep, exercise, and downtime to stay mentally and physically energized.
- **RECONNECT WITH JOY.** Engage in activities that bring you happiness, whether it's a hobby, time with loved ones, or moments in nature.

- **REFLECT OFTEN.** Periodically revisit your mission statement and evaluate how your efforts align with your purpose.

By maintaining balance, you ensure that your emotional fuel remains steady and sustainable, even during periods of intense effort.

Commit Fully to the Journey

Finally, emotional fuel is strongest when it's paired with resolute commitment. Purpose isn't something you stumble upon—it's something you build and reinforce every day through deliberate action and reflection. It must become fully integrated with your identity. Embrace the idea that your purpose is a journey, not a destination, and commit to evolving with it over time.

Here's an example of a mantra for purpose-driven pursuits:

> "I am in this for the long haul. My purpose is worth the effort, the challenges, and the growth. I'm *all in*."

By adopting this mindset, you transform your emotional fuel into an enduring force that propels you forward, no matter the circumstances.

Developing and maintaining emotional fuel is not a one-time effort; it's a continuous practice that evolves as you do. By connecting deeply with your values, cultivating rituals and resilience, and aligning your actions with your purpose, you create a cycle of emotional energy that sustains you through challenges and amplifies your impact—living with intention, embracing growth, and creating a meaningful legacy.

As you move forward, remember: Your emotional fuel is the fire that keeps your purpose alive. Protect it, nurture it, and let it guide you toward remarkable results.

GOING *ALL IN*

TO ACCESS YOUR ALL IN WORKSPACE,
VISIT APP.EXLR8.AI/ALL-IN

WHAT VALUES TRULY RESONATE WITH ME, AND HOW DO THEY ALIGN WITH MY PURPOSE?

Reflection

This chapter highlights how anchoring your purpose to your core values provides an enduring source of emotional fuel. Whether through grand pursuits or simple, authentic goals, aligning your actions with what truly matters to you creates a deep sense of meaning.

Action

Write down your top three values and consider how they show up in your daily life and work. Reflect on whether your current pursuits align with these values and identify one small adjustment you can make to bring your actions closer to your core beliefs.

HOW DO I CONNECT MY WORK OR PERSONAL GOALS TO A GREATER CAUSE OR IMPACT?

Reflection

We explored how purpose is more meaningful when it transcends self-interest and is tied to serving others. Whether through community acts, team leadership, or organizational goals, connecting to a greater cause strengthens emotional fuel and enhances resilience.

Action

Identify one way your current work or personal projects positively affect others. It could be as simple as supporting a team member's growth or as broad as contributing to a social cause. Commit to amplifying this impact by setting a specific, actionable goal tied to it.

HOW DO I MAINTAIN MY EMOTIONAL FUEL WHEN FACED WITH CHALLENGES?

Reflection

This chapter emphasizes the importance of authenticity and emotional connection in sustaining commitment to purpose, even when the journey gets tough. Emotional fuel is replenished by reconnecting with the why behind your actions and staying grounded in what truly drives you.

Action

Create a "purpose reminder" for yourself—this could be a written mission statement, a photo representing your goals, or even a daily affirmation. Place it somewhere you'll see it often, and use it as a touchstone to reconnect with your purpose during moments of doubt or fatigue.

These considerations will help you align your actions with your values, build resilience through connection to a broader purpose, and sustain the emotional energy needed for purpose-driven pursuits.

13

HARNESSING COMMITMENT DEVICES

A Fail-Safe Path to Purpose Fulfillment

In the pursuit of meaningful goals, good intentions are but whispers on the wind—easily carried away by distraction, doubt, or the pull of comfort. To transform aspiration into achievement, we must bridge the gap between what we *want* to do and what we *will* do and anchor ourselves to deliberate actions that keep us accountable when our resolve falters. This is where "commitment devices" emerge as indispensable tools: They are strategic mechanisms that bind us to our purpose and fortify our intentions. Much like Ulysses lashing himself to the ship's mast to resist the Sirens' seductive calls, these devices ensure that we stay the course even when temptation beckons or the road grows steep. The "Ulysses contract," as it is aptly named, is a self-imposed agreement we make that is designed to override impulsivity and safeguard our focus; such a contract transforms fleeting willpower into unshakable dedication.

This chapter marks a turning point, where mindset moves from theory to practice and determination evolves into disciplined action. We will explore the psychology behind commitment devices and why they are such powerful allies in the pursuit of purpose. More importantly, you'll discover actionable strategies to integrate these tools into your life: accountability partnerships, self-imposed boundaries, and reward-linked systems to lock in your intentions. Commitment devices act as guardrails for your goals, shielding you from procrastination, self-doubt, and the inertia of indecision. By employing these tools with intention, you'll create a foundation of resilience and clarity that ensures your aspirations are not just ideas but the blueprint for sustained, meaningful progress.

A MASTERCLASS IN COMMITMENT, EXCELLENCE, AND STAYING POWER

I've had to learn to fight all my life—got to learn to keep smiling. If you smile, things will work out.
—SERENA WILLIAMS

Serena Williams, one of the greatest athletes of all time, is a living, breathing manifesto of what it means to commit fully to one's purpose. Across two decades of dominance in tennis—a sport that demands not only physical prowess but also mental mettle—Serena has crafted a framework for excellence that transcends the boundaries of her profession. Through a symphony of public accountability, rigorous routines, and an inner circle of mentors and supporters, she has shown the world how to stay tethered to purpose, even when the stakes are astronomical and the challenges abundant.

But let's not sugarcoat her journey. To rise to this level and stay there, Serena has had to wrestle with more than just tennis opponents. She has faced public scrutiny, self-doubt, grueling injuries, and, oh yes, the inevitable critics who love to remind women—and especially women of color—that they're stepping into spaces where they weren't always invited. And yet, with a forehand as impressive as her presence, Serena has not only endured but also thrived. Let's unpack the magic behind her story: her public declarations of intent, the meticulous routines that keep her sharp, and the web of accountability she's spun around herself to ensure she's never drifting too far from her North Star.

From Compton to Center Court

To understand Serena Williams's mastery of commitment devices, we must first examine the force that shaped her path: her father, Richard Williams. Richard is not simply a determined parent; when Serena was growing up, he was a man driven by an audacious vision that many found incomprehensible. With no formal coaching background, he proclaimed—publicly and emphatically—that his daughters, Serena and Venus, would dominate the sport of tennis. This declaration wasn't born from blind hope but from a deeply rooted resolve, backed by a plan that would consume their family's lives. Yet behind Richard's unyielding push for his daughters' success lies a question that lingers: Was he filling his own void?

Richard Williams grew up in Shreveport, Louisiana, at a time and place where opportunities were scarce, particularly for a Black man with ambition. He witnessed firsthand the barriers of systemic inequality, the limitations placed on his potential, and the dreams that had no space to grow. Tennis—a sport steeped in privilege and exclusivity—became, in a sense, a vehicle for Richard to rewrite that story through his daughters. His drive wasn't solely about their success; it was also a battle against his own unrealized potential, an effort to conquer a world that had once excluded him. By pouring his ambition into Serena and Venus, Richard didn't just give them purpose but also anchored his own, turning personal voids into a sustainable sustenance for their pursuit of greatness.

Richard's early approach was Serena's first glimpse at her lifelong dance partner, accountability. From the moment she picked up a racket, her life was structured around purpose. Daily training sessions on cracked public courts, drilling forehands and backhands until the neighbors complained, didn't just build skills but also forged discipline. This well-crafted early regimen became the cornerstone of her commitment, showing Serena that excellence is not accidental but cultivated, often under circumstances far from ideal.

Public Declarations: Speaking Goals into Existence

Serena's knack for leveraging public accountability emerged early in her career and became a defining feature of her approach to greatness. Unlike many athletes who prefer to keep their ambitions close to the vest, Serena has consistently declared her goals to the world with an audacity that makes lesser mortals cringe. Whether it was proclaiming her intent to win all four Grand Slam titles in a calendar year or openly stating her desire to be the greatest tennis player of all time, Serena has never shied away from making her intentions known.

Why does this work? Publicly declaring your goals raises the stakes and turns them into a shared responsibility. You shift from internal accountability to a commitment that others are now invested in, which drives you to follow through with greater determination. And let's be honest, nothing motivates like the prospect of having to eat your words on the global stage. Serena has weaponized this dynamic to remarkable effect, using the weight of public expectation as a tool to sharpen her focus and keep her on track.

Take, for instance, her 2015 season, when she was chasing the "Serena Slam"—holding all four Grand Slam titles simultaneously. By openly stating her goal, she invited the pressure that comes with such a monumental pursuit. Yet, instead of crumbling under the weight, she rose to the occasion, leaning on her team and her unshakable routines to carry her through. This is Serena in a nutshell: bold, unapologetic, and unrelentingly accountable.

Routines: Anchoring Excellence in Daily Practice

If public declarations are Serena's megaphone, her routines are the quiet metronome keeping her grounded. And let's be clear, these routines aren't just related to crushing tennis balls on a court—they're a holistic system encompassing physical training, mental preparation, and even sleep. Yes, sleep. Serena is famously disciplined about her rest schedule, often declaring it as vital to her performance as any session on the court.

Her training regimen, meticulously planned and brutally executed, is a testament to her commitment. Conditioning workouts, strength training, and on-court drills are scheduled with the precision of a military operation, each session designed to address a specific aspect of her game. But it's not just volume—it's also intentionality. Serena's team tailors her workouts to ensure she's peaking at the right moments, whether that means building perseverance for long matches or fine-tuning her explosive power for a dominant serve.

And then there's her mental routine. Serena has spoken openly about the importance of visualization and mental rehearsal in her preparation. Before stepping onto the court, she imagines every possible scenario, from a perfect opening serve to the agony of fighting through a tiebreaker. This mental conditioning ensures that when the moment arrives, she's already lived it a hundred times in her mind. It's no wonder she often seems unflappable under pressure.

The Power of Mentorship and Team Support

Serena's individual brilliance often eclipses the fact that she operates within a carefully cultivated ecosystem of support. From her coaches to her fitness trainers, her physiotherapists to her family, Serena has built a network of accountability partners who push her, challenge her, and, when necessary, call her out.

One of the most notable figures in her orbit is Patrick Mouratoglou, her longtime coach. Known for his analytical approach and candid feedback, Mouratoglou has been instrumental in helping Serena adapt her game as she's aged—a reality even the greatest athletes must face. Together, they've redefined what it means to compete at the highest level well into one's thirties and, astonishingly, after becoming a mother.

Speaking of which, Serena's role as a mother has added yet another layer to her network of accountability. Her daughter, Olympia, often features prominently in her public declarations and personal reflections, serving as both a motivator and a reminder of why Serena's purpose extends beyond trophies. Serena has spoken about the desire to set an example for Olympia—not just as an athlete but also as a person who embodies resolve, determination, and grace under fire.

Mental and Physical Challenges: Resilience Redefined

Of course, no narrative about Serena would be complete without acknowledging the immense challenges she has faced. From life-threatening complications during childbirth to recurring injuries, she has encountered obstacles that would sideline even the most determined competitors. But here's where her commitment devices shine brightest.

When Serena tore her pectoral muscle at the 2018 French Open, she could have easily viewed it as a sign to step back. Instead, she leaned on her team to recalibrate her training and adopted new strategies to compensate for the injury. Similarly, when facing the emotional toll of returning to competition as a new mother, she relied on her routines and public accountability to stay anchored.

Even her critics—who, let's face it, seem to relish questioning her every move—have inadvertently fanned her already powerful flame. Rather than succumbing to the negativity, Serena uses it as motivation, channeling the doubters' energy into her unyielding drive to prove them wrong. In true Serena fashion, she doesn't just silence her critics—she outlasts them.

Lessons from Serena's Playbook

What can we learn from Serena Williams about locking in our purpose with commitment devices?

- First, don't be afraid to put your goals out into the world, even if they seem audacious. Public accountability can be intimidating, but it also forces a level of commitment that's hard to ignore.
- Second, build routines that align with your purpose. Whether it's a morning ritual, a fitness schedule, or a dedicated time for reflection, routines create the structure needed to sustain progress.
- Third, surround yourself with people who challenge you, support you, and hold you accountable—not yes-men but partners in growth.

And finally, embrace the challenges. Serena's career is a testament to the fact that resilience isn't about avoiding adversity—it's about meeting it head-on, armed with the tools and systems that keep you grounded. In her own words: "I don't like to lose—at anything. Yet I've grown most not from victories, but setbacks."

In the end, Serena Williams is more than a tennis legend; she's a master of commitment. Her journey reminds us that greatness often has little to do with talent and more to do with dedication, discipline, and the willingness to lock yourself into your purpose, no matter what life throws your way. And if she can do it under the spotlight of global scrutiny, what's stopping the rest of us?

BUILDING YOUR COMMITMENT BLUEPRINT

Commitment is doing what you said you would do,
long after the mood you said it in has left you.

—ANONYMOUS

Commitment to purpose is not something reserved for elite athletes or the extraordinary moguls of history; it's a framework anyone can adopt to achieve goals of any magnitude. Serena Williams's journey provides a masterclass in leveraging commitment devices—public accountability, structured routines, and strong support networks—to anchor purpose and fuel success. The good news? These tools are entirely adaptable to your life, whether your goal is to build a business, earn a promotion, write a book, improve your health, or strengthen personal relationships.

Now, let's explore practical, actionable strategies inspired by Serena's example. These tips and best practices will show you how to create your own commitment devices, craft systems of accountability, and transform your purpose into a nonnegotiable force in your life. Let's break it down into key areas.

Public Declarations: Turning Intention into Commitment

Serena Williams isn't shy about declaring her goals. She boldly announces her ambitions because she understands the power of public accountability. Once you share your goals, they're no longer just personal aspirations; they become commitments you've made to others, which raises the stakes for follow-through. I have found this tool immensely influential in my personal and professional lives—but these acts of declaration must be clothed in extreme humility, not boastful bravado.

PRACTICAL APPLICATION

Announce Your Goals

Share your objective with trusted friends, family, or colleagues. Better yet, post it on social media or within a professional network to add an extra layer of accountability if you feel particularly bold. Again, "public" can simply mean sharing goals and commitments with an accountability partner.

Here's an example: "I'm committing to running my first marathon in six months. Training starts tomorrow!"

Track Progress Publicly

Regularly sharing progress with others—through meetings, mentors, or loved ones—keeps your goals visible, reinforces commitment, and adds external accountability, encouragement, and constructive feedback.

Use whatever medium suits your purpose, such as sharing updates in a group chat, maintaining a progress journal shared with key supporters, and checking in regularly with a trusted accountability partner. The act of tracking and sharing, no matter the channel, keeps you focused, motivated, and connected to your commitments.

Create a Consequence or Reward

Tie your goal to a clear reward or consequence and share it with your accountability partner. For instance, treat a friend to dinner if you succeed, or tackle a dreaded chore if you fall short. This sharpens focus and strengthens commitment.

If your goal is to complete a challenging project by month's end, commit to treating your team to lunch if you succeed. If you fall short, everyone agrees to tackle a chore at home they have been avoiding. This blend of incentive and consequence keeps you motivated and accountable. Ensure that consequences drive both accountability and growth. In SEAL training, failing a two-mile ocean swim often means turning around and doing it all over again. The result? A meaningful consequence that also builds strength and resilience.

In your case, if the team falls short, you conduct a debrief to understand why, apply lessons learned, and as a bonus—you finally get that clean garage you've been hoping would magically organize itself.

Crafting Routines That Anchor Your Purpose

Once again—routines in action. Serena's success is built on the foundation of her meticulously designed routines. Deliberate systems align her daily actions with her long-term goals. Routines reduce decision fatigue, ensure consistency, and create a rhythm that sustains progress even on days when motivation wanes.

PRACTICAL APPLICATION

Start with a Morning Ritual

Begin each day with practices that align with your purpose. This could include listing your top five priorities, exercising, or setting intentions for the day.

If your goal is to improve your mental focus, your morning might include ten minutes of focused breathing exercises to center your attention and thirty minutes of deep work on a distraction-free task, such as reading a book that challenges you.

Schedule Nonnegotiables

Identify the activities most critical to achieving your goal and treat them with the same importance as a meeting with your boss or a doctor's appointment. These nonnegotiables should be fixed parts of your day or week, protected from interruptions or distractions.

While writing this book, I committed an hour every morning—5:30 to 6:30 a.m.—to focused, uninterrupted writing. This sacred, distraction-free time ensured consistency and progress. If you're working on developing soft skills as a manager, adopt a similar approach: Carve out intentional, early-morning time, shielded from excuses and distractions, to make progress inevitable.

Batch Related Tasks

Serena Williams's team often integrates fitness and skill building seamlessly into her training sessions—she hones physical perseverance while perfecting her technique. This principle of combining complementary activities can be just as powerful in a professional setting.

Combine brainstorming with walking meetings to boost creativity, and batch related tasks such as composing emails and reports into focused blocks to save time and enhance productivity.

Creating Accountability Networks

Serena's network of coaches, trainers, and mentors holds her accountable to her goals, acting as both her support system and driving force. These individuals provide honest feedback, challenge her to push past perceived limits, and reconnect her with her purpose when setbacks arise.

Although you may not have a professional team on standby—which would be pretty cool—you can build a network of accountability partners (for free) who share your commitment to growth and success. The right support system not only keeps you on track but also helps you navigate challenges with clarity and resilience.

PRACTICAL APPLICATION

Enlist the Aid of an Accountability Partner

Find someone with similar goals or challenges—whether a colleague, friend, or peer—and establish regular check-ins so that you can exchange insights, celebrate wins, and navigate obstacles together, fostering accountability and collective momentum.

Here's another example: Partner with a peer manager and exchange constructive feedback after meetings or presentations. Focus on communication, clarity, and engagement so that you each transform your daily interactions into leadership growth opportunities.

Join a Community

Surround yourself with like-minded individuals who share your ambitions and energy. Communities foster shared learning, inspiration, and a sense of belonging that keeps your motivation high. Look for mastermind groups, industry associations, or niche forums.

Our VP of Customer Success at EXCELR8 improved her presentation skills by joining Toastmasters, a club where she practiced speeches, received feedback, and honed her impromptu speaking skills. Similarly, joining a writer's group can provide structure, feedback, and motivation for refining your writing and communication skills because collaboration accelerates growth.

Hire a Coach or Mentor

For high-impact goals, seek a coach or mentor with real-world expertise in your field. I must emphasize—*with real-world expertise in your field*. Or at least real-world expertise in general! Their practical experience ensures that they can offer relevant, actionable feedback and guidance grounded in proven success.

For example, when you are launching a new business, working with a seasoned entrepreneur—someone who has successfully navigated the roller coaster of building and scaling companies—can save you years of trial and error. Similarly, if you're striving to optimize time management and workflow, don't just hire a productivity coach who has read books on the subject; find someone who has personally balanced demanding projects, tight deadlines, and complex work environments.

By building an intentional network of accountability and using the right tools, you create a system that helps you stay focused, motivated, and connected to your long-term purpose.

Visualizing Success: The Mental Game

As discussed in Chapter 4, visualization is an impactful tool used by icons like Michael Phelps and Serena Williams to mentally rehearse scenarios and prepare for success. Similarly, as a Navy SEAL, I used visualization to meticulously plan missions—picturing every step, contingency, and sensory detail. This mental preparation instilled clarity, calmness, and confidence, ensuring I was ready to perform under pressure.

PRACTICAL APPLICATION

Imagine the End Goal

Close your eyes and vividly picture yourself achieving your objective. Engage all your senses to make it as real as possible—what does success look, feel, and sound like? Visualize the path that gets you there, step by step, so you're mentally prepared for the journey.

If your goal is, let's say, juggling on stilts, visualize every step—mounting the stilts, steadying your balance, tossing each ball with surprising grace, and basking in applause as you defy expectations and gravity alike.

Rehearse Challenges

Anticipate roadblocks and mentally rehearse how you'll navigate them. This builds resilience by preparing your mind to stay focused and composed when challenges arise.

If you have a big presentation coming up, don't just imagine the highlight reel of success. Picture the tough moments—forgetting a line, a tricky question, or a moment of nervousness—and rehearse how you'll respond calmly and recover confidently. By the time you're onstage, you'll have already overcome those challenges in your mind.

Whether on the battlefield, on the tennis court, or in your own personal pursuits, visualization isn't just imagining success—it's the act of training your mind to face every scenario with clarity and confidence so that when the moment arrives, you're already prepared to perform.

Leveraging Incentives and Consequences

Serena's passion for the game drives her success, but the tangible rewards—trophies, titles, and financial gains—reflect her hard work and skill. Incentives, both intrinsic (personal growth) and extrinsic (recognition, financial success), sustain motivation, whereas consequences add accountability. Strategically balancing rewards and consequences ensures progress remains inevitable so that you can celebrate the well-earned fruits of dedication and discipline.

PRACTICAL APPLICATION
Reward Progress
Recognizing milestones with meaningful rewards not only reinforces your commitment but also provides moments in which you can recharge and reflect on your progress. The reward should feel proportionate to the effort and carry personal value—something that motivates you to keep pushing forward.

After completing a major project at work, treat yourself to a relaxing weekend getaway at one of your favorite spots, allowing yourself time to reset and celebrate your success. If your fitness goal is to run a half marathon, after months of hard training reward yourself with that high-tech smartwatch you've been eyeing or a massage to rejuvenate your body. The key is to create incentives that feel like earned victories. These reinforce the feeling that hard work yields meaningful benefits.

Set Consequences
Consequences, when thoughtfully applied, serve as effective motivators by introducing discomfort while still delivering value—much like SEAL training, where punishments, such as extra hundreds of burpees or brutal sand runs, made us mentally and physically stronger. The consequence should hold enough weight to push you toward positive action, but not derail you entirely.

If you fail to meet a self-imposed deadline for finishing a critical presentation, commit to waking up an hour earlier for a week to make up for lost time, which is slightly unpleasant but will strengthen your discipline. Alternatively, impose a public accountability measure: Share your setback and your plan to bounce back with a peer group or mentor. By pairing rewards with meaningful, growth-oriented consequences, you create a balanced system of motivation that fuels both progress and resilience.

Building Endurance for the Long Haul

Serena's ability to rise above injuries, defeats, and personal challenges highlights her extraordinary resilience. The path to success is rarely linear, and learning to navigate its inevitable twists requires both perspective and persistence.

PRACTICAL APPLICATION

Embrace Failure as Feedback

Reframe failures as valuable data points rather than accepting them as final verdicts. Each setback offers a chance to analyze, learn, and recalibrate your approach. Ask yourself what contributed to the result—was it a lack of preparation, an unexpected distraction, or an unrealistic goal? Then adjust your plan to address those triggers.

Here's an example: If you fail to stick to a morning workout routine, identify whether late nights are the culprit and commit to an earlier bedtime or schedule a more realistic workout time that aligns with your natural energy levels.

Focus on the Process

Shift your focus away from distant outcomes to celebrating the small, consistent efforts that build momentum. By valuing the process—showing up daily, pushing through discomfort, and dedicating time to improvement—you remove the pressure of immediate success and sustain long-term commitment.

If you're learning to play an instrument, celebrate the deliberate hours of practice rather than stressing over how quickly you can master a piece of music. Recognize that repetition and refinement are the keys to progress.

Develop a Growth Mindset

Understand that growth always resembles a series of peaks and valleys, not a straight climb. Progress may feel imperceptible at times, but every step—no matter how small—moves you forward. Trust that setbacks are temporary, and true heroism comes from staying the course even when progress stalls.

If a presentation for potential investors doesn't go as planned, reflect on what you learned, seek constructive feedback, and view it as a rehearsal for future success rather than as an endpoint.

By embracing failure as feedback, celebrating the process, and cultivating a growth mindset, you strengthen your resilience and create a foundation for lasting success. Like Serena, you'll learn to see challenges as opportunities to adapt, improve, and come back stronger.

Integrating Purpose into Daily Life

Serena's success is not simply the result of routines, habits, and accountability—it's deeply rooted in her ability to connect everything she does to a larger purpose. Purpose is the force that turns discipline into devotion and transforms challenges into opportunities for growth. When your actions are anchored to something bigger than the task at hand, commitment becomes a source of joy and fulfillment rather than a burden.

PRACTICAL APPLICATION

Align Actions with Values

Regularly evaluate whether your daily choices reflect your larger purpose and values. Small misalignments—skipping workouts, neglecting relationships, or delaying important tasks—can derail progress. Consistently bring your actions back into alignment.

If your purpose is to build a healthier lifestyle, ensure your choices reflect that goal: meal-prep nutritious food to avoid impulsive eating, schedule workouts like you would meetings, and make quality sleep a nonnegotiable priority.

Stay Inspired

Surround yourself with tangible reminders of why your purpose matters to keep your motivation alive during moments of doubt or fatigue. These reminders can take many forms: a vision board with personal or professional goals, photographs of loved ones you're working hard for, a playlist that energizes and inspires you, or quotes from role models who embody the values you aspire to live by.

A teacher might keep heartfelt notes from students as reminders of the lasting impact they have on young persons' lives; a business owner could integrate core values into meeting agendas and marketing materials to consistently anchor the team to a shared vision as a way to foster excellence and meaningful results.

Revisit Your Why

Regularly reconnect with the deeper why behind your goals to stay grounded and focused. Write it down and place it somewhere visible—a notebook, a sticky note on your desk, a tattoo on the back of your eyelid (most common), or even your phone wallpaper—so it serves as a constant reminder. Your why isn't just about the achievement itself; it's about what the goal represents, the values it reflects, and the lives it impacts. When challenges arise, this clarity provides the motivation and perspective you need to persevere.

An entrepreneur's why might be as follows: "I'm building this business to create financial security for my family, provide opportunities for my team, and inspire others to pursue their own dreams of independence." For someone returning to school after years in the workforce, their why might be, "I'm proving to myself and my children that it's never too late to invest in growth and rewrite your future."

By aligning your actions with your values, surrounding yourself with reminders of purpose, and regularly revisiting your why, you integrate meaning into every aspect of your daily life. This connection not only fuels motivation but also strengthens tenacity so that you stay focused and fulfilled on the quest to achieving your goals. Purpose is the compass that ensures every step you take moves you toward a life of impact and meaning.

GOING *ALL IN*

TO ACCESS YOUR ALL IN WORKSPACE, VISIT APP.EXLR8.AI/ALL-IN

HOW STRONG ARE MY COMMITMENT DEVICES?

Reflection

Serena Williams's success stems from her ability to create powerful systems—public declarations, structured routines, and a network of accountability—that lock her into her purpose, even when she is under immense pressure. Her father's audacious declaration about her and Venus dominating tennis was one of the first commitment devices that anchored their journey.

Action

Identify a goal that matters deeply to you and create a commitment device to support it. Share your goal with a trusted accountability partner, schedule nonnegotiable time to work toward it, and set a meaningful reward or consequence to keep yourself on track.

AM I SURROUNDING MYSELF WITH THE RIGHT SUPPORT SYSTEM?

Reflection

Serena's success isn't hers alone—it's a shared triumph of her coaches, mentors, and support team who challenge, guide, and hold her accountable. In your own pursuit of excellence, your network plays a critical role.

Action

Seek out an accountability partner, coach, or community that aligns with your goals. If you're developing leadership skills, pair up with a peer to exchange feedback. For bigger challenges, find a mentor who has "been there, done that" to provide guidance rooted in real experience.

DOES MY DAILY ROUTINE REFLECT MY PURPOSE?

Reflection

Serena's meticulous routines—physical, mental, and emotional—are intentional systems that align every action with her larger purpose. Success isn't a single act; it's a by-product of consistent, deliberate effort.

Action

Audit your daily schedule. Identify one nonnegotiable task that directly supports your goal, whether it's thirty minutes of skill development, an early-morning workout, or uninterrupted time to plan and reflect. Treat this time as sacred and anchor it into your routine.

Commitment devices bridge intention and action because they employ accountability, routines, and support to keep you anchored to your goals. Success stems from discipline and commitment. Like Serena Williams, declare your ambitions and let your systems guide you through challenges.

14

PURPOSE IN MOTION

Cultivating Perseverance and Adaptability

Purpose is often portrayed as a steadfast compass that guides us unerringly toward our goals. Yet, life is rarely so predictable. The journey toward meaningful achievement is not a direct path but an intricate dance between vision and circumstance. Landscapes shift without warning, and even our own motivations can waver in the face of uncertainty. It is in these moments that perseverance and adaptability emerge as the true guardians of purpose—transforming it from a static ideal into a dynamic force capable of driving us forward through any storm.

Perseverance—the silent force that propels us through adversity—infuses us with the grit we need to endure when progress seems unattainable. Adaptability, on the other hand, breathes flexibility into our resolve, allowing us to adjust course without losing sight of our ultimate objectives. Together, these twin pillars uphold purpose as a living journey rather than a fixed destination. Without perseverance, purpose risks crumbling under the weight of adversity. Without adaptability, it risks becoming brittle and unable to bend when life demands change.

Now, delving into the intricate interplay between persistence and flexibility, we will uncover the strategies that allow purpose to thrive through setbacks, surprises, and reinvention. Whether you're navigating a career pivot, personal growth, or life's unforeseen detours, you'll discover that purpose is not a passive ideal but an evolving partnership with life itself that, when nurtured by perseverance and adaptability, becomes an unbreakable force for transformation and fulfillment.

IF YOU'RE GOING THROUGH HELL,
KEEP CHUGGING ALONG

I have not failed.
I've just found ten thousand ways that won't work.
—THOMAS EDISON

Perseverance and adaptability transform purpose into mental steroids that enable us to endure adversity and evolve with changing circumstances. Achieving meaningful goals demands more than enthusiasm; it requires grit, flexibility, and the brain's ability to adapt through challenges. Neuroscience shows that setbacks can train cognitive flexibility, sharpening our focus and problem-solving while sustaining our purpose under pressure.

Few stories illustrate this better than Ernest Shackleton's infamous 1914 Antarctic expedition—a saga of triumph, not in achieving its original goal but in surviving against all conceivable odds. Shackleton's mission was ambitious, even by today's standards: He set out to traverse the entire Antarctic continent, a feat so audacious it seemed designed to taunt Mother Nature herself. To underscore his confidence—or perhaps to unwittingly foreshadow his challenge—he named his ship *Endurance*, a title that now drips with irony considering what would become of it. What began as a grand quest for exploration and glory soon spiraled into one of history's most extraordinary tests of human resilience, leadership, and adaptability.

Shortly after reaching the Weddell Sea, *Endurance* became trapped in a frozen labyrinth of pack ice. Shackleton and his men waited, hoping for a thaw that never came. For ten months, the ship, locked in a frozen vice, drifted aimlessly as the ice groaned and cracked ominously around it. By October 1915, the pressure of the sea ice became unbearable, and the *Endurance* was crushed—splintering like a toy ship in the firm grasp of the taunted Mother Nature. The sinking ship left Shackleton and his crew stranded on drifting ice, hundreds of miles from land, with no means of communication and no reasonable hope of rescue.

Pause here for a moment. Consider the reality Shackleton faced: His vessel—his very lifeline—was obliterated, his dream of Antarctic conquest reduced to rotting wood. Many leaders might have succumbed to despair;

Shackleton, however, did something remarkable. He let go of his original purpose and reframed his mission entirely. In that moment, his focus shifted to survival: He resolved to bring every single one of his men home alive. His ability to pivot so decisively—without losing his resolve or his leadership responsibility—would become the defining feature of his journey and a master-class in purpose-driven adaptability.

The next two years presented a gauntlet of hardships that tested the limits of human endurance. Shackleton led his men, hauling their lifeboats, across vast ice floes and over the jagged and unforgiving terrain. When the ice finally began to melt, they launched the boats into treacherous, icy waters and rowed for days on end—navigating the frigid sea with little more than determination and hope. Their first landing was on the desolate, uninhabited Elephant Island—better than the open water, but still far from salvation. Shackleton knew they could not survive there indefinitely.

In a move as bold as it was desperate, Shackleton and five men set off again, this time in a single lifeboat, to traverse eight hundred miles of the world's most violent ocean to reach the whaling stations of South Georgia Island. The journey, now considered one of the greatest feats of navigation and seamanship in history, was nothing short of harrowing. They endured monstrous waves, unforgiving winds, and the constant threat of capsizing. At times, the men had to chip away at ice that had accumulated inside the boat just to keep it afloat. After seventeen days at sea, Shackleton's group, battered and exhausted but alive, finally reached South Georgia Island.

The mission, however, wasn't complete. Shackleton still needed to cross the island's uncharted interior—mountainous and glacial—to reach the whaling station on the opposite side. With nothing but rudimentary tools and sheer grit, he and his men traversed the treacherous landscape and eventually stumbled into the station after thirty-six sleepless hours. Shackleton wasted no time. He immediately organized the rescue of his remaining crew. After four separate attempts to return to Elephant Island, Shackleton finally succeeded. He brought home every single crew member alive—a feat that defied all logic and expectations.

Let that sink in: Not a single life was lost. Against crushing odds, catastrophic setbacks, and the harshest environment on earth, Shackleton delivered on his redefined purpose. It wasn't the glory of crossing Antarctica that defined his legacy—it was his resolve to adapt his mission and lead his men through a nightmare that could have easily broken even the most hardened souls.

Shackleton's story demonstrates that purpose is not a fixed destination. It is, instead, a compass that adjusts to life's tempests to guide us through the unknown even when the path forward disappears. Perseverance, the dogged determination to keep moving forward, provides the engine that drives us through adversity. But it is adaptability—the ability to shift strategies without losing sight of the bigger picture—that ensures purpose does not shatter when challenges arise.

In modern times, we tend to view setbacks as signs to quit or indicators of failure, but the brain is far more adaptable than we give it credit for. Many studies have shown that humans are hardwired to grow stronger through adversity, provided we approach challenges as opportunities for learning rather than as threats to our success. Shackleton's ability to pivot was not a demonstration of blind optimism—it was grounded in psychological resilience. His leadership offered his crew a lifeline of hope, proving that the mind, when anchored to purpose, can endure conditions that the body alone might otherwise reject.

Your *Endurance* may not be a ship in the Antarctic ice, but the principle is universal. Whether you're experiencing a failed business launch, an unexpected health crisis, or a moment of professional stagnation, perseverance and adaptability are what will carry you through. Like Shackleton, you must allow your purpose to evolve when necessary so that you adapt your strategies without losing your commitment to the outcome that matters most.

Stay Agile: Balancing Flexibility with Focus

Winston Churchill's leadership during World War II is often hailed as one of history's most remarkable demonstrations of adaptability and purpose. Tasked with steering Britain through the gravest crisis it had ever faced, Churchill exhibited an extraordinary ability to shift strategies while maintaining a commitment to his ultimate goal: defeating Nazi Germany. Yet, behind the iconic speeches and resolute decisions lay a man deeply acquainted with struggle, failure, and personal challenges. His life's story, filled with setbacks and demonstrations of resilience, forged the very adaptability that made him the leader Britain so desperately needed during its darkest hour.

Churchill's journey to wartime leadership was anything but smooth. Born into privilege in 1874, he struggled personally early in life, including in a difficult relationship with his parents. His father, Lord Randolph Churchill, was a prominent but emotionally distant politician, and his mother, Jennie Jerome, an American socialite who was often preoccupied with her own ambitions. Young Winston's longing for approval from his parents gave him stamina but also left emotional scars. As a child, he battled a persistent speech impediment, often described as a lisp, which became a lifelong challenge. Ironically, this struggle shaped him into one of the most eloquent orators in history—a testament to his ability to transform weaknesses into strengths.

Churchill's career before the war was marked by a series of failures and public humiliations that would have ended the ambitions of a lesser man. As First Lord of the Admiralty during World War I, he championed the Gallipoli campaign, a military disaster that resulted in massive Allied casualties and damaged his reputation. Forced to resign from his position, Churchill retreated to the political hinterlands and spent much time in what he called his "wilderness years." Many wrote him off as a relic of the past, an overly ambitious politician whose best days were behind him. But Churchill used this time to reflect, write, and prepare for the challenges he sensed were on the horizon.

As the storm clouds of World War II gathered, Churchill's tenacity and foresight brought him back into prominence. While others were hesitant to confront Hitler's growing aggression, Churchill stood firm, warning of the dangers posed by Nazi Germany. In May 1940, as Germany swept across Europe, Churchill was appointed prime minister, and he inherited a nation on the brink of collapse. France was falling, and Britain stood alone against a seemingly unstoppable enemy. The situation was dire, yet Churchill's purpose never wavered. He famously told the nation, "I have nothing to offer but blood, toil, tears, and sweat," rallying a demoralized public with his indomitable spirit.

One of the earliest tests of Churchill's adaptability came during the evacuation of Dunkirk. With hundreds of thousands of British troops stranded on

French shores and German forces closing in, Churchill faced the possibility of catastrophic losses. Conventional military wisdom might have dictated surrender or negotiation, but Churchill thought differently. He launched Operation Dynamo, an unprecedented evacuation effort that relied on a flotilla of civilian boats—fishing vessels, yachts, and ferries—in addition to the Royal Navy. Against all odds, more than 338,000 soldiers were rescued, turning what could have been a devastating defeat into a symbol of British resilience.

Churchill's ability to adapt extended beyond military strategy. He understood the importance of alliances and shifted Britain's diplomatic efforts accordingly. Although initially skeptical of the Soviet Union, once Hitler invaded Russia Churchill recognized the necessity of forming an alliance with Stalin. Similarly, he cultivated a close relationship with President Franklin D. Roosevelt, ensuring that the United States would become Britain's indispensable ally. These alliances, though fraught with tension and compromise, were pivotal in turning the tide of the war.

Churchill's speeches became a cornerstone of his leadership, a way to reinforce his nation's shared purpose. His words weren't just rhetoric; they were carefully crafted tools of resilience. Phrases like "We shall fight on the beaches," "Never in the field of human conflict was so much owed by so many to so few," and "Let us go forward together" were more than morale boosters—they were rallying cries that united a nation. But what many don't realize is the painstaking effort Churchill put into crafting his speeches. Each word was deliberate, each phrase designed to inspire and galvanize, reflecting his belief that language could be as powerful a weapon as any in Britain's arsenal.

Churchill's adaptability also extended to his willingness to listen and learn from others. He surrounded himself with a diverse War Cabinet and encouraged debate and dissent to refine his strategies. This openness to alternative viewpoints, combined with his ability to make resolute decisions, exemplified Churchill's unique leadership style. He understood that true strength lies not in stubbornness but in the ability to pivot when circumstances demand it.

When the war ended in victory, Churchill's role as Britain's wartime leader became immortalized. Yet, in a twist of political fate, he was voted out of office shortly after the war's conclusion. Many might have viewed this as their final chapter, but for Churchill, it was merely another setback to overcome. He continued to write, speak, and he even returned to serve as prime minister from 1951 to 1955, proving once again that purpose doesn't retire—it evolves.

Churchill's story offers a symposium in adaptability paired with unflappable purpose. He understood that rigidity in the face of change was a recipe for failure and that true commitment to purpose requires constant recalibration. In your pursuits, whether you're navigating professional challenges, personal struggles, or the occasional unexpected ambush, take a page from Churchill's playbook. Regularly assess your progress, pivot when necessary, and never lose sight of your ultimate goal. Adaptability, as Churchill demonstrated, isn't a sign of weakness—it's the strength that turns adversity into triumph.

Build Perseverance: Cultivating Mental and Emotional Resilience

When Malala Yousafzai was just fifteen years old, the Taliban made a brutal attempt to silence her voice—a voice that had already become a beacon of hope for girls and women in Pakistan. Growing up in the Swat Valley, Malala witnessed firsthand the Taliban's oppressive regime, which sought to strip women and girls of their basic rights, including access to education. For most, the threats made against her would have been enough to force their compliance, but not for Malala. Encouraged by her father, Ziauddin Yousafzai, a passionate advocate for education himself, Malala began speaking out at a young age. At just eleven, she started writing an anonymous blog for the BBC Urdu service, detailing life under Taliban rule and the struggles of girls denied education. Her bravery quickly drew international attention and, with it, the ire of the Taliban.

By the time Malala was fifteen, her identity was well known, and her activism had made her a target. On October 9, 2012, while riding in a school bus with friends, Malala was shot in the head at point-blank range by a Taliban gunman. The bullet entered her left temple, traveled down her neck, and lodged in her shoulder. Two other girls were injured in the attack. The world watched in horror as Malala was airlifted to a hospital in Peshawar and later transferred to the United Kingdom for further treatment. Her survival was nothing short of miraculous. Doctors performed multiple surgeries to remove the bullet and repair the damage, including reconstructive procedures to restore her skull and hearing. Her recovery, though grueling, started a new chapter in her life—one defined by her determination to go all in for the cause that nearly killed her.

Malala's decision to continue her activism after the attack was an act of extraordinary courage. She could have retreated into anonymity, shielding herself from further threats. Instead, she used her platform to amplify her message on a global scale. In 2013, she delivered a stirring speech at the United Nations on her sixteenth birthday, declaring, "One child, one teacher, one book, one pen can change the world." Her words resonated worldwide, inspiring millions and solidifying her role as a global advocate for education.

What many don't know is the immense personal sacrifice and constant danger that Malala continues to face. Even after surviving the attack, she remains a target for extremist groups who view her advocacy as a direct challenge to their ideology. Her family, too, has had to endure threats and displacement. Despite this, Malala remains steadfast, refusing to let fear dictate her life. Her purpose—to ensure that every girl has access to education—has become her shield and lends her the strength to endure physical recovery, psychological trauma, and ongoing hostility.

Malala's advocacy isn't limited to speeches and symbolic gestures. In 2014, at the age of seventeen, she became the youngest-ever recipient of the Nobel Peace Prize, that year sharing the honor with Indian children's rights activist Kailash Satyarthi. The recognition was not just a personal triumph but a spotlight on the millions of girls worldwide who are still denied education. She has also founded the Malala Fund, which invests in education initiatives, particularly in areas where girls face the greatest barriers. Through the fund, she has helped rebuild schools in Gaza, supported education for Syrian refugees, and provided scholarships for girls in countries like Pakistan, Afghanistan, and Nigeria.

Behind the scenes, Malala's life is a balance of advocacy and normalcy. After surviving an attack that could have ended her life, she went on to complete her education at the University of Oxford, earning a degree in philosophy, politics, and economics in 2020. This milestone, more than an academic achievement, was a testament to her enduring belief in the transformative power of education. She remains deeply committed to her work and balances her public role with the quiet determination of a scholar who knows that knowledge is power.

Malala's ability to transform pain into progress is a reminder that resilience is born from purpose. For Malala, every challenge—whether physical recovery, ongoing threats, or the uphill battle of changing global attitudes—has only deepened her commitment. She has shown the world that even in the face of unimaginable adversity, it is possible to rise, to fight, and to inspire.

In your life, the challenges may not involve global advocacy or acts of violence, but the principle remains the same. Connect your struggles to a larger purpose. Like Malala, remember that resilience is not about avoiding the storm but about learning to dance in the rain, knowing that your purpose can weather anything life throws at you. Malala's journey reminds us that even in the darkest moments, perseverance and purpose can light the way forward.

HOW PURPOSE ENDURES BEYOND LIFE'S GREATEST TRIALS

The warrior who trusts their purpose doesn't need to
prove the battle is worth it;
they simply fight because they know it is.
—UNKNOWN

Shenell Malloy, my wife's best friend, was a radiant force of love, determination, and unyielding strength. A devoted wife and mother, Shenell's life revolved around her family, and when glioblastoma cast its dark shadow over her world, she responded not with despair but with an extraordinary sense of purpose. Her mission became clear: survival, not for herself alone but for her husband and children—the family she cherished above all else. In the face of an aggressive and pitiless disease, Shenell demonstrated courage and resilience that left everyone who knew her in awe. Her journey, though tragically cut short in 2024, is a story of love's power to endure even in life's harshest moments.

An aggressive cancer, glioblastoma is a cruel opponent. For Shenell, the diagnosis was devastating, but she refused to let it define her. Through multiple surgeries, rounds of chemotherapy, radiation, and the exhausting toll of countless medical appointments, Shenell remained steadfast. Her body bore the weight of the disease, but her heart held true to her family. Each moment she spent with them became a declaration of her love, a testament to her will to be there for them, even when the odds felt insurmountable.

As a mother, Shenell's purpose shone brightest. She made it her mission to create moments of joy and normalcy for her children, even when the illness left her drained. Whether it was helping with homework, attending a school event, or simply sitting at the dinner table hearing about their day, Shenell found a way to show up. These small moments, though seemingly ordinary, were acts of extraordinary courage. They were her way of saying, "I am still here for you," even as her body fought against her. For her children, those moments are forever etched in their hearts as proof of their mother's unfailing love.

Her husband, too, was her anchor. Their relationship was a partnership in every sense of the word, built on mutual respect, love, and a shared determination to face the unthinkable together. He stood by her side during the grueling treatments, the sleepless nights, and the endless uncertainty, a rock-solid presence in a storm that would have crushed many. Together, they found pockets of joy, moments where laughter broke through the heaviness, and moments of quiet strength where words weren't needed—only love.

Shenell's friendship with my wife was a buoy of support for both of them. They shared not just conversations and laughter but also the kind of connection that goes beyond words. My wife was a source of comfort for Shenell, a shoulder to lean on when the weight of the fight felt unbearable. In turn, Shenell's courage and grace left an indelible mark on my wife, teaching her lessons about strength and love that will last a lifetime. Their bond was a reminder that in life's darkest moments, we don't endure alone—we endure together.

Through it all, Shenell's purpose gave her strength. Her family was her reason to fight, her reason to push through the pain, and her reason to endure when others might have given up. Her illness may have stolen time from her, but it never stole her spirit. She used every ounce of her energy to ensure her family felt her love and created memories that will be cherished forever. Her passing on May 18, 2024, left a void that can never be filled, but her legacy is one of resilience, love, and the power of purpose.

Shenell's story resonates deeply, reminding us of the enduring power of purpose and love. Her journey teaches us to hold strong to what truly matters, even in the face of unbearable challenges. Through her strength, she showed that, although we cannot dictate the number of our days, we can shape their meaning and infuse each moment with love and significance. For her family, friends, and all who had the privilege of knowing her, Shenell Malloy is remembered as a warrior whose unwavering spirit and purpose illuminated even the darkest of battles.

GOING *ALL IN*

TO ACCESS YOUR ALL IN WORKSPACE, VISIT APP.EXLR8.AI/ALL-IN

HOW DO I RESPOND WHEN LIFE DOESN'T GO ACCORDING TO PLAN?

Reflection

Ernest Shackleton's story teaches us that purpose must be flexible if we are to endure life's storms. When the *Endurance* was crushed, he didn't let failure define him; instead, he recalibrated his mission to focus on survival. Shackleton's ability to adapt his strategy without compromising his leadership became the very reason his men lived to tell the tale.

Action

Think of a goal or plan in your life that has recently been disrupted. Write down three ways you can adapt your approach while remaining committed to the outcome that matters most. Start by identifying one small, actionable step you can take today to regain momentum.

WHO ARE THE ALLIES IN MY JOURNEY, AND HOW AM I LEVERAGING THEIR SUPPORT?

Reflection

Winston Churchill's leadership during World War II was strengthened by his willingness to collaborate with his War Cabinet, listen to dissenting perspectives, and refine his strategies.

Action

Identify one person in your life—whether a peer, mentor, or friend—who can serve as an accountability partner or sounding board. Schedule a conversation to share your current challenges or goals and invite their honest feedback and perspective. Commit to regular check-ins to track your progress and stay accountable.

WHAT ANCHORS MY PERSEVERANCE DURING LIFE'S MOST DIFFICULT MOMENTS?

Reflection
Malala Yousafzai's unshakable belief in education and Shenell Malloy's love for her family demonstrate that purpose becomes an anchor when life feels unbearable. Both women connected their struggles to something far greater than themselves, which enabled them to endure unimaginable adversity with strength and grace.

Action
Reflect on what gives you strength and keeps you grounded during challenging times. Write a statement that connects your perseverance to a larger value, goal, or relationship. For example: "I stay committed to building this business because it will create opportunities for my family and inspire others." Place this statement somewhere visible as a daily reminder of the purpose that anchors you.

PART 4

SYSTEMS AND PROCESSES AND HOW THEY DRIVE REMARKABLE RESULTS

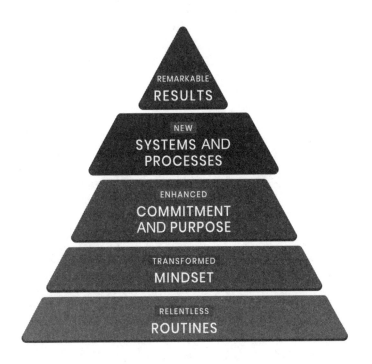

THE REMARKABLE RESULTS PYRAMID (RRP)

15

THE BLUEPRINT OF SUCCESS

Systems That Drive Outcomes

Routines are the quiet rhythm of our daily lives, the repeated actions that give structure to our days and form the scaffolding of our habits. They have the power to be the discipline that transforms fleeting intention into consistent behavior, the steady beats that move us continuously in the direction of progress. But, although routines are invaluable in setting us on the right path, they alone are not enough to sustain us during life's most demanding challenges. To achieve the extraordinary, to reach the summit of ambition, we must look beyond routines and embrace the power of systems.

Systems are the grand design, the blueprint that connects individual efforts to meaningful outcomes. They provide the architecture that turns routine actions into transformative results, ensuring consistency and alignment with a greater purpose. A well-crafted system doesn't just guide what you do—it defines how, why, and when you do it by organizing your efforts into a cohesive strategy that amplifies impact and drives sustained success. Systems, which weave routines into a framework of purpose, adaptability, and progress, bridge intention and achievement.

As we ascend to the top of the Remarkable Results Pyramid, the interplay between routines and systems reveals an insightful reality: Whereas routines build the foundation, systems create the structure that allows for growth and flourishing. They optimize effort, eliminate inefficiency, and provide clarity in moments of uncertainty. Whether you are striving for personal mastery, professional achievement, or the realization of a bold vision, embracing systems is the key to unlocking your potential. By moving from habit-driven repetition to systematized purpose, you transcend the ordinary and position yourself for truly extraordinary outcomes.

UNDERSTANDING SYSTEMS: THE UNSUNG HEROES OF SUCCESS

You don't rise to the level of your goals;
you fall to the level of your systems.

—JAMES CLEAR

Systems are the framework that supports the towering ambitions of every high performer, from elite organizations to everyday achievers. Routines lay the bricks; systems form the blueprint that ensures those bricks construct something meaningful—like a skyscraper, not a random pile of rubble. Yet, the term *system* often conjures images of overly complex processes, sterile corporate flowcharts, or rigid rules that stifle creativity. In truth, a well-designed system is anything but. Systems are the dynamic frameworks that connect your actions to your outcomes, providing both structure and flexibility so you can handle the chaos that life inevitably throws your way.

In many circles, Navy SEALs are celebrated not only for our physical prowess but also for our unyielding commitment to well-designed systems. Every SEAL mission is underpinned by a meticulously crafted framework: mission planning, training and rehearsals, execution, and debriefing. We don't just wing it with bravado and biceps. Our success hinges on the fact that no action is random. Every step, from reconnaissance to postmission analysis, fits into a larger structure designed to maximize success and minimize risk. One of our mantras, "Slow is smooth, smooth is fast," embodies the essence of systems thinking: structured processes executed with precision creating seamless, adaptable outcomes even under extreme pressure.

The Anatomy of a System

So, what exactly is a system? Think of it as a living, breathing road map for achieving your goals. Unlike routines, which build singular habits performed regularly (think morning workouts or journaling), systems connect multiple elements—habits, resources, tools, processes, and strategies—into a cohesive framework. They're not about checking boxes but about achieving outcomes efficiently and sustainably.

Consider this analogy: If routines are the gears of a machine, systems are the mechanism that brings those gears together and converts movement into output. Routines alone might keep you spinning your wheels; systems ensure you're moving forward, building momentum toward something greater.

For a writer working on a novel, a routine might involve writing for two hours every morning—great for building consistency. But a system integrates that habit with an outline, character development frameworks, progress-tracking tools, and scheduled feedback sessions with an editor. It ensures that those two hours don't just produce words but also meaningful progress toward a finished manuscript.

Why Systems Matter More Than Ever

In our hyperconnected, distraction-heavy world, systems have never been more critical. The modern workplace (whether remote, hybrid, or in-office)—and let's face it, life in general—is a hotbed of interruptions, conflicting priorities, and constant demands for attention. Without systems, even the most disciplined routines can falter under the weight of chaos. Systems act as a buffer, providing structure so you can navigate complexity and clarity so you can focus on what truly matters.

In the SEAL Teams, we trained relentlessly, not to memorize every possible scenario but to ingrain systems that prepared us to handle the unexpected. Our approach was equal parts structure and flexibility. When a mission inevitably deviates from the original plan, those systems—supported by mindset—enabled us to adapt without losing sight of the objective. That's the beauty of high-performance systems: They aren't rigid; they're dynamic frameworks designed to evolve with changing circumstances as a way to ensure precision and effectiveness no matter the challenge.

The same principle applies to you, whether you're leading a business, training for an Ironman, or trying to survive another day of parenting—which, let's be honest, is its own kind of battlefield. Systems don't constrain you; they free you. They eliminate decision fatigue, streamline priorities, and provide a reliable fallback when things go awry.

Learning from High Performers:
The SEALs' Systematic Approach

Special operators excel at understanding and implementing systems, but the real genius lies in how we approach adaptability. Every mission begins with meticulous planning. Objectives are defined, roles are assigned, and contingencies are prepared. But we know better than to trust a plan blindly because, as Dwight D. Eisenhower famously quipped, "Plans are useless, but planning is indispensable."

A pivotal aspect of our systems framework that distinguishes special operators and elite military units is their reliance on a postmission process: the debrief, a practice we'll explore further later in the chapter. After every training scenario or operation, regardless of the outcome, we gather to analyze what worked, what didn't, and what could be improved. This structured feedback loop ensures constant learning and refinement of the system. It's never about blame; it's always about building. Each debrief feeds into the next mission, creating a continuous cycle of improvement that sharpens both our individual and collective performance. And here's the secret: As this system is used consistently, behavior shifts toward increased individual and collective accountability. A shared understanding of success and failure. A common bond through transparency and rapid learning.

Now, take this principle into your world. Imagine running a sales team using a similar feedback system. Instead of berating your reps for missed targets, implement a structured postcampaign review. What strategies hit the target? Which ones missed the mark? What can you tweak for next time? Remind the team that a no is simply a yes in the making. This transformative process requires data, analysis, and actionable insights. A debriefing system solves immediate problems and simultaneously elevates the team's long-term performance by creating a culture of continuous improvement.

Why Systems Build Trust—in Yourself and Others

Here's another, and perhaps the most underrated, benefit of systems: They build trust. When you have a system in place, you don't have to question whether you're on the right path. You trust the process. This trust is essential not only for ensuring your own peace of mind but also for building credibility with others.

Look at championship sports teams. They don't dominate the battlefield by relying on individual talent alone. They operate within a system that emphasizes teamwork, adaptability, and consistent execution. Each player knows their role—and the roles of teammates—and trusts the process, even when the scoreboard doesn't initially reflect their efforts. Trusting the system allows you to keep moving forward, even when progress feels slow or uncertain. It shifts the focus from immediate outcomes to long-term consistency, which, ironically, is what drives success faster than frantic effort ever could.

Systems are the unsung heroes of success. They are the engine that transforms good intentions into great outcomes, connecting your daily actions to your overarching goals. The world's highest-performing people, teams, and organizations rely on systems to achieve extraordinary results.

In your journey, understanding what systems are and why they matter is the first step. They aren't just tools—they're your formal guide, your safety net, and your accelerant. Embrace them, adapt them when necessary, and you'll find that no goal is too ambitious when supported by a well-designed system.

SYSTEMS DESIGN: TAILORING THE BLUEPRINT TO YOUR GOALS

Give me six hours to chop down a tree
and I will spend the first four sharpening the axe.
—ABRAHAM LINCOLN

In my combat experience, the backbone of every mission was a well-designed system tailored to the objective. Whether it was a high-stakes direct-action capture-or-kill mission or a strategic reconnaissance operation, nothing was left to chance. Systems were not just a nice-to-have; they were a matter of survival. These systems were meticulously crafted blueprints designed to align every moving part—people, tools, resources, and processes—with the mission's goals.

That's the key to designing effective systems in any domain: tailoring them to fit the unique demands of your goals. A system is not a rigid checklist; it's a dynamic framework that ensures every effort made contributes meaningfully to the desired outcome. And although your system likely won't involve HALO (high-altitude low-opening) insertions or a bubbleless underwater breathing apparatus (unless your line of work is far more exciting than most people's), the principles remain the same. A well-designed system ensures efficiency, clarity, and a cohesive path to success, whether you're running a business, managing a team, or trying to grapple your personal goals into submission.

Start by Clarifying the Objective

Again, the first step in designing any system is defining your mission objective. In the Teams, every operation began with a crystal-clear understanding of the objective. Or at least *some* understanding. You never want to get caught in the nasty snare of overplanning or analysis paralysis.

Was our goal to capture high-value targets, to provide sniper overwatch, or to neutralize a threat? Clarity dictated every subsequent decision, from personnel assignments to resource needs and logistics. Without a clear objective, even the best tools and processes amount to little more than noise. Systems can quickly become cluttered, creating more work instead of simplifying it. Define your objective, and let it serve as the North Star for every aspect of your system design.

Break Down the Mission into Components

Eat that elephant one tasty morsel at a time. During my deployments to Iraq, for example, we approached no mission as a monolithic task. Instead, we broke it down into manageable components—reconnaissance, intel analysis, planning, multiple points of execution, and extraction. Each phase had its own mini-system that ensured every detail was accounted for. This modular approach not only made the overall mission less daunting but also allowed for pinpoint focus on each critical element.

Similarly, when designing your own systems, break down your goals into actionable steps with specific key performance indicators (KPIs). Let's say you're leading a marketing team tasked with supporting the launch of a new product. Instead of treating the entire campaign as one massive to-do list, create systems for each component: market research, content creation, distribution, and analytics. Assign ownership, set milestones, and ensure each piece of the puzzle aligns with the bigger picture.

Integrate the Right Tools and Resources

Even a meticulously well-designed system will falter if it doesn't leverage the right tools. Pipe hitters use tools ranging from advanced technology—like drones, GPS systems, and surveillance equipment—to less sophisticated but equally critical instruments: basic communication devices, weapons, ammo, and the occasional tomahawk (obviously). Every tool is chosen with purpose, enhancing efficiency and minimizing the chance of error.

In your systems, whether personal or professional, the tools you choose can make or break your process. If you're managing a team, platforms like Slack and ClickUp can help streamline task assignments, project management, and progress tracking. At EXCELR8, our platform offers AI-powered software solutions that seamlessly integrate rapid learning with efficient execution to drive measurable improvement for individuals and teams. Our tools are designed to amplify productivity, foster deeper engagement, and drive cross-team collaboration by empowering users to continuously learn, adapt, and perform at their best. Regardless of the tools, they are only as good as the consistency and proficiency with which they are used.

If you're tackling personal fitness goals, apps like MyFitnessPal or Strava can provide the data and insights you need to stay on track. The key is to select tools that simplify and enhance your efforts, not complicate them with unnecessary bells and whistles. And remember, tools are only as effective as how consistently they are used.

Establish Feedback Loops

No system is flawless from the outset; even the most meticulously designed frameworks require ongoing evaluation and refinement. This is where debriefing methodology comes into play: It is a critical component for fostering constant and immediate improvement in both individuals and teams. In special operations, debriefs or after-action reviews (AARs) hold a nearly sacred status because they serve as structured forums in which we would dissect missions and evaluate every aspect of performance. Debriefs are not about assigning blame; they are about learning. The focus is on understanding what worked, identifying what didn't, and developing actionable steps to improve for the next iteration. Continual feedback and adaptation ensure that systems evolve to meet new challenges and environments effectively.

The principles of AARs translate seamlessly to other domains. In corporate settings, debriefing can take the form of regular team check-ins, project post-mortems, or performance reviews. These sessions create a collaborative environment where team members can openly share insights, address roadblocks, and brainstorm solutions. For teams, the structured methodology ensures that discussions remain productive and forward-looking and avoid the pitfalls of defensiveness or unconstructive criticism. Each debrief becomes an opportunity to align team goals, sharpen strategies, and enhance the overall effectiveness of the system.

For individuals, debriefing can be equally transformative. It might involve a daily self-reflection process, where you review progress toward your goals, identify areas for improvement, and celebrate small wins. Journaling or using apps to track milestones can help make this process more structured and actionable. The key is to approach personal debriefs with the same level of objectivity and commitment to growth as a team would.

Ultimately, debriefing is for creating a continuous feedback loop that drives iterative improvement. Whether applied to teams or individuals, it transforms the system from a static framework into a dynamic, responsive engine for growth. By embracing this methodology, you not only refine your current systems but also build the resilience and adaptability to tackle future challenges with confidence.

Make Systems Adaptable

Here's the paradox of systems design: The best systems are structured enough to provide consistency but flexible enough to adapt to change. Military units plan for contingencies because through experience we understand that no mission has ever unfolded exactly as expected. A system that can't be adjusted on the fly is useless.

This principle applies to every system you design. If you've implemented a time-blocking system to improve productivity, what happens when an urgent task throws off your carefully planned schedule? A rigid system might leave you scrambling, but a flexible one allows you to reprioritize without losing sight of your goals.

High-performance teams in the workplace thrive on this level of adaptability. Their workflows are designed to evolve and adapt, ensuring that systems remain relevant even as organizational priorities shift. For individuals or teams, this means regularly revisiting your systems and asking: *Does this still serve my purpose?* If not, tweak it. Systems should grow with you, not hold you back.

Applying This to Your Life and Work

Whether you're leading a team, running a business, or managing your own goals, the principles of system design are universal. Start by defining your mission, breaking it into actionable components, and integrating tools that enhance efficiency. Build feedback loops to refine your approach and ensure your system is adaptable to changing circumstances. And remember, no system works unless you commit to using it consistently. Accountability is critical.

SEALs, high-growth organizations, and championship sports teams share a common trait: They achieve success by designing systems aligned with their unique goals while maintaining the agility to adapt when necessary. Your systems don't need to be perfect—they just need to work for *you*. And with the right design, they will. After all, a great system doesn't increase complexity; it drives simplification, focus, and results.

GREAT SYSTEMS AND THE REMARKABLE RESULTS THEY CAN DELIVER

Success is nothing more than a few simple disciplines,
practiced every day.
—JIM ROHN

Designing an exceptional system is an achievement in itself, but adhering to it—day in and day out—is where true transformation occurs. This is the crucible in which intentions are tested, discipline is forged, and results are ultimately realized. Yet, this is also where many falter, derailed by distractions, fatigue, or the allure of comfort. Adherence to systems demands you unleash the uncelebrated trio of discipline, focus, and follow-through. It's not the initial spark of excitement that accompanies new beginnings; it's about the commitment to persist when the novelty fades, when obstacles arise, and when the process feels tedious or inconvenient.

This principle is precisely why the foundational layers of the Remarkable Results Pyramid emphasize cultivating a mindset that enhances both resilience and commitment to purpose. I can't emphasize this enough—systems are only as effective as the consistency with which they are executed. They do not thrive on sporadic enthusiasm but on quiet, persistent effort, on showing up especially when it's hardest. Discipline is the oxygen that keeps the system running, that turns lofty aspirations into sustainable action and, ultimately, tangible success.

Systems only work if you work the systems. Every day.

Amancio Ortega's journey, intertwined with the rise of Zara, transcends business success to reveal a narrative of vision, perseverance, and transformative innovation. Born in 1936 in the modest Spanish town of Busdongo de Arbas, Ortega grew up in humble circumstances as the youngest of four children in a household marked by scarcity. A pivotal moment in his youth—overhearing a shopkeeper refuse his mother credit for food—fueled his determination to ensure his family would never face such indignity again. It also sharpened his awareness of the disconnect between human needs and the societal systems that serve them, an insight that later inspired his revolutionary retail approach.

Leaving school at fourteen, Ortega began working as a delivery boy for a local shirtmaker and immersed himself in the garment trade. He quickly recognized inefficiencies in traditional supply chains, such as delays and waste, which sparked an idea that would reshape the industry. After years of learning every facet of the business, in 1963 Ortega founded Confecciones Goa, a company that produced affordable bathrobes; he cut out middlemen to maintain quality and reduce costs. This commitment to vertical integration would become the cornerstone of Zara's future success.

When Ortega opened the first Zara store in La Coruña in 1975, it marked the debut of a revolutionary retail model. Unlike traditional retailers, Zara prioritized adaptability so that it could respond to customer demand with speed and precision. Ortega orchestrated seamless integration across design, production, and distribution, reducing the time from concept to shelf to mere weeks—a groundbreaking feat. His vision democratized high fashion and shifted focus from exclusive runways to accessible, trend-driven streets. Under his leadership, Zara pioneered fast fashion by creating a customer-centric model, and that transformed this small Spanish retailer into a global powerhouse with stores in more than ninety countries. Guided by innovative systems, a growth mindset, and a commitment to purpose, Ortega redefined the fashion industry by setting a standard of adaptability and customer-driven success.

Centralized and Decentralized Components of Systems

The most effective systems have both centralized and decentralized components. As Zara expanded, Ortega's vision for a vertically integrated supply chain became the company's superpower. Traditional fashion retailers operated on a fixed schedule, producing collections months in advance on the basis of predictions of future trends. Ortega's system turned this approach on its head. Zara's model thrived on decentralization and agility, which enabled the brand to design, produce, and distribute new products in as little as two weeks. This lightning-fast cycle was supported by advanced technology and a culture of collaboration that spanned every level of the organization.

However, the backbone of Zara's success was its centralized logistics hub in La Coruña, Spain. Here, Ortega implemented a distribution system akin to a precision-engineered machine. Every piece of clothing passed through this hub, ensuring consistency, quality, and speed. Stores around the world communicated daily sales data back to headquarters, which allowed designers and planners to react almost in real time to customer preferences. This ability to adapt swiftly to market demands created an unprecedented sense of relevance and keeps Zara perpetually aligned with its customers.

Zara's success was not without hurdles. Rapid growth introduced logistical complexities, competitive pressures, and environmental scrutiny. Critics questioned the sustainability of fast fashion; competitors aimed to replicate

Zara's efficiency. Ortega viewed these challenges as opportunities to refine the systems that defined the brand.

Global expansion posed one of the toughest tests because it required Ortega and his team to adapt to diverse cultural and economic landscapes. While they maintained core systems, the Zara team tailored product lines to local tastes, blending scalability with customization. Ortega's commitment to listening to customers reinforced Zara's customer-first philosophy.

Environmental concerns also demanded attention as awareness of fast fashion's impact grew. Ortega responded by steering Zara toward sustainable practices, such as incorporating ecofriendly materials, reducing waste, and improving energy efficiency. This pivot not only addressed criticism but also positioned Zara as a leader in sustainable fashion, showcasing that innovation and responsibility can coexist.

Lessons in Leadership: Adaptability and Humility

Ortega's leadership style was a critical factor in Zara overcoming these challenges. Known for his humility and preference for staying out of the public eye, Ortega focused on empowering his team rather than seeking personal recognition. He fostered a culture where innovation was celebrated and mistakes were treated as opportunities for learning. This mindset permeated every level of the organization, creating a workforce that was resilient, creative, and deeply committed to the company's vision.

One of the most profound lessons Ortega demonstrated was the importance of adaptability. He understood that to stay relevant in a rapidly changing world even the best designed systems require constant refinement. Embracing technology, addressing environmental concerns, adapting to new markets—Zara's ability to evolve was a direct reflection of Ortega's belief in continuous improvement.

The Legacy: A Testament to Purpose and Systems

Today, Zara stands as a testament to the power of purpose-driven innovation. As of March 2025, Inditex, the parent company of Zara, has a market capitalization of approximately €139.78 billion. This valuation reflects the combined worth of all Inditex brands, including Zara, Massimo Dutti, Bershka, and others. Zara itself holds a valuation of approximately $15 billion. From its humble beginnings in a small Spanish town, it has grown into a global icon, celebrated for its ability to make high fashion accessible to millions. Ortega's journey from a teenage delivery boy to one of the wealthiest people in the world is not just a story of personal triumph but a masterclass in building systems that scale.

At its core, Zara's success is a reminder that greatness is achieved not through shortcuts or luck but through clarity of vision, disciplined execution, and a commitment to creating value. Ortega's legacy extends far beyond the fashion industry; it serves as an enduring inspiration for entrepreneurs, leaders, and dreamers everywhere who seek to make a meaningful impact on the world.

Through the systems he and his team designed and the values he upheld, Amancio Ortega proved that it is possible to balance profitability with purpose, efficiency with empathy, and ambition with humility. This is the true essence of Zara's story—a story that will continue to inspire generations to come.

GOING *ALL IN*

TO ACCESS YOUR ALL IN WORKSPACE, VISIT APP.EXLR8.AI/ALL-IN

HOW CAN I DESIGN SYSTEMS THAT ALIGN WITH MY LONG-TERM GOALS AND DAILY ACTIONS?

Reflection
Amancio Ortega's success with Zara highlights the importance of creating systems that integrate routines into a broader, purpose-driven framework. His vertically integrated supply chain and rapid-response production model were not just about efficiency but about staying aligned with his vision of delivering relevance and immediacy to customers.

Action
Identify a major goal in your life or work and break it down into smaller, actionable components. Develop a system that integrates these actions, ensuring they are aligned with your overarching purpose.

HOW ADAPTABLE ARE MY SYSTEMS WHEN FACED WITH CHANGE OR UNEXPECTED CHALLENGES?

Reflection
Ortega's ability to navigate Zara's global expansion and address environmental concerns exemplifies the power of adaptable systems. His approach ensured that Zara's operations could evolve without losing sight of its core mission.

Action
Evaluate one of your current systems and test its adaptability by introducing a hypothetical challenge or change. For instance, if you have a time management system, simulate a scenario where unexpected tasks disrupt your schedule. Adjust your system to handle these disruptions effectively without losing productivity.

AM I FOSTERING A CULTURE OF CONTINUOUS IMPROVEMENT IN MY PERSONAL OR PROFESSIONAL SYSTEMS?

Reflection
Zara's success was fueled by Ortega's emphasis on constant learning and refinement. The company's feedback loops, such as analyzing sales data and adapting to customer trends, ensured continuous growth and improvement.

Action
Implement a feedback mechanism within your systems. If you're managing a team, conduct regular debrief sessions to assess performance and identify areas for improvement. For personal goals, schedule weekly reflections to evaluate progress, celebrate wins, and adjust your approach as needed.

These questions and their associated actions empower you to not only understand the principles behind Ortega's success but also apply them in practical and transformative ways to create systems that drive meaningful outcomes in your life.

16

SYSTEMS IN MOTION

Aligning Purpose and Execution

S ystems, by their very nature, are designed to simplify the complex and bring order out of chaos. But let's be real: No system—no matter how meticulously crafted—runs itself. The true test of a system lies in its execution. This is where theory meets reality, where plans must be put into action and adjusted along the way. A system in motion is a living, breathing entity that requires your engagement, your discipline, and your willingness to adapt. Without consistent implementation, even the best systems are nothing more than elegant models gathering dust.

The power of a system lies in its ability to align your purpose with actionable steps, yet the path is rarely smooth. Obstacles, bottlenecks, and shifting priorities are inevitable. In this chapter, you'll discover how to ensure your systems not only endure disruptions but also thrive once past them. By executing daily actions, tracking key metrics, and mastering adaptation, you can transform a static plan into a dynamic engine of progress that maintains alignment with your goals while it builds unstoppable momentum for meaningful achievements.

COMMITMENT TO CONSISTENT EXECUTION

We are what we repeatedly do.
Excellence, then, is not an act but a habit.

—ARISTOTLE

To understand the transformative power of consistent execution, look no further than Tony Dungy, the legendary NFL coach whose steadfast belief in systems not only silenced skeptics but ultimately delivered a Super Bowl championship. When Tony Dungy took over as head coach of the Tampa Bay Buccaneers in 1996, the team was, in a word, dismal. They had a long history of mediocrity and losing records, and many believed the franchise was beyond redemption. But Dungy had a different vision—one rooted in methodical systems, not flashy plays or dramatic overhauls. His philosophy was simple: Build a system, commit to it with consistency, and the results would follow.

Dungy's system revolved around two core principles: *simplicity* and *repetition*. One more time—simplicity and repetition. His defensive strategy, famously known as the "Tampa 2," emphasized disciplined positioning, clear roles, and a focus on fundamentals. It wasn't a strategy designed to dazzle; it was designed to win. "We don't need to outsmart anyone," Dungy would say. "We just need to execute better than everyone else." Critics scoffed. They said his approach was too rigid, too basic. But Dungy didn't flinch. He knew that the brilliance of his system lay in its simplicity—and in the consistent execution required to make it work.

Dungy's approach wasn't just about Xs and Os; it was about culture. He emphasized consistency in plays as well as in mindset, commitment, and behavior. He believed that a team's habits—on and off the field—would determine its success. Practices were regimented, drills were repeated endlessly, and players were held to a standard of discipline that left no room for shortcuts. There were no fiery locker room speeches or over-the-top theatrics. Instead, Dungy cultivated a quiet, steady confidence in his players, teaching them to trust the system and trust themselves.

It wasn't an overnight transformation—it rarely is. In his first season, the Buccaneers finished with a losing record. Skeptics pointed to the scoreboard as evidence that Dungy's methods wouldn't work. But he remained steadfast. "It's not about quick fixes," he told his team. "It's about building something that lasts." And build he did. In his second season, the Buccaneers had their first winning record in over a decade. The team continued to improve and made the playoffs repeatedly under Dungy's leadership. His system had turned a perennial loser into a legitimate contender.

Dungy's belief in consistent execution ultimately reached its pinnacle when he became the head coach of the Indianapolis Colts. With quarterback Peyton Manning leading the offense, Dungy implemented the same disciplined systems that had defined his career. Again, there was skepticism. Could Dungy's understated style succeed in an era dominated by larger-than-life personalities and explosive offenses? The answer came in 2007, when the Colts defeated the Chicago Bears to win Super Bowl XLI. Dungy became the first African American head coach to win a Super Bowl, a milestone that underscored not just his personal achievement but also the power of a system executed with discipline.

What makes Dungy's story so compelling is that he never wavered in his belief, even when the results weren't immediate. He trusted the process, and in doing so, he taught his players to do the same. His legacy, beyond the championships, is the lesson his systems imparted: Success is the result of small efforts, repeated consistently over time.

For anyone looking to apply this principle, the idea is clear. Design a system that aligns with your goals, and then commit to it with relentless consistency. Show up, day after day, even when the novelty has worn off and the results feel distant. Trust the process, as Tony Dungy did, and you'll find that the grind of execution becomes the foundation for greatness. Whether you're building a business, leading a team, or pursuing a personal goal, the path to success isn't glamorous—it's disciplined, deliberate, and deeply rewarding.

MEASURE WHAT MATTERS

What gets measured gets managed.
—PETER DRUCKER

Peter Drucker's oft-quoted wisdom may feel like the kind of platitude tossed around in MBA programs, but in reality, a system without measurement is little more than a shot in the dark. To keep a system in motion, you need to know whether it's actually working. And that requires meaningful metrics—not an endless spreadsheet of irrelevant data, but sharp, focused indicators that align with your purpose and signal whether you're on the right track or veering off course.

Measurement does not mean drowning in analytics or obsessing over vanity metrics; the goal is clarity. The best systems—whether applied by individuals, teams, or organizations—are underpinned by a commitment to measuring what truly matters. This is the art of continuous improvement, the philosophy of *kaizen*, applied to modern systems. By tracking the right metrics, evaluating progress, and recalibrating as needed, you transform your system into a dynamic powerhouse of adaptability and growth.

Change for the Better

Kaizen, meaning "change for the better" in Japanese, has become a cornerstone of continuous improvement across industries and personal development alike. Born out of Japan's post–World War II recovery, kaizen was inspired by a fusion of Japanese cultural values and American management techniques introduced during the occupation. Its application in manufacturing—most famously in Toyota's production system—revolutionized the industry because it showcased how small, incremental improvements could create extraordinary results.

This philosophy aligns seamlessly with systems thinking. Both emphasize process optimization, adaptability, and the power of compounding improvements over time. Kaizen is not about dramatic overhauls; it is about fostering a culture in which progress becomes a habit and is measured and refined continuously.

Kaizen in Systems: Measurement as the Catalyst

Kaizen thrives on measurement, which serves as the feedback loop connecting actions to outcomes. In high-performing systems, measurement is not a static activity but an ongoing process that informs adjustments and guides future actions. Small, incremental changes rooted in accurate data ensure that systems evolve without losing efficiency or focus:

- **STANDARDIZATION:** Establishing a clear baseline ensures progress is measurable. Without it, improvement lacks direction.

- **INCREMENTAL CHANGES:** Instead of overhauling entire processes, kaizen emphasizes manageable adjustments that, over time, lead to profound transformations.
- **FEEDBACK AND REFINEMENT:** Continuous evaluation ensures that systems remain effective, adaptable, and aligned with their objectives.

For example, Toyota's legendary success lies in its ability to identify inefficiencies, apply targeted improvements, and measure the results. This feedback loop ensures every element of the production system contributes to overall performance. Similarly, high-performing teams and individuals can apply these principles by tracking key metrics, analyzing outcomes, and making steady refinements.

Kaizen in Daily Life and Work

Kaizen is not limited to manufacturing or corporate systems—it is a transformative philosophy for personal goals, too, that fosters growth in productivity, relationships, and beyond. By emphasizing small, consistent improvements, kaizen enables you to create sustainable systems to make progress while avoiding the overwhelm often associated with drastic, sweeping changes.

Let's consider the pervasive challenge of procrastination. Meet "Procrastination Pete," the human embodiment of charm cloaked in the warm embrace of mediocrity. Pete is the kind of guy who lights up the room—virtually, of course, because his work-from-home status has rendered his actual presence as rare as his completed to-do list. Leisure is his modus operandi.

But here's the rub: Pete wouldn't know productivity if it showed up with a neon sign and a personal assistant. He's mastered the art of *performative busyness,* which confuses frenetic activity with actual results. Need a color-coded spreadsheet of the team's coffee preferences? Pete's on it. Want someone to spearhead the quarterly report? Well, Pete's got "something urgent" on his plate, like brainstorming names for next year's management offsite.

Pete's greatest talent is his ability to rationalize. He waxes poetic about how he's saving the "big tasks" for the perfect moment—when the stars align, and his inbox reaches inbox-zero nirvana. He can argue, with Shakespearean flair, that reorganizing the apps on his phone is "strategic planning," and somehow, you almost believe him. So, we can only imagine what his personal life must look like.

How Pete landed his midlevel management gig remains one of life's enduring mysteries. Some suspect nepotism; others think it's his uncanny knack for convincing people that he's "a big-picture guy." Whatever the case, the guy operates in a time zone entirely of his own making, where deadlines are "suggestions" and productivity tools are mere suggestions *about* suggestions.

Here's where you come in. Pete *really* wants to be your friend. He sends you memes, pings you on Slack for "quick chats," and invites you to meetings that are not even remotely relevant to your role. And sure, his charisma is disarming, but deep down, you know the truth: Prolonged exposure to Pete's methods might infect *you* with this same ailment. A missed deadline here, an overlong brainstorming session there, and soon you'll be singing Pete's anthem: *Why do today what you can reschedule indefinitely?*

So, although Pete's an absolute delight at the (virtual) party, perhaps it's best to admire him from a distance—preferably the safe, productivity-preserving kind. After all, you've got things to do...unlike Pete.

Don't Be Like Pete: The Best Way to Start Is to Start

Tackling procrastination often feels daunting because it involves changing ingrained habits and overcoming internal resistance. Kaizen provides a practical, incremental approach to dismantling this barrier. To Pete, Kaizen is a boring inconvenience. An unnecessary effort far less desirable than doing, let's say, nothing. But for you, it's a superpower.

Instead of aiming to eliminate procrastination overnight, start small. If you struggle to begin a task, commit to working on it for just a few minutes. The effort required to "just start" is minimal, yet it breaks the inertia of inaction. Over time, you can gradually extend this period—five minutes, ten minutes, or more. Each step builds confidence and establishes a habit of starting tasks without hesitation.

Over time, this approach rewires your response to tasks and transforms procrastination into productivity. By focusing on incremental progress rather than perfection, you reduce overwhelm, build consistency, and create a system that supports sustained success.

The strength of kaizen lies in its adaptability. Systems rooted in this philosophy are designed to evolve with changing circumstances while staying true to their overarching goals. This flexibility reflects the ethos of another legendary Japanese discipline: the samurai. The samurai's Bushido code provided them with a structured framework for life and combat, one that emphasized honor, discipline, and loyalty. Yet, their success in battle relied just as much on their adaptability. Samurai like Miyamoto Musashi, mentioned in Chapter 2, who adapted his techniques depending on the opponents he faced, demonstrated that preparation combined with flexibility is the basis of resilience. Musashi's approach—constant training to cultivate fluidity and improvisation—mirrors kaizen's principles of continuous improvement within a dynamic framework.

Applying Kaizen in Your Systems
MEASURE WHAT MATTERS
Begin with clarity. Identify the metrics that reflect progress toward your goals. Whether in personal development or business, focus on meaningful data that guides improvement.

EMBRACE SMALL CHANGES
Identify one small adjustment to make within a system—whether you are automating a repetitive task, optimizing your workflow, or dedicating five extra minutes to a priority. Measure the impact and refine as needed.

FOSTER FEEDBACK LOOPS
Regularly evaluate what works and what doesn't. Treat inefficiencies as opportunities for growth. Like Toyota's production teams or a samurai's battlefield adaptations, make refinement part of your process.

Kaizen reminds us that success is neither the result of sporadic nor grand efforts but springs from steady, consistent progress. Whether you are optimizing a corporate workflow or tackling personal goals, this philosophy instills a mindset of improvement and empowers your systems so that you can evolve and thrive. With kaizen as your guiding principle, systems become living frameworks—disciplined yet adaptable, structured yet fluid. In this balance lies the secret to long-term success.

GOING *ALL IN*

TO ACCESS YOUR ALL IN WORKSPACE, VISIT APP.EXLR8.AI/ALL-IN

ARE MY SYSTEMS DESIGNED FOR CONSISTENT EXECUTION?

Reflection
Tony Dungy's commitment to his system demonstrates that success is not about fleeting motivation but about showing up and executing consistently. A system gains its power through disciplined adherence, even when results aren't immediate.

Action
Identify one system in your personal or professional life and commit to executing it consistently for the next thirty days. Track your adherence daily and reflect on how persistence, rather than perfection, shapes your outcomes.

AM I MEASURING WHAT TRULY MATTERS?

Reflection
Peter Drucker's principle, "What gets measured gets managed," highlights the importance of focusing on meaningful metrics. Whether in personal goals or organizational performance, measuring the right things ensures you have clarity into the process and guides progress.

Action
Select a goal or system you are working on and identify two or three key metrics that reflect its success. For example, if tackling procrastination, track how often you "just start" tasks and how this influences your productivity. Review these metrics weekly and adjust your system based on your findings.

HOW ADAPTABLE IS MY SYSTEM IN THE FACE OF CHANGE?

Reflection
The philosophy of kaizen teaches us that systems must evolve to remain effective. Like the samurai, who combined disciplined preparation with battlefield adaptability, we must create systems that respond to challenges without losing sight of our purpose.

Action

Test the flexibility of one of your systems by introducing a hypothetical challenge. For example, if you're using a time management system, simulate a day with unexpected interruptions. Adapt your approach while keeping your core priorities intact. Reflect on what worked and refine the system for greater resilience.

By considering these questions and taking deliberate action, you can align your systems with your purpose, ensuring they remain dynamic, effective, and capable of driving meaningful progress. These small, thoughtful adjustments—rooted in reflection and action—transform systems from static plans into engines of sustained success.

17

THE INFINITE EDGE

Avoiding the Plateau

As we near the conclusion of our time together, we must now step back and reflect—not just on what you've learned but also on how you'll carry it forward. Transformation isn't a destination; it's a way of life. The pursuit of remarkable results isn't defined by a singular milestone or a final triumph but by a mindset that embraces growth as a perpetual process. Whether it comes through the steady rhythm of small, incremental changes or the seismic shifts of bold decisions, reinvention requires a commitment to continuous improvement. It's about achieving and sustaining. Succeeding and evolving.

As tenor Robert Brault says, "We are kept from our goal not by obstacles but by a clear path to a lesser goal." This final chapter is a call to action, an invitation to see your routines, mindset, commitment, and systems as part of a living framework that adapts, refines, and grows with you. Life's most meaningful pursuits—fulfilling work, faith in your higher power, thriving relationships, good health, personal accomplishment—are not achieved in static moments but through ongoing evolution. This is where the pieces of the puzzle come together: the rituals that shape your days and hone your warrior mindset, the purpose that fuels your efforts, the systems that drive your progress toward remarkable results, and the resilience that keeps you moving forward. Together, they form the foundation for a life of continuous achievement, a life where your impact extends beyond your ambitions to the lasting influence you leave behind. This is your infinite edge—your path to remarkable results. Go all in and never stop fighting.

NEVER OUT OF THE FIGHT

Under the bludgeonings of chance.
My head is bloody, but unbowed.
—WILLIAM ERNEST HENLEY, "INVICTUS"

Okay, fine. One more crazy story. As this book continually reinforces, pursuing purpose-driven goals requires relentless forward motion—a principle Lt. Gen. Sir Adrian Carton de Wiart embodied quite literally. If sheer grit were a currency, de Wiart would have retired as the wealthiest man on earth. His life wasn't just about marching forward—it was about doing so while missing body parts, defying the laws of probability, and leaving a trail of medics wondering whether he was even human. Unlike Hugh Glass, the frontiersman, de Wiart did it all without the performance-coaching wisdom of Angela Duckworth! Can you imagine? So, buckle up, because this is no ordinary tale of perseverance; this is the absurd, utterly insane story of a man who treated war wounds as if they were mosquito bites and viewed overwhelming catastrophes as mildly inconvenient occupational hazards.

Fresh out of Oxford (which he apparently found to be quite boring), Carton de Wiart joined the British Army to fight in the Second Boer War (1899–1902). Early in his career, he was shot in the stomach and the groin. Yes, the groin. Did he let that stop him? Of course not. Most men would be clutching pearls, but Adrian dismissed it as a "minor inconvenience" and went right back to the battlefield. This was just the warm-up. Fast-forward to the Western Front in World War I, where de Wiart was practically a magnet for bullets and shrapnel. He was shot in the head (losing his left eye), shot in the face (because one headshot wasn't dramatic enough), shot in the ear (apparently a ricochet from a bullet that had temporarily missed its mark—probably his other ear), and had his nose rearranged by shrapnel. He and Justinian II would have been fast friends. And let's not forget the time he lost his left hand. When doctors hesitated to amputate his hand after it had been mangled by shrapnel, he took matters into his own hands—pun intended—and *bit off his two remaining fingers*. Why wait for surgery when you have teeth and determination? The surgeons ultimately had no choice but to perform a complete amputation of the hand. He reportedly remarked, "Frankly,

I enjoyed the war." Clearly, war enjoyed him too, because it kept throwing him back into the mix.

By World War II, Carton de Wiart wasn't just battling enemies—he was battling captors. Taken prisoner by the Italians in North Africa, he decided captivity wasn't for him. Over the course of two years, he made several escape attempts. On one occasion, he tunneled out of a POW camp with a spoon. Yes, a spoon. Move over Shawshank legend, Andy Dufresne—Adrian did it first, faster, and with one less hand. When he finally escaped in 1943, he was sixty-three years old. Yet there he was, missing an eye and a hand, riddled with gunshot wounds, trudging through enemy territory, making every Italian guard rethink their career choices.

Post-escape, you'd think the British government might want to keep him out of harm's way. He was, to say the least, accident prone. Instead, they sent him to Poland, Romania, and eventually China, where he represented British interests. On his way to China, his plane crashed into the Indian Ocean! Everyone else panicked. But not this nut job. He calmly swam to shore, once again, mildly inconvenienced by this travel delay. I have a total man-crush on this guy.

de Wiart's story defies reason and borders on farce, yet it's a testament to an unshakable sense of purpose. He wasn't just a man of resilience; he was resilience personified—a walking, one-eyed, one-handed reminder that purpose-driven goals demand forward motion, no matter the odds or injuries. For de Wiart, there was no plateau. No end.

He finally retired from military service in 1947. He settled in County Cork, Ireland, where he spent his later years fishing, writing his memoir, not surprisingly titled *Happy Odyssey* (published in 1950), and enjoying a quieter life—a sharp contrast to his action-packed career.

Carton de Wiart passed away peacefully on June 5, 1963, at the age of eighty-three. Despite his remarkable exploits, he remained humble and understated about his adventures, famously writing in his memoir after one particular battle, "We had a few drinks to celebrate, and I found myself more optimistic about our chances of survival." Love it. His legacy endures as a symbol of fortitude, courage, and indomitable spirit and has inspired generations to face adversity head-on and live with a sense of purpose and determination.

For those of us navigating far less perilous endeavors, let Sir Adrian's absurdly inspiring life serve as a call to action: Whether you're metaphorically tunneling through a challenge with a spoon or patching yourself up after a setback, keep moving forward. And remember—if someone can endure multiple gunshot wounds to the head and still *bring it* on the battlefield, you can definitely handle your next Monday morning meeting.

MAINTAINING MOMENTUM

Momentum begets momentum,
and the best way to start is to start.
—GIL PENCHINA

Achieving a goal is often seen as the pinnacle of success—the finish line after a long and arduous race. But, in truth, conquering a goal is only the beginning. Real fulfillment lies not just in reaching the summit but also in what comes after: sustaining the momentum, evolving the journey, and ensuring the victory becomes a pathway rather than a final destination.

Achieving a goal often brings a surge of euphoria, a moment when effort and aspiration align in the glow of accomplishment. Yet, this triumph can also leave an unsettling void. The driving force of momentum that was propelling you forward begins to wane, replaced by a sense of "What now?" This phenomenon—the achievement plateau—can feel like you're standing at the edge of the mesa, unsure where to go next. To get past this plateau, you must shift your mindset from one of finite goals to one of infinite growth, where the journey itself becomes the destination.

Momentum is not a perpetual force; it must be sustained by intention, effort, and care. The first step in maintaining it is to redefine your horizon. The accomplishment of a goal is not an endpoint but a gateway, an opportunity to envision new possibilities. Ask yourself: What's next? How can the foundation you've built serve as a platform for greater impact? Success, after all, is not a static monument but a dynamic, evolving process. Each new pursuit should stretch your capabilities, deepen your purpose, and invite you to explore the uncharted territories of your potential.

Instead of pursuing outcomes alone, you build true momentum by committing to growth. Shift your focus from simply achieving to mastering. Growth, unlike results, is intrinsically fulfilling; it sharpens your sense of curiosity, hones your expertise, and broadens the ways you can contribute to the world. With this mindset, achievements—not simply trophies to collect—are milestones along an endless path of self-discovery and service to others.

Consistency becomes your anchor. The routines and habits that carried you to success must not be discarded but refined and repeated. They are the rhythms that keep your momentum alive and prevent you from drifting toward complacency. In showing up daily, even when the excitement fades, you transform discipline into a quiet strength that sustains your forward motion. These small, deliberate actions are anything but mundane—they are sacred, the embodiment of your commitment to continual progress.

Celebrate not only the culmination of your efforts but also the incremental victories along the way. External validation may affirm your achievements, but lasting fulfillment is rooted in the internal recognition of your growth. In honoring progress—no matter how modest—you remind yourself of your inherent capacity to rise, to improve, and to create. This celebration fuels the joy that makes each step worthwhile, even when the path feels steep.

Ultimately, momentum finds its truest expression in purpose and legacy. Once you've conquered a goal, look outward. How can your success inspire others, uplift communities, or contribute to a greater good? When you share your achievements, they ripple outward, creating waves of impact. Purpose-driven action transforms momentum from a personal force into a collective one, multiplying its power and sustaining its energy.

Remember, achievement is not an arrival; it is an evolution. Maintaining momentum requires you to see every conquered summit as the starting point for a new ascent. The joy of the journey lies in its continuity. Momentum is not a prize to win but a state of being to cultivate, a force that grows with intention and purpose. With a vision that evolves, a heart that gives, and a soul unafraid of the unknown, you build not just a life of achievement but also a legacy of impact. Each step forward is an act of creation, a testament to your resilience, and an offering to the world. The infinite path stretches before you. Walk it boldly, move with intention, and never look back.

GOING *ALL IN*

TO ACCESS YOUR ALL IN WORKSPACE, VISIT APP.EXLR8.AI/ALL-IN

HOW DO I REDEFINE SUCCESS AFTER ACHIEVING A GOAL?

Reflection

Achieving a goal often brings a surge of satisfaction, but it can also lead to the "achievement plateau." The completion of one journey is not an end-point but a gateway to new possibilities. Success, as this chapter reminds us, is a dynamic and evolving process.

Action

Reflect on a recent goal you've achieved and ask yourself: What's next? How can this success be a foundation for greater impact? Set a new goal that stretches your capabilities and aligns with your deeper purpose, ensuring that your journey of growth continues.

AM I FOCUSING ON GROWTH OVER RESULTS?

Reflection

Although outcomes are important, true momentum and fulfillment come from an intrinsic commitment to personal growth and mastery. Achievements become more meaningful when you see them as milestones along an infinite path of self-discovery and contribution rather than as endpoints.

Action

Identify one area of your life—personal, professional, or relational—where you can shift focus from achieving a specific outcome to deepening your growth. For example, rather than aiming for a promotion, focus on developing a key skill that will enhance your long-term potential.

HOW DO I SUSTAIN MOMENTUM THROUGH CONSISTENCY AND PURPOSE?

Reflection

Momentum is not a force that sustains itself; it is fueled by discipline and intentional effort. The routines and habits that brought you to success must be refined and repeated. Purpose provides the emotional fuel that turns consistent action into a source of resilience and inspiration.

Action

Revisit the routines and habits that have contributed to your past successes. Identify one that may have slipped or that needs refining and commit to incorporating it into your daily life. Pair this with a renewed connection to your purpose—ask yourself how your actions today serve your larger goals and legacy.

By considering these questions and engaging with the reflections and actions, you can sustain momentum, deepen your growth, and allow each achievement to bring you closer to a life of lasting purpose and impact. The infinite edge is not just a path—it's a way of being. Walk it boldly.

EPILOGUE

Dream Big, Start Small, Act Now

The only limit to our realization of tomorrow
will be our doubts of today.

—FRANKLIN D. ROOSEVELT

The journey to greatness does not begin with certainty or ease; you must take a single, courageous step into the unknown. As our time together comes to a close, allow me to reinforce the profound truth that achieving remarkable results demands action in the face of fear, the discipline to embrace temporary discomfort over lifelong regret, and the urgency to begin today. The battlefield of your highest potential awaits—and it is only by stepping boldly onto it that you can transform, create, and leave an endowment of impact.

Fear and suffering are the twin flames that forge the steel of human greatness. Yet, in this modern era, we are conditioned to avoid both and seek instead the comfort of familiarity, the ease of mediocrity. But greatness, as history repeatedly teaches us, is born not in comfort but in the crucible of discomfort, where fear dances alongside potential, and suffering becomes the ink with which our masterworks are written. Leonardo da Vinci's *Mona Lisa*, Beethoven's Ninth Symphony, and the towering cathedral of Notre Dame—all were birthed from pain, perseverance, and an unyielding drive to manifest beauty amid adversity.

To embrace fear is to acknowledge our humanity, to stand on the precipice of uncertainty and take that first tremulous step forward. Fear whispers the possibility of failure, of ridicule, of loss. Yet, it is in this very whisper that we find the voice of purpose. Without fear, there is no bravery; without adversity, no triumph. To create something remarkable, we must be willing to wade through the waters of doubt and discomfort, trusting that the current will carry us closer to the shores of our aspirations.

Suffering, far from being a curse, is a purposeful teacher. It demands of us our fullest engagement, calls us to dig deeper, work harder, and rise stronger. The path to fulfilling our highest potential is paved with days when every muscle aches, every thought questions, and every fiber of our being cries out for retreat. But it is in those moments of near surrender that the seeds of greatness are sown. The Spartan warriors of ancient Greece, the samurai of feudal Japan, military service women and men, modern-day entrepreneurs, and the visionaries who dare to defy convention all embrace this truth: Suffering is the price of mastery. And what we create in those moments—the innovations, the breakthroughs, the contributions to humanity—become our gift to the world, testaments to our courage and a source of inspiration for those who follow.

THE MINDSET OF DISCIPLINE OVER REGRET

Discipline and regret are the two governing forces of every human life. One we choose; the other chooses us. To make the mindset of discipline our daily mantra is to acknowledge that although the path of resistance may be arduous, the alternative is far more painful—a life tinged with the bitterness of unfulfilled potential and the haunting echoes of "what if." Regret is the shadow that looms over every opportunity forsaken, every dream deferred.

Remember that the pain of discipline is temporary, a fleeting companion in the pursuit of mastery. It is the early mornings, the sacrifices, the hours spent perfecting a craft while others sleep or indulge in distraction. It is the deliberate choice to embrace the struggle, to face the obstacle head-on. But this pain, this self-imposed hardship, is also the architect of achievement. It sharpens our focus, strengthens our resolve, and molds us into individuals capable of transcending the ordinary.

Regret, on the other hand, is eternal. It lingers long after the opportunity to act has passed, a persistent reminder of the moments we let fear dictate our choices. It is the lament of the artist who never picked up the brush, the entrepreneur who never launched the idea, the warrior who never stepped onto the battlefield. To live with regret is to carry the weight of unfulfilled potential, a burden far heavier than the temporary discomfort of discipline.

This philosophy—that it is far better to endure the pain of discipline today than the sting of regret tomorrow—must become a way of life. It demands that we approach each day with intentionality and view every challenge as a chance to grow, every setback as an opportunity to learn, and every moment as a precious fragment of time that will never return. The mindset of discipline is not about perfection; it is about persistence. Showing up, day after day, in the pursuit of something greater than ourselves.

THE IMPERATIVE TO BEGIN TODAY

Time is the most precious currency we possess. It is also the most fleeting. We spend it freely while never knowing the balance of our account. We know not what tomorrow holds, nor can we count on its arrival. All we have is this moment, this singular opportunity to step boldly into the arena and begin the work that calls to us. The fear of failure, the voices of doubt—both internal and external—are but distractions from the truth: that action is the only path forward.

Starting today does not require perfection; it requires courage. It is the willingness to be vulnerable, to stumble, to fail, and to rise again. It is recognizing that every great journey, every monumental achievement began with a single step. The world's most celebrated innovators, creators, and leaders did not wait for the perfect moment or the guarantee of success—they began, often imperfectly, and allowed the process to refine them.

Procrastination, that insidious thief of dreams, preys on our fears and feeds on our doubts. It whispers the lie that there will always be more time, that tomorrow will be more favorable. But tomorrow is not promised, and the cost of waiting is often the loss of opportunity. To delay is to risk the erosion of ambition, the dulling of passion, and the forfeiture of the remarkable results we are all capable of achieving.

To those who hesitate, who linger on the precipice of their potential, hear this: Today is the day to begin. Step confidently into the light of possibility, for within you lies the power to shape the world in ways both profound and beautiful. Write the first sentence of the story only you can tell. Take the first step toward the dream that has whispered to you in quiet moments. Begin the practice that will lead to mastery, the conversation that will heal wounds, the effort that will ignite hope in others. Do not let fear or doubt tether you to inaction—stand firm, for the battlefield of your aspirations awaits.

The path ahead will not be without trials. They will test your resolve, challenge your patience, and at times demand more of you than you think you can give. Yet within these trials lies the opportunity to grow, to rise above limitations, and to become something greater than you ever imagined. Have no fear, for you are not alone. Lean on your faith—faith in God, faith in yourself, faith in a higher purpose, and faith in the goodness of others. Let that faith be your anchor in storms and your compass in uncertainty.

As you walk this road, carry joy with you. Not as a fleeting emotion but as a deliberate choice, a steady flame that brightens your path and warms those around you. Project love into the world with every step—love for what you do, for the people you encounter, and for the journey itself. Let kindness guide your actions, for it is the quiet strength that transforms even the smallest gestures into acts of greatness.

And above all, remember this: You are capable of extraordinary things. The infinite edge of your potential is not a destination to be reached but a horizon to be pursued. It stretches endlessly before you, each step revealing new possibilities, each effort deepening your impact. The choice to walk this path begins now.

So, rise. Begin. With faith in your heart, kindness in your actions, and love in your purpose, step forward without fear. You are here to create, to inspire, to build a legacy that will endure. The first step is waiting—you must take it. The world needs what only you can offer.

And once you commit to going *all in*, always remember this line from the Navy SEAL Ethos:

I am never out of the fight.

ACKNOWLEDGMENTS

First and foremost, I must extend my deepest gratitude to my wife, Nicole, and our four incredible children, Tyler, Parker, Ryder, and Walker. Your support, patience, and understanding have been my anchor throughout this journey. Nicole, your love and belief in me have been my greatest source of strength, and to our children, your curiosity and boundless energy remind me daily of the importance of living with purpose and intent. This book exists because of the moments you selflessly allowed me to steal away for early mornings of writing and reflection—thank you for being my inspiration and my foundation. Only a few days ago, as I made my final edits to this manuscript, our family endured yet another heartbreaking loss. We said goodbye to Pappa Beau—Nicole's father, my father-in-law, and our children's beloved grandfather. He was a beacon of light, and his warmth, wisdom, and spirit will forever guide us.

Beau, thank you for your kindness, generosity, love, and support over the years. This book stands as a tribute to your resilience, your love of life, and the profound truth that each of us has something extraordinary to share with the world.

I am grateful for my agent, Farley Chase, whose steadfast belief in my vision and tireless commitment to these projects have been instrumental in bringing them to life. To the team at Hachette Book Group, thank you for championing my work and allowing this book to find its voice. My heartfelt appreciation goes to my brilliant editors, Dan Ambrosio, Nana Twumasi, and Christina Palaia, whose keen insights and thoughtful guidance elevated every word on these pages. To my team at EXCELR8, your understanding and flexibility during the early hours of this creative process made this endeavor possible. Finally, to the extraordinary thought leaders whose wisdom and ideas I have drawn upon in this book, your work has provided the foundation on which these concepts stand. It is with humility that I acknowledge the collective effort, wisdom, and encouragement of so many who made this book a reality—none of this could have been done alone.

SELECTED BIBLIOGRAPHY

Abbott, Jim. *Imperfect: An Improbable Life*. Ballantine Books, 2012.

Aurelius, Marcus. *Meditations*. Various translations.

Bigelow, Kathryn, dir. *Point Break* (1991).

Bondeson, Jan. *Buried Alive: The Terrifying History of Our Most Primal Fear*. W. W. Norton & Company, 2001.

Byrne, Rhonda. *The Secret*. Atria Books, 2006.

Carlson, W. Bernard. *Tesla: Inventor of the Electrical Age*. Princeton University Press, 2013.

Carton de Wiart, Adrian. *Happy Odyssey*. Pen and Sword Military, 2007.

Chapman, Marina. *The Girl with No Name: The Incredible Story of a Child Raised by Monkeys*. Pegasus Books, 2013.

Churchill, Winston. *The Churchill War Papers*, edited by Martin Gilbert. W. W. Norton & Company, 1993.

Clear, James. *Atomic Habits: An Easy & Proven Way to Build Good Habits & Break Bad Ones*. Avery, 2018.

Copeland, Misty. *Life in Motion: An Unlikely Ballerina*. Touchstone, 2014.

Coram, Robert. *American Patriot: The Life and Wars of Colonel Bud Day*. Back Bay Books, 2007.

Darwin, Charles. *On the Origin of Species by Means of Natural Selection*. John Murray, 1859.

Deci, Edward L., and Richard M. Ryan. *Intrinsic Motivation and Self-Determination in Human Behavior*. Springer, 1985.

Doidge, Norman. *The Brain That Changes Itself: Stories of Personal Triumph from the Frontiers of Brain Science*. Viking Penguin, 2007.

Drucker, Peter. *The Practice of Management*. Harper Business, 2006.

Duckworth, Angela. *Grit: The Power of Passion and Perseverance*. Scribner, 2016.

Duhigg, Charles. *The Power of Habit: Why We Do What We Do in Life and Business*. Random House Trade Paperbacks, 2014.

Dungy, Tony. *Quiet Strength: The Principles, Practices, and Priorities of a Winning Life*. Tyndale, 2007.

Durant, Will. *The Story of Philosophy*. Wisehouse Classics, 2023.

Dweck, Carol S. *Mindset: The New Psychology of Success*. Ballantine Books, 2006.

Easwaran, Eknath. *The Upanishads*. Nilgiri Press, 2007.

Ericsson, K. Anders. *Peak: Secrets from the New Science of Expertise*. Eamon Dolan / Houghton Mifflin Harcourt, 2016.

Erikson, Erik H. *Identity and the Life Cycle*. W. W. Norton & Company, 1959.

Fogg, B. J. *Tiny Habits: The Small Changes That Change Everything*. Houghton Mifflin Harcourt, 2019.

Franklin, Benjamin. *The Autobiography of Benjamin Franklin*. Various editions; originally published in 1791.

Franklin, Jonathan. *438 Days: An Extraordinary True Story of Survival at Sea*. Atria Books, 2015.

Gladwell, Malcolm. *Outliers: The Story of Success*. Little, Brown, 2008.

Gleeson, Brent. *Embrace the Suck: The Navy SEAL Way to an Extraordinary Life*. Hachette Books, 2020.

Goggins, David. *Can't Hurt Me: Master Your Mind and Defy the Odds*. Lioncrest Publishing, 2018.

Goldsmith, Marshall. *What Got You Here Won't Get You There: How Successful People Become Even More Successful*. Hachette Books, 2007.

Heifetz, Ron. *Leadership Without Easy Answers*. Harvard University Press, 1998.

Henley, William Ernest. "Invictus." Originally published in *A Book of Verses*, 1888.

Herbert, Frank. "Litany Against Fear," in *Dune*. Chilton Books, 1965.

Hill, Napoleon. *Think and Grow Rich*. Ralston Society, 1937.

Imai, Masaaki. *Kaizen: The Key to Japan's Competitive Success*. McGraw-Hill Education, 1996.

Inazō, Nitobe. *Bushido: The Soul of Japan*. East India Publishing Company, 2022.

James, William. *Principles of Psychology*. Henry Holt and Company, 1890.

Jeffers, Susan. *Feel the Fear… and Do It Anyway*. Ballantine Books, 1987.

Jiang, Jia. *Rejection Proof: How I Beat Fear and Became Invincible Through 100 Days of Rejection*. Harmony, 2015.

Lally, Phillippa, Cornelia H. M. van Jaarsveld, Henry W. W. Potts, and Jane Wardle. "How Are Habits Formed: Modeling Habit Formation in the Real World." *European Journal of Social Psychology* 40, no. 6 (2010): 998–1009.

Lansing, Alfred. *Endurance: Shackleton's Incredible Voyage*. Basic Books, 2015.

Liker, Jeffrey K. *The Toyota Way: 14 Management Principles from the World's Greatest Manufacturer*. McGraw-Hill, 2004.

Macmillan, Malcolm. *An Odd Kind of Fame: Stories of Phineas Gage.* MIT Press, 2002.

Milligan, Ben. *By Water Beneath the Walls: The Rise of the Navy SEALs.* Bantam, 2021.

Mischel, Walter, et al. "Cognitive and Attentional Mechanisms in Delay of Gratification." *Journal of Personality and Social Psychology* 21, no. 2 (1972): 204–218.

Musashi, Miyamoto. *The Book of Five Rings,* translated by Thomas Cleary. Shambhala, 1993.

Nietzsche, Friedrich. *Beyond Good and Evil.* Various editions.

Nilsson, Magnus. *Fäviken.* Phaidon Press, 2012.

O'Brady, Colin. *The Impossible First: From Fire to Ice—Crossing Antarctica Alone.* Scribner, 2020.

O'Shea, Covadonga. *The Man from Zara: The Story of the Genius Behind the Inditex Group.* Lid Pub Inc., 2012.

Ries, Eric. *The Lean Startup.* Crown Currency, 2011.

Roberts, Andrew. *Churchill: Walking with Destiny.* Viking, 2018.

Senge, Peter. *The Fifth Discipline: The Art & Practice of the Learning Organization.* Broadway Business, 1997.

Shackleton, Ernest. *South: The Endurance Expedition.* Signet Books, 1999.

Sharma, Robin. *The 5AM Club: Own Your Morning. Elevate Your Life.* HarperCollins, 2018.

Skinner, B. F. *The Behavior of Organisms: An Experimental Analysis.* Appleton-Century, 1938.

Stockdale, James B., and Jim Stockdale. *In Love and War: The Story of a Family's Ordeal and Sacrifice During the Vietnam Years.* Harper & Row, 1984.

Willink, Jocko. *Discipline Equals Freedom: Field Manual.* St. Martin's Press, 2017.

Willink, Jocko, and Leif Babin. *Extreme Ownership: How U.S. Navy SEALs Lead and Win.* St. Martin's Press, 2017.

Womack, James P., Daniel T. Jones, and Daniel Roos. *The Machine That Changed the World.* Free Press, 1990.

Yousafzai, Malala. *I Am Malala: The Girl Who Stood Up for Education and Was Shot by the Taliban.* Back Bay Books, 2015.

INDEX

ABOUT THE AUTHOR

Brent Gleeson is a Navy SEAL combat veteran, award-winning entrepreneur, founder and CEO of EXCELR8, and the author of *Embrace the Suck: The Navy SEAL Way to an Extraordinary Life.*

EXLR8.ai
INSTAGRAM: brent_gleeson
X: @brentgleeson

RAISING READERS
Books Build Bright Futures

Thank you for reading this book and for being a reader of books in general. We are so grateful to share being part of a community of readers with you, and we hope you will join us in passing our love of books on to the next generation of readers.

Did you know that reading for enjoyment is the single biggest predictor of a child's future happiness and success?

More than family circumstances, parents' educational background, or income, reading impacts a child's future academic performance, emotional well-being, communication skills, economic security, ambition, and happiness.

Studies show that kids reading for enjoyment in the US is in rapid decline:

- In 2012, 53% of 9-year-olds read almost every day. Just 10 years later, in 2022, the number had fallen to 39%.
- In 2012, 27% of 13-year-olds read for fun daily. By 2023, that number was just 14%.

Together, we can commit to **Raising Readers** and change this trend. How?

- Read to children in your life daily.
- Model reading as a fun activity.
- Reduce screen time.
- Start a family, school, or community book club.
- Visit bookstores and libraries regularly.
- Listen to audiobooks.
- Read the book before you see the movie.
- Encourage your child to read aloud to a pet or stuffed animal.
- Give books as gifts.
- Donate books to families and communities in need.

BOB1217

Books build bright futures, and **Raising Readers** is our shared responsibility.

For more information, visit **JoinRaisingReaders.com**

Sources: National Endowment for the Arts, National Assessment of Educational Progress, WorldBookDay.org, Nielsen BookData's 2023 "Understanding the Children's Book Consumer"